Th Glovebox
Transporting Horses

JOHN HENDERSON

J. A. ALLEN · LONDON

Important Phone Numbers

This checklist has been placed at the start of *The Glovebox Guide* for instant access in the event of breakdown or other emergency. Readers are advised to add their own details to the table below, and to update them in the event of any change. Do not rely on programming these numbers into a mobile phone in case it is lost or damaged.

	Name/address	Phone numbers
UK Emergency services	Police, Fire Brigade, Ambulance	999
Home*		
Stable yard*		
Vet		
Breakdown service (warranty)		
Breakdown service (other)		
Insurers		

*You know these but emergency services do not.

Name/address   **Phone numbers**

Insurance policy   Company name and address:

_____

_____

_____

Policy number: _____

Expires: _____

Farrier   _____

_____

_____

Friend with horse transport   _____

_____

_____

_____

Friend with horse transport   _____

_____

_____

_____

Friend with horse transport   _____

_____

_____

_____

Talking _Yellow Pages_   In case you need services away from home   118 247

Owner's Notes

© John Henderson 2004
First published in Great Britain 2005

ISBN 0 85131 8789

J.A. Allen
Clerkenwell House
Clerkenwell Green
London EC1R 0HT

J.A. Allen is an imprint of Robert Hale Limited

The right of John Henderson to be identified
as author of this work has been asserted by him
in accordance with the Copyright, Designs and
Patents Act 1988

A catalogue record for this book is available
from the British Library

Photographs by the author, except photo
on page 57 courtesy of Mercedes-Benz

Edited by Martin Diggle
Design and typesetting by Paul Saunders
Line illustrations by Rodney Paull

Printed by New Era Printing Co. Ltd Hong Kong

Contents

Acknowledgements   xii
Introduction   1

1. What's What   5

Trailer and Towcar Parts   6
Lorry Parts   10
Lorry and Trailer Floors   11
    Stress on the Floor

2. Licences and Legal Requirements   13

Insurance   13
The Authorities   13
Licence Categories   15
    Licences for Pre-1997 Drivers; Licences for
    Post-1997 Drivers
LGV Medical Requirements   17
Driving Tests   17
    Reversing; Braking; On the Road; Uncoupling and
    Recoupling; Marking
Training   21
Vehicle Testing   22

Tachographs   23
Livestock Laws   24

3. Choosing a Towcar and Trailer   26

Weights   26
Choosing a Towcar   30
    4WD Terms; Electronic Aids; Engines; Diesel Terms;
    Gearboxes; Towing Equipment
Buying Used Towcars   40
Choosing a Trailer   44
    Thinking Ahead; Features to Look For; Running In
Buying Used Trailers   50
Getting Acquainted   53

4. Buying a Lorry   55

Whatever You Want   57
Weights and Payloads   59
Engines   60
Bodywork   60
Technology   63
Horses' Accommodation   65
Living Section   68
Security   71
Buying a Used Lorry   72

5. Preparing for the Worst   77

Buyer Beware   77
    Taking Action
Security   79
Fire Risks   82
Tool Kits   83

First Aid Kits 84
Kits for Humans; Kits for Horses
Breakdown Cover 86
Horse Equipment 87
Coping with Emergencies 87
Motorway Emergencies; Accidents; Breakdowns;
Punctures

6. Pre-drive Checks 93

Tyres 93
Under the Bonnet 96
Trailer Checks 98
Where Are You Going? 99
Final Checks 99

7. Basic Driving Skills 100

Hitching and Unhitching 101
Reversing 107
Reversing Lorries; Reversing Trailers
Pulling Away 112
Use of Mirrors 113
Changing Gear 114
Using 4WD 116
Using Electronic Driving Aids 118

8. On the Road 120

Vehicle Size 120
Speed Limits 121
Observation 121
Steering 122
Manoeuvres 123

Cornering; Roundabouts; Left and Right Turns;
Passing Obstructions; Passing Animals; Overtaking

Bridges	128
Town Driving	128
Minor Roads	130
Motorways and Dual-carriageways	131
Roadworks	134
Bad Weather	135

Wind; Rain; Fog; Snow and Ice

Rough Ground	140
Snaking	141

9. Loading Horses   143

Travelling Gear	143
Preparing the Vehicle	148
Right Approach	150
Securing the Horse	152
Unloading	153
Loading and Unloading Dangers	154
Problem Loaders	155

10. Travelling Horses   159

Driving Breaks	159

What to Check

Very Long Trips	162
Consideration for Others	163

11. Trailer Maintenance   164

Storage	165
Cleaning	166
Wheels	166

General Maintenance 167
 Bodywork; Bolts; Brakes; Floors; Hinges and
 Catches; Ramps; Hitches and Towballs; Lights;
 Wheel Nuts; Servicing Axles

12. Lorry Maintenance 183

Storage 183
Cleaning 185
Floors and Ramps 187
Bodywork 188
 Body Lubrication
Servicing 189
 Oil Changes; Brakes; Lights

Checklists

Buying a Trailer 194
Buying a Towcar 196
Buying a Lorry 199
First Aid Kits 202
Car and Trailer Checks 203
Lorry Pre-drive Checks 204
Things to Take 205
Trailer Maintenance 206
Lorry Maintenance 207

Further Information 208
Index 209

Acknowledgements

Thanks are due to the following people and companies for their help with this book: vets Andy Bathe and Karen Coumbe; horsebox owners Katie Moore, Jill Jerram, Rob Walker, Sallie Walrond and those met at shows who welcomed photography; my wife Carolyn and various horses for patient help with photography; companies Ifor Williams Trailers, Equibrand, Land Rover (especially Roger Crathorne), Hyundai Cars UK, Mercedes-Benz (picture of a lorry chassis in Chapter 4), Bulldog, M and M Leisure, Mid Norfolk Canopies and Trailers and Bussens and Parkin.

Also thanks are due to everyone who, on hearing that I was writing this, said 'Oh, you ought to mention...' and came up with useful tips, potential problems and handy reminders.

Introduction

Every time you get into a driving seat you take on certain responsibilities. You must obey the law, show consideration for others and be responsible for ensuring the safety of all those in and around your vehicle.

When you drive a horsebox (or lorry – see start of Chapter 1) or tow a horse trailer you add a further dimension. You become responsible for the well-being of an animal which, unlike human passengers, has to totally trust you to ensure his environment and transport are safe. A human passenger at least has the option to refuse to get into an unsafe vehicle; your horse does not. In addition, the size and weight of the vehicle means that if anything goes wrong it will be harder to keep it under control and the resulting accident will be far more damaging and dangerous for all parties involved. An off-roader towing a trailer with two horses weighs around three times more than a car the size of a Ford Focus, and even a non-LGV (Large Goods Vehicle) lorry can weigh five times more than the car.

The aim of this book is to help you to understand all that is necessary to make transporting your horse as safe and stress-free as possible – for both you and them. We will cover both trailers and lorries, though in some cases the advice will apply to both. Where there are differences, these will be explained.

This book is aimed at private horse owners, not those who transport horses professionally. There is a whole raft of extra rules and regulations for people who transport horses 'for hire or reward', which it is not the remit of this book to cover – things like tachograph rules, operators' licences and public and employers' liability insurance. If transporting horses might be considered to be part of your business, or something which you or an employee are being paid to do, seek legal advice about whether you would be considered to be doing it for hire or reward. For example, a groom paid to drive a vehicle transporting horses to a show might be considered to be doing it for reward and even a friend contributing more than their actual share of the fuel costs for their horse going to a show with yours could be considered to be paying you. Checking now could save you a lot of trouble later.

Lorry or Trailer?

If you do not already own horse transportation, your first concern is deciding what to buy. Many people make the mistake of buying a lorry purely because they think it will be easier to drive but, whatever you choose, its driving characteristics are different from a car, so there are things you will have to learn, or get used to. Yes, when reversing a lorry you steer the same way as with a solo car, but reversing a large vehicle with no rear windows, using mirrors alone, is very different from even the biggest car.

Trailers are popular because they are cheap to buy and run, but you must add the cost of buying and running a car capable of towing one if you do not already own something suitable. Of course, unlike a lorry, that car can be used for personal transport, but because of its size it will almost certainly cost more to run than the more modest car you would be able to use if you did not tow. However, trailers require less space than lorries to store, have lower maintenance cost, carry no road tax and currently require no annual safety testing in the UK (which is unfortunate, and is not the case in the rest of Europe).

Long-distance travel is probably less tiring for horses in a good lorry than in a trailer because they generally have more

Many horse owners dream of owning a mobile stable yard, like show horse producer Katie Moore's seven-horse Oakley.

An Ifor Williams HB505 and Toyota Landcruiser make an ideal outfit for two-horse towing.

room, better insulation and give a better ride. They should provide more protection in the event of an accident. If you have to stay overnight at events, you can cut costs by having a lorry with living accommodation, and in most you have the space to carry extra equipment and clothing. But lorries have to be taxed, maintained and tested, you need specialist breakdown back-up and you still have to run a car.

An important consideration is the amount of use the vehicle will get. A lorry will still have to be taxed and maintained even when it is standing still, which can work out expensive if you only use it three or four times a year. You could cut costs with a lorry by only taxing it during the show season, but what happens when you need to get your horse to a vet in an emergency in the winter? Trailers also need some maintenance when not in use to prevent deterioration, but with no battery, engine or gearbox, they do not need as much care as lorries and you are not paying road tax on something that is not on the road.

Whatever you have, it will have to be insured at all times because of the risk of theft. Because trailers are not registered, their theft is a bigger problem than lorry theft, but do not let that sway your decision. Lorries are often stolen because thieves can separate the body from the chassis, which bears all the identification numbers, then put the body onto a cheap, legitimate chassis. So, lorries need to be guarded as fiercely as trailers.

All the things you need to know to help you make your personal decision are in the next few chapters. The biggest mistake anyone ever makes when buying a trailer or lorry is to buy first and research later. Horse magazine problem pages frequently get queries from people asking 'Can my car tow this?' or 'Do I need to pass a test to drive that?' after they have bought it – which means they then have the unexpected expense of buying a new car or paying for tuition and testing while the vehicle remains unused. In addition, the more you know about the subject before you buy, the less likely you are to be misled by the untrustworthy.

It should also be remembered that, if you drive a vehicle for which you do not have the necessary licence, you are committing very serious motoring offences, which not only carry hefty fines but could make insurance more expensive or harder to get in the future.

This book has been designed to be dipped into for reference so you may find some important information repeated in different sections. It was felt that this would be more helpful than having constant cross-references.

1

What's What

Strictly speaking, a horsebox is a lorry (i.e. a lorry specially adapted to transport horses), but some people also use the word 'box' to describe a horse trailer so, in this book, we will generally use the terms 'lorry' and 'trailer'.

The classes of lorry and trailer are differentiated by their maximum authorized mass (MAM) which is the maximum laden weight laid down by the manufacturer and is sometimes called gross weight. Other important weights are *unladen, kerb, nose, maximum towing* and *gross train weights* plus *payload*.

Unladen weight is the weight of a trailer or vehicle totally empty. With cars and lorries, strictly speaking this means without any of the fluids necessary to drive it, including coolant, brake fluid and fuel. It should be obvious that vehicles do not even leave the production line like that, so it is a difficult weight to obtain, but that did not stop those drawing up the licence regulations from using the car's unladen weight to establish what drivers can tow. It would have been more realistic to have used *kerb weight*, which is the weight of a vehicle ready to be driven –

one method of calculating this even includes a 75 kg allowance for a driver.

Nose weight is the downward pressure a trailer exerts on the car's towball and a maximum is quoted by the manufacturer for all vehicles.

Maximum towing weight is the maximum laden trailer weight laid down by the vehicle's manufacturer – though it is usually only based on its ability to pull away on a slope. There are three types of maximum towing weight. Horse trailers come under the one for trailers with overrun brakes, applied when the trailer pushes against the slowing car's towball (this may just be called 'braked trailer weight' for cars) and the legal maximum weight for such a trailer is 3.5 tonnes. Lorries and some specialist vehicles, like Land Rover Defenders, can tow heavier trailers with hydraulic brakes linked to the vehicle's braking system. Finally, the maximum towing weight for an unbraked trailer is half the towing vehicle's weight up to 750 kg so, for a 900 kg car it is 450 kg, but for a 2-tonne off-roader it is only 750 kg.

Gross train weight is the maximum

weight for the laden vehicle and trailer combined: it is an offence to exceed this, though in most cases it is the vehicle fully loaded while towing a trailer to the maximum towing weight.

Payload is the amount of weight a vehicle or trailer can carry and it includes people as well as horses and luggage. If it is not quoted, you simply subtract the kerb weight from the gross (MAM) weight to get it.

Lorries fall into three categories nowadays: those up to 3,500 kg are in the same licence category as ordinary cars; those between 3,500 kg and 7,500 kg are called medium goods vehicles and those weighing more than that are large goods vehicles (formerly heavy goods vehicles or HGV). We will deal with who can drive what in the next chapter.

Horse trailers, though having the potential to be heavy, are in legal terms light trailers because they have MAMs of up to 3,500 kg. When making inquiries of licensing and testing authorities about trailers it is important to stress that you are talking about a trailer weighing under 3,500 kg, or you may be given information relevant only to the large trailers used by articulated lorries. Also, make sure you quote the trailer's MAM, not its unladen weight.

Trailer and Towcar Parts

Trailers usually consist of a substantial chassis with a framework built onto it to take the bodywork. These days the chassis and frame are galvanized, which greatly improves longevity. Body panels on modern trailers are usually of composite materials for the body sides, with light-weight aluminium, glass fibre or both for the roof.

Trailers have overrun braking systems which harness the action of the trailer

A weighbridge is the most accurate way of checking the weight of your trailer.

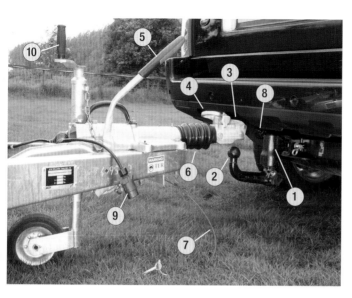

1: Towbar
2: Towball
3: Tow hitch
4: Hitch locking handle
5: Handbrake
6: Drawbar

7: Breakaway cable
8: Electrical socket
9: Electrical plug
10: Jockey wheel handle
11: Rear ramp
12: Front ramp

13: Groom's door
14: Ramp counterbalance
    spring
15: Side reflectors
16: Upper doors
17: Galvanized chassis

18: Breast bar
19: Partition
20: Breeching bar
21: Tie-up ring
22: Ventilator
23: Interior light
24: Rear lights
25: Slip-resistant
    flooring
26: Rear reflector

trying to overtake the car when it slows down. As the car slows, the trailer pushes against its towball which slides the drawbar, to which the hitch is attached, backwards against a lever which is connected to the brakes by rods and cables. The system is lightweight, simple and easily maintained, though it does not allow the use of self-adjusting brakes like those on most cars. Looking to the future, some caravan companies have experimented with electronic braking systems where electric motors, activated by the car's brake light circuit, apply the

brakes. This arrangement is said to react more quickly than a mechanical system and it could even pave the way for anti-lock brakes on trailers.

Any braked trailer must have a breakaway cable to apply the handbrake if it becomes unhitched. This is a cable attached to the bottom of the handbrake lever and has a clip on the other end for attaching to a substantial part of the car or a purpose-made ring on the towbar. It is supposed to break after it has applied the handbrake.

The hitch is a cup with a locking

mechanism that clamps round the towball. The handle on top holds that locking mechanism open while the ball enters the cup. On some trailers it must be held up while the hitch is lowered onto the ball, while on others it only needs to be held up to unhitch. Other types lock open when the ball is removed and automatically click down to lock when the ball is engaged. One type of hitch has a pop-up indicator on the cup to show when the ball is engaged. Modern hitches usually have some sort of towball wear indicator and most have a key lock, allowing the locking handle to be secured as a theft deterrent.

To tow anything, a car has to have a towbar fitted. A traditional towbar has a towball bolted to it. These towballs are cheap and easy to replace and allow for things such as stabilizers to be bolted behind them. Many manufacturers now use removable swan-neck towballs, in which the ball is on a long neck attached to the bar. Swan-neck towballs may be necessary in some cases to clear the car's bodywork.

Trailers have to show two white lights to the front, while the rear lights are the same as a car's except that there is usually no reversing light and trailers must also have red triangular rear reflectors. Trailers manufactured since late 1998 have to have orange side reflectors – although some built before that also have them.

In the UK, we use seven-pin plugs and sockets for electrical systems for towing, which means one plug to power the trailer or caravan's road lights and another to supply a caravan's auxiliary power to charge its battery and run its fridge while on the move. The latter socket has a white

above **A traditional bolt-on towball.**

right **A swan-neck towball: note the correct amount of cable slack.**

or pale grey sprung flap covering it and the pins are in a different pattern to prevent the wrong plug being used. However, many European car manufacturers' towing wiring systems have a single multi-pin socket to do both jobs and allow a reversing light to be added to the trailer.

Lorry Parts

Horseboxes as such are not built by the manufacturer whose name is on the cab – Mercedes-Benz do not build horseboxes on the production line. The lorry manufacturer builds a cab and chassis – the 'ladder' of metalwork onto which the cab, engine and running gear are mounted – then a specialist coachbuilder adds whatever bodywork the customer wants. Thus a horsebox body can be added to a new chassis or to a second-hand one from which the original body has been removed.

Old-fashioned boxes used to be made from hardwood, which offered good insulation, was kick-resistant and easily repaired, but was often very heavy and needed to be revarnished or teak-oiled to keep it in good condition. These days, the body is more likely to be made from a composite laminate comprised of layers that may be any combination of wood, fibre, plastic, resin or metal. These

left top **A British seven-pin towing socket.**

left centre **Twin towing sockets: the white-capped one is for running caravan electrical systems.**

left below **A European thirteen-pin towing socket.**

offer strength and insulation but are lightweight and easy to maintain. They may be on a steel or aluminium framework.

In a lorry, horses may face the front or back (sometimes both), in which case they have to have a breast and breeching bar, like in a trailer, to give them something to lean against during acceleration and braking. A few large lorries have horses standing horizontally across the floor, but it is far more common to have them arranged at an angle across the lorry – an arrangement called herring-bone.

On a lorry, there is usually a pair of flaps or gates that swing out to either side of the lowered ramp. Surprisingly, these ramp loading guards are not a legal requirement, even though a horse falling from the top of a ramp would not only seriously injure itself but could crush its handler!

Lorries have the same lights as cars front and rear, but also have side reflectors or side position lights.

In general, lorries have all the parts cars have, but bigger. They may additionally have a tachograph fitted, especially if the chassis and cab have had a previous life as something other than a horsebox. This is a device mated to a calibrated speed-ometer and is designed to record the lorry's speed, hours travelled and hours stationary and it is a legal requirement on trucks used for hire or reward (see Chapter 2).

The living section of a lorry is like a caravan, so it may have an auxiliary battery to supply power, a petrol generator and gas heating and cooking appliances. If it has gas appliances, the lorry will also have vents to ensure they get enough air to burn without producing deadly carbon monoxide. Any stowage for a gas cylinder must also have vents to allow gas to escape in the event of a leak.

Lorry and Trailer Floors

Horse lorry and trailer floors used always to be made of wood. The traditional method was a double skinned floor of hardwood planks, each floor being laid in at ninety degrees to the other. In recent years, many manufacturers have switched to using some form of heavy-duty, waterproof plywood, often with fibre reinforcing and resin coating. Also, for some years now, many lorry manufacturers have been using floors made of thick aluminium planking or box sections and, more recently, Ifor Williams Trailers have started using aluminium flooring in their horse trailers. Aluminium is lighter than wood and does not rot, but it may eventually corrode, especially where it comes into direct contact with steel, as a consequence of an electrolytic reaction, so it still needs to be checked.

Floors and ramps always have some form of slip-resistant surface, but it is does much more than provide grip. Thick rubber matting is usually used and this has the important jobs of helping to spread the load (by allowing the horseshoes to sink in), and of helping to absorb the impact of horses stamping or kicking.

Lorries often have a Granulastic rubber coating on the floor, which looks a little like tarmac (it is sometimes seen in trailers, too). It is made up of rubber chips in a rubber-like solution which is spread on the floor and then sets, sticking to the floor. If spread thickly it does a good job and seals the floor against moisture but its drawback is that you cannot examine the floor from above and any moisture that does get in cannot get out.

Stress on the Floor

Horses are not an ordinary load and they put an immense amount of stress on the floor of a trailer or lorry – far more than a similar weight on a pallet – because their weight is passed down through four relatively small areas. Even if a horse has the whole sole of every hoof on the floor, the total ground area covered is less than an A4 sheet of paper and the average horse is putting more than half a tonne down through that area. But a shod horse on a hard surface is putting all that weight down through the area of his shoes alone, which means that a 550 kg horse exerts a ground pressure of 3.3 kg per square

centimetre – the same as a fully laden military Land Rover weighing about six times more!

That is extreme stress for a floor to cope with, particularly when you remember that the horse does not always have all his feet on the floor and may add to the stress by kicking and stamping. When a floor gives way, horses are likely to suffer horrendous injuries that often result in them having to be put down. Even if the vehicle is stationary, they can have muscles and tendons stripped from the bone as they pull against the 'bear trap' of the broken floor. In moving vehicles, horses can have hooves or whole limbs wrenched off by contact with the road or moving parts of a lorry.

This is why, throughout this book, emphasis is put on the construction and maintenance of floors. This matter should be obvious to all horse owners, but vets estimate that more than 1,000 horses a year are seriously injured in transport accidents and faulty floors and ramps are to blame for the majority of these injuries.

2

Licences and Legal Requirements

The driving licence regulations changed in 1997, bringing in new rules about what people can drive on our increasingly busy roads. However, these new rules were not retrospective so they apply only to people who have passed their driving test since 1 January 1997.

Always make sure that you are entitled to drive a particular class of vehicle before doing so, because if you do not you will be committing serious offences that will have expensive repercussions for years to come. You will be driving without a licence for the relevant class of vehicle, probably failing to show L-plates, and, because insurance policies require drivers to have the right type of licence, you will be driving uninsured. Courts take a particularly serious view of insurance offences because they not only mean that you may be unable to pay for damage to property, but you would almost certainly be unable to meet the hefty personal injury claims that would result from a serious accident. A conviction would also mean that vehicle insurance will become expensive and difficult to get in future.

Before allowing anyone else to drive your lorry or trailer, check that they have the correct licence categories and are insured. Employers have a legal duty to ensure that their employees hold the appropriate licence so they should keep regularly updated photocopies of staff licences on file and be clear about who can drive what. Failure to do this can result in prosecution and ignorance of the law is not a defence.

Insurance

You are legally required to have a minimum of third party insurance to drive any vehicle on the public highway – which is anywhere the public has a legal right to drive, including byways and even car-parks.

Car insurance usually extends at least third party cover to a trailer while it is attached to the car. This means that if you, say, clip another car with the trailer while towing, your insurer will pay for the repair of the other car, but not for the damage to your trailer. Third party cover also means that your trailer is not covered for theft or damage while it is parked.

Most car insurance policies allow you to add a trailer (or caravan) extension which expands the comprehensive cover to the trailer, so that accidental damage and theft are covered. However, a dedicated horse trailer policy from a specialist insurer may offer better cover and give you an insurer more understanding of the demands that horses put on trailers. A policy of this sort is essential if you plan to tow with more than one towcar, or with a borrowed one.

Your car insurance may also cover you for driving other vehicles, but usually this only gives the legal minimum third party cover, even if you have fully comprehensive insurance for your own car. So, while you may legally be able to drive a lorry on your car insurance (unless the policy has weight restrictions) you would, again, only be covered for damage you did *with* the lorry and not damage *to* it. Neither would it be covered for theft.

Several firms, mostly equestrian insurance specialists, offer dedicated horsebox lorry policies which take account of the lower-than-average mileage that many horseboxes do compared to other lorries, and they often include equestrian breakdown services as part of the package, or as a low-cost option. These firms can also help with finding specialist repairers should the worst happen. In many cases, specialist insurers offer reduced rates if you insure both your horses and your trailer or lorry with them.

When buying insurance always seek more than one quote, even if you use a broker. Never lie to an insurance company (doing so is fraud) and always read the policy document when you get it to ensure that you understand what is required of you and that the policy provides the level of cover you require. The time to raise queries is when you take the policy out, not when you make a claim and find the insurer expected you to wheel clamp the parked trailer!

The Authorities

Working out which government agency is responsible for what can be difficult for the uninitiated, but this is who does what.

DVLA: The Driver and Vehicle Licensing Agency in Swansea is responsible for the administration of driving licences and vehicle registration and taxation. It publishes booklets explaining all aspects of its work. It has two inquiry units: one for drivers on 0870 240 0009 and one for vehicles on 0870 240 0010. The website is at www.dvla.gov.uk.

DSA: The Driving Standards Agency is responsible for conducting all driving tests. It also publishes the manual *Driving*, which is the standard textbook for the driving test, as well as books explaining the content of the driving tests. Its head office in Nottingham is on 0115 901 2500, though your normal point of contact is through your local DSA office in the phone book. (If inquiring about the trailer towing test, make sure you ask about the B+E towing test or they may think you mean the annual MOT-style test on lorry trailers, which is a Vehicle and Operator Services Agency responsibility.) The website is at www.dsa.gov.uk.

Vehicle and Operator Services Agency: The body responsible for 'construction and use' matters and for vehicle testing. Their national phone number is 0870 6060440 but your usual point of contact is through the local office or testing station listed in your phone book. The website is at www.vosa.gov.uk.

Licence Categories

The current licence categories relevant to horse transport are shown below. Licences issued before 1997 show the previous categories, where all shown here are covered by category A except the current C-categories, which were various classes of HGV. *All weights below, and referred to elsewhere in this chapter, are maximum*

authorized mass (gross weight) unless otherwise stated.

These categories where introduced in 1997 and have been applied to all drivers without altering their rights to drive. That is, if your pre-1997 licence said you could drive Class A, which included cars and

9. Cat.		10. From	11. To
B		13-03-74	05-06-22
BE		13-03-74	05-06-22
C1		13-03-74	05-06-22
C1E		13-03-74	05-06-22
D1		13-03-74	05-06-22
D1E		13-03-74	05-06-22
f k l n p		13-03-74	05-06-22

Licence categories as shown on a driving licence for a pre-1997 driver.

B	Vehicles up to 3,500 kg with up to eight passenger seats plus a 750 kg trailer or a larger trailer provided the combined weight is no more than 3500 kg and the MAM* of the trailer does not exceed the unladen weight of the vehicle.
B+E	B-class vehicle with a larger trailer.
C1†	Goods vehicles with a MAM between 3,500 kg and 7,500 kg with a trailer of up to 750 kg.
C1+E	A C1 vehicle with a trailer heavier than 750 kg up to a combined weight of 12,000 kg. For post-1997 drivers, the trailer's MAM must not exceed the truck's unladen weight.
C	Large goods vehicle with a MAM exceeding 7.5 tonnes with a trailer not exceeding 750 kg. (Formerly HGV Class Two or Three.)
C+E††	LGV with a trailer exceeding 750 kg. This can be an articulated lorry (formerly HGV Class One) or it can be restricted to LGVs with drawbar trailers.
D1	Minibus with between 9 and 16 passengers seats plus a 750 kg trailer (this includes the Land Rover Defender 110 Stationwagon).
D1+E	Minibus with a trailer heavier than 750 kg up to a combined weight of 12,000 kg. The trailer's MAM must not exceed the minibus's unladen weight.

*Maximum authorized mass – see Chapter 1. †Minimum age 18: ††Minimum age 21.

minibuses with all sizes of trailers, it will now show Classes B and D1 plus the E trailer classification for both. (Note that Class B can be restricted to automatic gearboxes only.)

Licences for Pre-1997 Drivers

If you passed your car driving test before 1 January 1997 you should be entitled to drive vehicles with up to 16 seats and trucks up to 7.5 tonnes. Your licence includes towing large trailers with a car. Curiously, with minibuses, you are not restricted to trailers weighing less than the car's unladen weight, even though your towing skills are untested.

The normal licence classifications for a pre-1997 driver are: B, B+E, C1, C1+E, D1 and D1+E. You only need to take an extra test to drive LGVs.

If you passed your test before 1997 you are also deemed to be a qualified person to accompany a post-1997 driver driving a car and trailer or medium goods vehicle with L-plates.

Licences for Post-1997 Drivers

If you passed your car driving test after 1 January 1997, you have class B entitlement, so are only entitled to drive vehicles weighing up to 3,500 kg with up to eight passenger seats. You are allowed to tow a trailer of up to 750 kg with a 3,500 kg vehicle or a larger trailer provided that the combination does not weigh more than 3,500 kg and the trailer's MAM is not more than the car's unladen weight.

Almost all horse trailers fall outside these limits (contrary to what the DSA's driving manual has said since 1997). At the time of writing, there was only one single horse trailer on the market that could just scrape under these rules with the right towcar – and even then it would be very close to the limits. Most horse trailers have MAMs of around 2 tonnes so they have the potential to weigh more than all but the largest off-roaders and, when combined with any vehicle suitable for towing them, the outfit's MAM would be over 3,500 kg.

Post-1997 drivers need to take extra tests to drive categories B+E, C1, C1+E, D1, and D1+E as well as LGVs. To drive a minibus they must be over 21 years of age and must have held a class B licence for at least two-years. (You do not need to take the minibus driving test if you are a volunteer driver for a non-commercial organization.) You must follow the minibus test with a minibus towing test before you can tow trailers over 750 kg.

You can practise driving these additional classes of vehicles if you display L-plates and are accompanied by someone who has held the relevant licence class for three years and is over 21. With cars and trailers, accompanying drivers can be those who passed their driving test before 1997, but with minibuses they have to have passed a minibus driving test. However, check that the insurance covers you, because a few policies have restrictions about provisional licence holders (your car licence becomes a provisional licence for other classes of vehicles).

LGV Medical Requirements

The medical and eyesight requirements for the LGV licence are much more strict than those for car licences. New LGV drivers, and those over 45 years of age renewing their licences, must have a medical examination at which their doctor completes a report form. It covers vision, the nervous system, general and cardiac health, psychiatric illnesses and diabetes mellitus.

In addition to the numberplate sight test, you have to undergo a visual acuity test which must show acuity, with glasses or contact lenses, of at least 6/9 in the good eye and 6/12 in the other. You must also have an uncorrected acuity of at least 3/60. If you held an LGV licence before January 1997 you may in some circumstances be able to continue to hold it if your sight is below these standards.

There is a long list of illnesses and conditions that could mean being refused an LGV licence. They range from those which would obviously make you a danger, like a liability to epilepsy and disorders causing vertigo, to less obvious risks such as serious difficulty in communicating by phone, and insulin-dependent diabetes, in which the sufferer is usually able to tell if problems are imminent. So, if you have a medical condition, it is sensible to check with the DVLA before going to the trouble and expense of applying for a test.

Driving Tests

If you have to take a test, think about the future to save time and money. For example, taking the medium goods vehicle test enables you to drive boxes of up to 7.5 tonnes, so if you want to drive bigger ones in future you will have to pay and train to take the large goods vehicle test as well. But if you take the large goods vehicle test, you can drive a lighter truck now but would not have the expense of taking a further test in the future if you moved up to truck weighing more than 7.5 tonnes.

The medium and large goods vehicle and minibus tests all include a theory test, like the modern car driving test. As well as testing your knowledge of *The Highway Code*, these test your understanding of everything from drivers' hours and vehicle loading to environmental issues. Sample questions can be found on the DSA's website (see Chapter 1), as can the current test fees. You will also have to have a medical, including an eye test.

The B+E test does not involve a theory test or a medical but includes an eyesight test similar to the car test. You must be able to read an old-style numberplate with letters 79.4 mm high from 20.5 metres or the new style plates introduced in 2001, with two prefix letters, from 20 metres. If

You must be able to read old-style numberplates (top) from 20.5 metres and new ones (bottom) from 20 metres.

you need glasses or contact lenses to do that, you have to wear them while driving.

You will be asked to sign a declaration that the vehicle you take your test in is insured and it must be roadworthy. When you arrive for your test you must have your driving licence (including the paper counterpart for a photo licence), valid road tax, L-plates and, if the vehicle is old enough to warrant it (see Vehicle Testing, later this chapter), the MOT or lorry plating certificate. If you fail to take any of these, the test will be cancelled and you will lose the fee.

For the lorry tests, the vehicle must be the correct type for the test you intend to take, and capable of 50 mph. For the trailer test you must have a trailer of at least 1 tonne MAM (in effect, any horse trailer) and it must have a legally compliant numberplate matching the car's – a number written on a piece of card is not good enough. Note that, if you take your towing test in a car with an automatic gearbox you will only be able to tow with an automatic, even if your solo car test was taken in a manual.

Since 1 September 2003 all driving tests, including the ordinary car test, have included the examiner asking 'show me, tell me' questions on vehicle maintenance and safety matters. Examples of the questions examiners can choose from can be found on the DSA's website (see Chapter 1). You might be asked to show the examiner where you would check brake fluid levels, or how you would check tyres. A few of the possible questions do not have relevance to horse transport (for example, there is one on how to correctly

distribute the load on a cargo trailer), but the examiner should take account of that in choosing the questions.

The trailer and lorry practical tests are basically the same, though the lorry test includes a gear changing exercise, not included in the towing test, as part of the general driving section to show that you can shift smoothly up and down the gearbox.

The tests begin at a DSA lorry driving test centre. Key parts of the test are as follows.

Reversing

A reversing area is laid out according to the length and width of your vehicle or outfit (see diagram). You provide these details on your application form but, if you have to use a different vehicle, let the examiner know before you start.

The A cones are 1 metre in from the edge of the reversing area and are one and a half times the width of the widest part of the vehicle (excluding door mirrors). Cone B is twice the length of the vehicle or outfit from cone A and the manoeuvring length is five times the vehicle or outfit length. The bay you end the manoeuvre in is also based on vehicle or outfit length, but the examiner can vary it by up to plus 1 metre or minus 2 metres. The examiner will show you a map of the area and explain the exercise to you.

You drive straight up to the A cones, stopping with the nose of the vehicle in line with them. You must then reverse back, without any part of the vehicle going over the area's yellow border, going to the left of cone B and into the bay. The vehicle

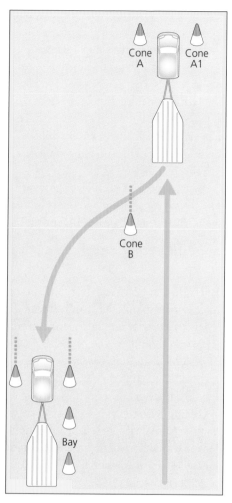

The towing test reversing exercise.

must be stopped with the tail over a 90 cm wide yellow box at the end of the bay. No part of the lorry or trailer must go beyond that box, so remember that the ramp feet stick out! Also. in the lorry test reversing exercise, the bay you back into has a barrier at the end to simulate reversing up to a loading platform.

You are not allowed to get out of the vehicle once the exercise has started and may only pull forward to get a better view, not to stop a trailer jackknifing. You can assume that the reversing area is a safe area, but the examiner will still expect to see you watching both mirrors as if you were checking for people or vehicles on the site.

Braking

This is not an emergency stop, but is intended to show that you can stop quickly and under full control in a restricted space. You will be asked to stop and shown two cones on either side of the road about 61 metres ahead. You must accelerate to about 20 mph and brake as you pass between the markers, stopping as quickly as possible without skidding or stalling, and in a straight line. *It should be stressed that this is exactly the sort of braking you would strive to avoid when transporting horses.*

On the Road

The road drive takes about an hour and should cover a variety of roads. You will have to show that you can pull away

left **The reversing manoeuvre is an important part of the towing test.**

safely, including up and down hill, from the side of the road and at an angle (for example, from behind a parked car).

The examiner expects to see that you can meet and cross the paths of other vehicles safely, overtake, keep a safe distance from the vehicle in front and exercise lane discipline. You must be able to negotiate all types of junctions correctly, including roundabouts, and follow correct procedures at traffic lights, pedestrian crossings and level crossings. You are expected to show courtesy to other road users, especially vulnerable ones like pedestrians, cyclists, motorcyclists and, of course, horse riders.

Great emphasis is put on observation and road awareness, so the examiner will be expecting to see good use of the mirrors, anticipation and correct use of signals. Not only do examiners want to see speed limits observed, but they want to see the correct use of speed – it is not always safe to drive at the speed limit, especially in a large vehicle. The examiner also wants to see care in the way you use the controls to reduce mechanical wear and tear, which in turn will make life more comfortable for the horses you transport.

Uncoupling and Recoupling

This is part of the B+E test only. An Equibrand Trailer Coupling Mirror (tel: 01327 262444 www.equibrand.co.uk) makes this exercise easier because it enables you to see hitch and towball coming together. It is permitted in the test as it is permanently fitted to the trailer.

The examiner wants to see you use a safe sequence so that you forget nothing. You will not fail if, say, you undo the breakaway cable before unplugging the lights, but you will if you unhitch before applying the trailer handbrake. If you use a stabilizer you must remove and refit it, so it may be easier to leave it at home. Tell the examiner if you have any disabilities that prevent you from carrying out any part of this exercise.

You will be asked to unhitch the trailer, park the car alongside it and then hitch up again. The process the DSA prefers is explained in Chapter 7: Basic Driving Skills.

Marking

The examiner has a marking sheet with a series of tick boxes for the various aspects of the test. Most have a box which is marked each time you show a fault, plus boxes to be ticked in the case of a serious or dangerous fault. A serious fault is something potentially dangerous, like changing lanes without looking. A dangerous fault is where there was actual danger and the examiner may have had to intervene, like a lane change forcing another driver to swerve.

Serious or dangerous faults result in immediate failure, though you continue the test because that is the service you have paid for and it will show you what you need to work on for next time.

Ordinary driving faults are added up at the end of the test and if you get more than 15, you fail. Whatever happens, the examiner will debrief you, explaining any problems.

Training

Even if your licence already allows you to drive lorries and trailers, it is still well worth seeking training, because they are very different from driving a car and a few lessons will make the transition easier and safer. You will need training to pass the driving tests, especially for the theory tests that are part of the lorry and minibus tests. There is nothing particularly difficult about the practical exercises on the handling area once you have mastered the basics of reversing a trailer or lorry, but they do require practice.

Professional training is essential, not least because driving instructors know what the examiners are looking for. They should also have the patience to teach an awkward learner and a lesson is far less likely to end in a row, as it usually does with a spouse or relative. They have also been trained to teach, which is very different from just knowing how to do something. Driver training is expensive, but it is an investment in your future safety and the safety of your horse.

There are plenty of lorry driving schools about the country, who are listed in your phone book or *Yellow Pages*. The DSA has a list of its approved lorry driving schools, though many respected schools have not yet gone through their selection process. Check what facilities the school has, especially classrooms and manoeuvring areas. As with choosing a car driving school, it pays to ask around locally to find out who has the best reputation.

Many lorry driving schools now offer B+E training, though in most cases you will have to provide a car and trailer, which means you will also have to have a suitably qualified person to accompany you to the school. Ifor Williams Trailers has a nationwide list of schools doing B+E training on its website at www.iwt.co.uk. This appears in the 'frequently asked questions/legal section' but, although all areas are covered, this is by no means a list of all of the schools.

The BHS website has a list of lorry driving schools showing which offer trailer lessons at www.bhs.org.uk

Another big advantage of professional tuition is that the instructors are kept fully up to date about changes to the test and to test vehicle requirements. At the time of writing, new standards are being established regarding weights and mechanical specifications of vehicles used in the test. By 2010, lorries used in the test will have to have anti-lock brakes and modern gearboxes with a minimum number of gears, which may render older lorries unsuitable as test vehicles – so you will have to find a more modern vehicle to take the test in, which driving schools provide.

There was also an EC driving test harmonization directive produced that required a minimum actual weight for trailers in the B+E test of 1 tonne by 2010, instead of the current requirement for a minimum MAM of a tonne. But the practical problems of adding, say, 250 kg to something like a horse trailer without risking damage to the trailer or test candidate are so huge that, at the time of writing, it looks as if this will not be implemented.

However, even if you are taking professional tuition, it is useful to put in additional practice. Once you have learned the basics of reversing, it may be possible to practise the reversing exercise at home or on your livery yard, especially with a trailer. For example, with a Land Rover Discovery and Ifor Williams HB 505R outfit 8.9 metres long, the reversing manoeuvre is 44.5 metres long, and with a shorter Land Rover Defender 90 it would be 40 metres long, so you would not need a very big field. However, it should be fairly level and not too rough, or the exercise will become more difficult, especially with a trailer which goes its own way if it drops a wheel in a hole. If you do not have the space to lay out a full reversing area, you can at least practise the separate elements of it. The important thing is to get a feel for the vehicle or outfit.

You can practise driving on the road if you display L-plates and are accompanied by someone who has held the relevant licence class for three years and is over 21 years of age, but check your insurance cover first. If you want to practise the braking exercise on the road, choose somewhere very quiet where you can see what is coming from a long way off and do not do it if anyone is in sight behind you – other drivers are not expecting you to stop suddenly for no apparent reason!

Whatever you do, do not transport horses until you are entirely familiar with the vehicle and can drive it competently. Even then, remember that lorries and trailers feel very different when carrying horses compared to the way they feel when empty. They accelerate more slowly, they handle differently on bends and hills and take longer to stop, and you will be surprised by how much you feel the horses moving. Trailers also become harder to reverse because they respond more slowly when laden.

Vehicle Testing

We all know that cars have to have an annual MOT test of their roadworthiness once they are over three years old. In fact, this applies to all motor vehicles weighing up to 3 tonnes. It is a check of all the factors affecting the safety of the vehicle on the road and if you use a car without one you are committing an offence and may invalidate your insurance. Sadly, in the UK, trailers do not require any kind of annual test, as they do in the rest of Europe.

Vehicles between three and 3.5 tonnes are subject to an annual Class VII test once they are three years old. This looks at all the things that are examined for a car MOT test, but there are differences in the brake and emissions tests and tyre and seatbelt examinations to take account of the vehicle's larger size and different layout.

Vehicles of over 3.5 tonnes undergo an annual test from a year old which is colloquially known as 'plating' because a certificate or plate is attached to the vehicle by the Vehicle and Operator Services Agency test centre if it passes. VOSA test centres can be found in the phone book or by looking on their website at www.vosa.gov.uk. Officially, the test is known as the HGV Test and vehicles are examined according to regulations laid out in the VOSA *Inspectorate Heavy Goods Vehicle Inspection Manual*. This is a very thorough test of a vehicle's safety on the road and is generally very strict. You will need to get the lorry thoroughly checked by an expert before presenting it – not least because, unlike the MOT, it is not carried out by a garage who often fix things and retest with no extra test fee.

Part of the HGV Test also includes the bodywork and its suitability for the purpose intended, so a horsebox with a dodgy floor should not get through. However, the VOSA says vehicles are judged individually, so this assumes that the inspector examining that vehicle understands the stresses horses may put on a floor.

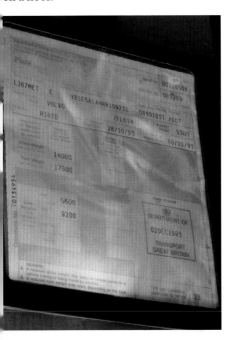

A lorry plating certificate is usually displayed in the cab.

None of these tests should be viewed as a guarantee of the condition of a vehicle. They simply show that it met test standards on the day it was examined, and only show that the parts required to be examined were in good order that day. For example, a car could pass the MOT with its clutch on its last legs so long as it still allowed gears to be engaged and disengaged on the day.

Tachographs

A tachograph is a calibrated device which records things like driver hours, vehicle speeds and distance travelled. It has to be fitted to any vehicle over 3.5 tonnes MAM, including car and trailer outfits, if used for hire or reward. Drivers of any vehicles to which they must be fitted face restrictions on driving hours.

Horse transporting vehicles are generally exempted from having tachographs unless they belong to businesses like professional horse transport companies (which also require an operator's licence). However, this is a very complex area and, if you have any doubts about whether your use might be considered as being 'for hire or reward', you would be sensible to take legal advice. If you take a horsebox or trailer abroad it would also be wise to check the regulations for the countries you are going through, because there are variations in tachograph rules even within the European Union.

Tachographs normally have to be tested periodically at cyclical intervals of two and six years but, where they are fitted to a horsebox as a speedometer, they are exempted from this as long as the seals are intact. This is because tampering with the instrument can affect the accuracy of the speedometer and stop any speed limiter fitted working properly.

Tachographs are the responsibility of the VOSA whose local offices can provide pamphlets about them and drivers' hours. These pamphlets are also available online at www.dft.gov.uk.

Livestock Laws

The rules and regulations governing the transport of livestock are complicated and fill volumes. Fortunately, because horses are not classified as 'farm animals', they are not covered by the same transport regulations and movement restrictions as cattle, pigs and sheep. In addition, most horse owners are concerned enough about their animals' welfare not to need the law to compel them to feed, rest and water them on long journeys.

However, there are still rules and regulations governing the transport of horses. Many of these should be looked after by the builder of the vehicle, but there are a few that it is wise to be aware of.

All vehicles used to transport equines must have 'adequate' headroom. By adequate, the EU requires that the animals are able to stand naturally. The Brussels bureaucrats have also been consulting on new regulations for the long-distance transport of all livestock and, as part of that process, proposed minimum headroom for horses that vehicle

manufacturers have objected to as excessive. If the new regulations came in, they would apply when transporting animals for over eight hours. The existing regulations require the ramp and floor to provide 'reasonable grip' and there must be no more than a 20 cm step between the two, even though horses will walk over much higher steps once they know they are there. Indeed, some owners of trailers with American doors, which open sideways, say there is often no need to pull out the slide-out ramp, as many horses step in happily from the ground. However, the regulation does mean that there is less chance of a horse or handler tripping as they enter the vehicle.

In trailers and in lorries with stalls facing front or rear, a breast bar is a legal requirement because it gives the horses something to brace against during braking. Without it, they would only be able to brace by pushing their noses against the bodywork! It is also usual to have a breeching bar behind the horse, simply to keep the animal in place while you raise and lower the ramp. This does not seem to be a legal requirement, but it would be unwise not to have these bars, not least because of the risk of the animal getting out if you had to lower the ramp at the roadside in an emergency.

When you are transporting more than one horse you are legally required to have a partition between them, unless they are mare and foal.

Anyone transporting animals at night has to have a means of illuminating them. Trailers and lorries have internal lighting for that purpose, but it is also wise to carry a good torch. Leaving interior lights on also seems to help horses who are worried by the lights of other vehicles, especially in trailers with the rear top doors open.

If you are going on a long journey, you are required to have food and water for the animals, but the journey times between rest periods laid down for farm animals are far longer than most horses owners would want to subject their horses to. In most horse lorries it is also possible to go through from the cab, allowing an assistant to feed and water horses on the move. However, it is best for drivers and horses to take a break every two or three hours, because that keeps drivers alert and gives horses a rest from keeping themselves steady in the trailer or lorry. It also gives you the chance to check that the horses are all right and do not need the ventilation or rugs adjusted.

3

Choosing a Towcar and Trailer

Do not buy a towcar or trailer without first doing your homework. There is no point buying one that will not suit the other and, if you have looked into things, you will not be misled by ill-informed or dishonest vendors. Car dealers are not horse towing experts, so may not fully realize what it involves and many will go only by the car's maximum towing weight. However, if a dealer tells you that a particular car is not suitable, take their word for it, because they have nothing to gain from saying that. Similarly, trailer dealers cannot know every car's towing abilities, though they probably get a lot of feedback from customers on the more common types of towcars' foibles. Whoever you buy a towcar from, whether new or used, make it clear that you want it to tow a particular weight of trailer. The Sale of Goods Act not only says that goods must be of reasonable quality and suitable for the use intended, but includes any special requirement made known by the purchaser to the vendor, such as the need to tow a trailer of a stated weight.

Weights

The most important consideration in buying a towcar and trailer is weight, or, rather a whole host of weights. But before you start looking up car and trailer weights, think about your horses' weights because this is the key to working out what sort of outfit you need. Also, take into consideration whether this is likely to change in the time you own the outfit. There is no point buying a lightweight towcar on the basis that your daughter only has a pony if, in eighteen months time, she is likely to progress to a horse.

Horses' weights are important in calculating both what sort of towcar you need and what sort of trailer you buy. The main consideration is that their weight has to be added to the trailer's weight when calculating towing capacities. But if you have very large horses, you also have to make sure that the trailer has the weight capacity to carry them. Most manufacturers produce larger trailers intended for big horses, which not only offer more headroom but have an increased maximum weight.

Many equine veterinary practices have specialist weighing machines to get the horse's exact weight, which is the ideal way of checking it. Weigh tapes provide a useful guide but, if you use one, leave a good margin for error and remember that they are based on horses of average conformation. Another good guide is the calculation below, in which the horse's length is measured from the withers to the point where the tail joins the body.

(Girth in cm, squared x length in cm) ÷ 8717 = weight in kilograms

Always work in kilograms because, since the motor industry is metric, all the weights quoted by manufacturers are in kilograms.

You must add together the weights of the heaviest horses you are likely to transport as a joint load, and add this

figure to the unladen weight of the trailer. If you only plan to transport one horse, and thus use a lighter towcar, make sure that you do not fall into the trap of

above **A weigh tape gives a good guide to a horse's weight.**

left **A trailer's chassis plate gives the chassis number as well as the MAM and axle loadings.**

offering someone else a lift to a show –
even if it is only a short journey.

Many people make the mistake of
thinking that the only weight they have
to consider when choosing a towcar, or
matching a trailer to their car, is the
maximum towing weight – but that should
only be seen as a maximum. It is based on
the car's ability to pull away on a slope,
usually an 8 per cent gradient, but
sometimes 12 per cent, and does not even
mean that you would be safe coming back
down the slope. Maximum towing weight
is usually more than the car's unladen
weight and, in the case of off-roaders with
additional low ratio gears, it can be
considerably more. That is because a good
off-roader in low ratio first gear would be
capable of pulling away with your stable
attached, never mind a trailer, but that
doesn't help when something weighing
1.5 tonnes more than the car is pushing
you into a downhill bend.

The ideal maximum weight for a trailer

is 85 per cent of the towcar's unladen
weight, as long as that is below the car's
maximum towing weight (there are a few
cars for which the maximum is lower).
That gives the towcar a substantial weight
advantage over the trailer and thus lessens
the risk of the tail wagging the dog.
However, if you are transporting two
horses, this can be difficult to achieve. For
example, two average sized horses in an
average sized trailer weigh around 1,880
kg, which puts them slightly above the 85
per cent weight of even a Land Rover
Discovery. Indeed, the only cars currently
on the UK market able to keep above the
85 per cent figure with two horses are the
Range Rover and Toyota Landcruiser
Amazon, which both weigh around 2.5
tonnes.

For this reason, if you want to tow a
trailer with two horses aboard, your
choice of safe towcars is limited to a
full-size off-roader – vehicles like the
Discovery, Land Rover Defender, Range

**The Land Rover Defender
110 stationwagon is
legally a minibus, so
drivers who have passed
their test post-1997 have
to take two tests to drive
and tow with it.**

Rover, Landcruiser, Mitsubishi Shogun, Isuzu Trooper, BMW X5, Jeep Grand Cherokee and Mercedes Benz M-Class. Small leisure sports utility vehicles, like the Land Rover Freelander, Nissan X-Trail, Honda CR-V and Toyota RAV4 do not have the weight to cope with two horses.

If you only plan to transport one horse or pony you will get away with an ordinary car, though it will have to be a large one to handle a horse and trailer safely. An average horse and trailer together weigh about 1,330 kg so, if we stick to the 85 per cent rule, that means towcars like the BMW 5-series, large MPVs (people carriers), Lexus GS300, most four-door, four-wheel drive pickups, Rover 75, Saab 9-5, Skoda Superb, Vauxhall Omega and the Volvo V70.

But, if you have the choice – and the budget – the more leeway you can give yourself on weight, the better, because horses have a far from ideal weight distribution to ensure trailer stability. Put it

this way: caravan and box trailer owners are advised to stow the heaviest luggage low down and evenly around the axle then secure it, but a horse has the opposite effect because his weight is up high with 60 per cent towards the front, and he moves. This is why it is important to give yourself as much margin for error as you can.

The final weight to consider is maximum noseweight, which is the downward pressure a trailer exerts on the car's towball. All car manufacturers quote a maximum, though often not in their brochures – you may have to ask the dealer or the manufacturer's customer service department to look it up. If the noseweight exerted by the trailer is too great it will push the back of the car down and lift its nose; if it is too low it can raise the back of the car. In either case, this seriously affects the outfit's stability and braking ability.

With caravans and trailers carrying static loads you can adjust noseweight by the way you load the vehicle and check it with nothing more sophisticated than a piece of wood and bathroom scales. However, you cannot do that with horses, and it would be very dangerous to try, because the trailer has to be unhitched to do it, so you risk the horses tipping the trailer on its tail.

So, horse owners need a towcar with a maximum noseweight of at least 75 kg, preferably more. Many off-roaders have maximum noseweights of more than double that and cars with self-levelling

left **A large car like this BMW 525i is suitable for towing a trailer with one horse.**

suspension, like many upmarket estate cars, also have higher-than-average nose-weights.

Incidentally, always avoid putting heavy objects, like water containers, in the front or back of the trailer, because this affects the noseweight. It is much safer to carry them in the car.

Choosing a Towcar

For many people, the natural choice is an off-roader because, as well as having good towing characteristics, they offer practical load-carrying ability for all the tack and other equipment horse owners need to take with them. They are also usually large vehicles with plenty of weight and it is this, not the four-wheel drive (4WD) that makes the difference. That said, 4WD is worth having because it makes it easier to pull away on loose or slippery surfaces. If the system is of a type that can be used on the road, you also have the advantages of extra traction when pulling away on steep hills and cornering and, with some systems, of more even engine braking when descending steep hills.

But make sure you understand what you are buying, because not all 4WD systems can be used on the road. Some manufacturers add to the confusion by using more than one system. For example, Jeep have road-going and off-road only 4WD in the Cherokee and mark one Grand Cherokee, according to both engine type and trim level.

Part-time off-road only 4WD, as found in pre-1984 Land Rovers, Daihatsu Fourtraks, Isuzu Troopers, most pickups

and mark one Mitsubishi Shoguns, simply engages the front wheels to the transfer gearbox, which splits the drive front-to-rear. The problem is that it does not include a central differential, which is a system of gears that allows the front and back wheels to travel different distances when cornering. Without that, taking a corner in 4WD on tarmac 'winds up' the transmission, and the tension this creates can break expensive parts. It is also dangerous because, if a car with a 'wound up' transmission hits a slippery patch – even just a puddle – all the tension goes out through the first wheel to slip, resulting in unpredictable handling.

Cars with full-time or road-going part-time 4WD have a central differential, usually with some way of locking it manually or automatically for off-road use. Cars with part-time road-going 4WD usually feel more reassuring when towing in 4WD. If you buy a car with 4WD it is essential that you read the handbook to make the best of the system and avoid costly mistakes.

One drawback with off-roaders is that they are usually more expensive to run than large cars. Not only do their weight and poor aerodynamics hit fuel consumption, but maintenance costs are usually higher, simply because there is more to maintain and many parts are heavy-duty items. However, many people, particularly country dwellers, who try an off-roader never want to change back to a car because of the practicality, commanding driving position and ability to get you there in all weather conditions. But, that said, don't let 4WD give you a false sense of security. For example, on snow and ice, it feels a lot more reassuring than a 2WD car, but when you want to stop the same laws of physics apply, so stopping will be just as difficult.

4WD Terms

Differentials are systems of gears that allow driven wheels to turn at different speeds and all cars have at least one on the driven axle, but full-time 4WD requires three. Differential locks (diff locks) lock the gearing so that power is not wasted on spinning wheels in off-road driving – never drive on hard surfaces with the differential locked. A limited slip differential, which may also be found on some powerful 2WD cars, is set up to allow only a limited amount of difference in speed (slip) between two wheels and is normally used on the rear axle.

Dual-ratio gearboxes allow you to select high ratio gears for road use and low ratio for off-road work. You can use low ratio get a very heavy trailer moving, or when crawling in traffic, though you can only do that if you can change to high on the move (check the handbook). With some full-time systems (like Land Rover's) you can use low ratio on the road, perhaps for towing in very hilly places, but other systems automatically lock the centre differential.

Viscous couplings are simple fluid-filled devices in which the fluid becomes more viscous (flows less easily) if plates attached to different drive shafts start moving at different speeds. They are used either to progressively lock a centre differential, or in place of one, when they allow the amount of power going to the front or rear wheels to be varied according to grip. Many 4WD systems now use electronic controls to do this job (see below).

Electronic Aids

Electronic driving aids used to be exclusive to luxury cars but have worked their way down to the most mundane models. Many of these aids have significant benefits when towing and some are worth paying extra for.

ABS prevents skidding when braking by monitoring the rotational speed of each wheel and making sure it matches the car's forward speed and the rotational speed of other wheels. As soon as it senses a wheel slowing down it will ease the brake pressure on that wheel to allow it to rotate instead of locking up. This retains stability and directional control under braking. In a solo car it does not significantly reduce braking distance but, when towing, it has been shown to reduce the stopping distance by as much as half. It also seems to stabilize the outfit under heavy braking, possibly because it senses the trailer trying to push the car to the side.

Since 1 July 2004, all new car models must have ABS. Most cars suitable for towing horse trailers would long have had it as standard but if you have a choice of used cars with and without, you would be foolish not to choose ABS because of the major contribution it makes to your safety. Unfortunately, it cannot be added to a car after manufacture.

Recent additions to ABS are electronic brake force distribution, which modulates the brake pressure according to the load, and emergency brake assist, which senses the driver's sudden move from throttle to brake in an emergency and applies extra braking force – making it feel as if you braked a fraction earlier than you did! Both of these are an asset in any car.

The ABS wheel sensors have also been used to create a number of other aids. Electronic stability programmes (ESP) sense the sideways movement of the car when cornering hard (understeer) and use the brakes to counter it. Cornering brake control stops braking in bends from destabilizing the car. You should never need these if you tow considerately enough for your horses, but they could save you if you are caught off guard or the trailer's braking is not as good as it should be. ESP must be turned off when driving off-road because it mistakes the slightest sideways movements caused by driving on slippery, uneven ground for the car becoming unstable. It will then brake wheels when you least need it, which is unhelpful when you are trying to get the trailer moving on a muddy showground.

BMW's X5 was the first car with electronic trailer stability control as part of its ESP. This recognizes when a trailer's electrical circuitry is plugged in and monitors any sideways 'yaw' movement caused by the trailer snaking. If that happens, it then brakes in a way that will stabilize the car, giving you a better chance of bringing the outfit back under control. Other manufacturers are now offering this.

Electronic traction control (ETC) prevents or reduces wheel spin caused when pulling away or through applying too much throttle in slippery conditions. It does the opposite from ABS by sensing when a wheel is starting to spin and applying the brake. This can be very useful when towing, especially when pulling away on hills and poor surfaces. It could be the difference between you getting off a muddy showground unaided and being towed off. You need to experiment with it, though, because some systems operate better if you gradually ease off the throttle, to give them a chance to work, while others need more power to give them something to work with.

ETC is often now combined with 4WD and may be linked to the system which electronically distributes drive to the wheels most able to use it. One drawback with electronically controlled 4WD systems like this is that, because they rely on braking the wheels to maintain traction, they can lose momentum in situations where you would rather they didn't, like in deep snow or mud.

Hill descent control first appeared in the Land Rover Freelander but something like it is now found in many off-roaders. This is intended for letting the car gently down steep muddy slopes under control, again using the ABS sensors and brakes. You are unlikely to use it for that when towing, but some HDC systems, including Land Rover's, can assist the traction control at low speeds.

Volkswagen's Touareg and post-2003 Landcruisers have electronic systems designed to stop the car rolling back or spinning its wheels during hill starts, which would obviously be useful when towing.

Electronic aids are often initially unique to one car manufacturer but usually spread to others, as ABS has done. This is because they are usually developed by a car maker in conjunction with electronics specialists, like Bosch, on the condition that the car company gets exclusive use for a certain time. But one problem with understanding electronic aids is that, while there are many industry-wide acronyms, like ABS and ESP, some manufacturers invent their own, so ETC becomes A-TRC (Active Traction Control) on a Landcruiser.

While electronic aids are intended to increase your safety margin, do not erode this function by driving up to it. If you feel the ABS pulse through the brake pedal when you brake normally, or an ESP warning light comes on, it is a hint that you were going too fast for the conditions. Electronics cannot defy the laws of physics so, while ABS may normally allow you to steer away from danger while braking hard, it cannot do so at 60 mph on ice!

Engines

The most powerful engines do not necessarily make the best towing engines. This is because torque, the engine's twisting or pulling power expressed in Newton metres (Nm) or pounds-feet (lb ft), is more important than outright power, expressed either as horsepower (bhp, or the German equivalent PS) or in kilowatts (kW). More importantly, a good towing engine normally has its torque peak at fairly low engine speeds (measured in revolutions per minute – rpm or revs) and maintains a good percentage of that peak over a wide rev band – such an engine is said to have a good spread of torque. However, you occasionally find engines where the peak torque is fairly high, say 4,000 rpm or more, but the engine develops such a good 'spread' that it still shows excellent flexibility at low speeds.

So, you might think that say, a mark one Honda CR-V's 145 bhp 2-litre petrol engine would tow better than the Land Rover Discovery's 136 bhp TD5 turbodiesel, but the Honda develops only 134 lb ft of torque at a high 4,500 rpm, while the Discovery manages a beefy 221 lb ft at just 1,950 rpm. In fact, the TD5 engine is producing more than the Honda's peak figure from just 1,000 rpm. This indicates that the Land Rover would be the much more relaxed towcar of the two, requiring much less gear changing and being able to hold higher gears longer.

This is one reason why many people choose turbodiesels as towcars. These engines almost always develop masses of low rev torque and many of the latest generation engines with advanced common rail direct fuel injection (see below) hold their peak torque over wide rev ranges. For example, the Mercedes-Benz ML 270CDi's 295 lb ft peak is maintained from 1,800–2,600 rpm.

Turbodiesels also have the advantage of being much less thirsty than large petrol engines. With older diesel technology it used to be reckoned they were about 30 per cent less thirsty than petrol engines of equivalent performance, but the latest common rail technology (see Diesel Terms) is generally even more frugal.

Diesel is also a much safer fuel than petrol because it has to reach quite high temperatures before it will ignite.

Diesel Terms

Diesels are called compression ignition engines because, instead of using a spark plug, the fuel is ignited by the heat from extreme pressure created in the cylinder. This means they have no ignition system, so older ones used no electrical power when they were running, though modern ones usually have electronic fuel injection control and an electric fuel pump. This makes them much more reliable in damp conditions, though they do need hefty battery power to turn them over for starting.

Most diesels now are turbocharged. A turbo is an exhaust gas driven turbine which spins a compressor to force-feed air into the engine. It increases power without a great increase in fuel consumption and, in diesels, usefully boosts their performance at higher engine speeds. Most turbodiesels have an intercooler which looks like a small radiator, is sometimes mounted on top of the engine and is used to cool the air after it has been through the turbo, increasing its density and, therefore, the amount of oxygen in a given volume.

Diesel engines have advanced a great deal in recent years and many now offer similar refinement to petrol engines, especially those using the latest diesel technology, which are also cleaner and more economical. Large cars with modern turbodiesel engines also tend to hold their value better than petrol models because

those who can afford, say, a BMW X5 4.4i petrol's 21 mpg solo and 14 mpg towing can generally afford to buy a new one!

Most advances in turbodiesels have centred on the way the fuel is injected. The first step was direct injection, which first appeared on a passenger car in the 1989 Land Rover Discovery. Old diesels used indirect injection, whereby the fuel is squirted into a pre-ignition chamber set off the engine cylinder. Direct injection squirts fuel straight into the cylinder which provides better control of the quantity and timing of fuel injection and allows higher injection pressure. The higher the pressure the better the fuel vaporizes and the more efficiently it burns.

The next step was common rail injection. Instead of having individual pipes from the fuel pump to each injector, with fuel delivered to them in turn, common rail uses a single pipe to supply the injectors and the fuel is maintained at a constant, very high pressure (usually around 20,000 psi). Electronics open the injectors with extremely precise timing that can be varied to suit all sorts of mechanical, physical and even atmospheric conditions. This makes common rail very efficient and clean. Peugeot-Citroën say this technology made their HDi turbodiesels around 15 per cent more economical than their same size direct injection engines.

The Volkswagen Group have gone a step further with their pump-injector (PD or *pumpe düse system*), in which each injector has its own high-pressure fuel pump so that the fuel pipes are not under pressure. This allows even higher fuel injection pressures (about 30,000 psi) because there is no risk of pipes stretching under the force. These engines are extremely efficient and capable of combining high performance with extreme economy, so even the sporty 150 bhp Golf GT TDi, capable of 134 mph, does 52 mpg!

Toyota has its D-4D turbodiesel technology which is a superb range of diesels, mating common rail to four valves per cylinders with variable valve timing. Valves let the air into the cylinder and exhaust gasses out and the timing of their opening and closing affects the engine's behaviour. Timing is usually a compromise because the ideal for low engine speeds is different from that for high engine speeds, but electronically controlled variable timing gets round that.

Diesels used to need more frequent servicing than petrol engines because they are harder on their oil, but new mechanical and oil technology has changed this. For example, the Land Rover 2.5 TDi engine needed servicing every 6,000 miles but the common rail 2.5 TD5 turbodiesel that replaced it is serviced every 12,000 miles. That is because it has a centrifugal oil filter, which spins at 15,000 rpm, and synthetic or part synthetic oils are specified. *This makes it essential that the correct grade of oil is used when servicing or topping up modern turbodiesels.*

Most of the information here also applies to lorry turbodiesels, though some of the technology now used in cars was used much earlier in the slower-running truck engines.

Gearboxes

Whether you tow with a manual or an automatic gearbox is largely a matter of personal choice – though one important consideration for anyone taking the towing test is that, if you pass it in an automatic, you will only be able to tow with an automatic even if your ordinary licence allows you to drive manuals.

Manuals are cheaper and generally offer better control, but towing will exaggerate bad gear changing technique. Manuals can also make traffic jams and hilly areas hard work when towing, especially in working off-roaders with clutches heavier than those in ordinary cars.

Automatics make smooth towing easier, but many people feel that they do not offer the same control as a manual. These days, however, automatics are getting so sophisticated that the difference in terms of control, performance and economy is getting smaller all the time. There are even automatics that 'learn' from the driver's use of the throttle and brakes and alter their changing pattern to suit the driving style. Many adapt to the extra load a trailer creates and some recognize when the car is going downhill and do not change up, so that engine braking is maintained. Pulling away and hill starts are also easier in automatics.

Most automatics now have 'normal' and 'sports' or 'power' modes. In the latter, they shift down more readily on modest throttle pedal pressures and hold gears longer, which can be helpful for towing, though you must take care. Some of these boxes can be a little over-willing to shift down when towing, sometimes shifting down two gears with little provocation, and many show a marked reluctance to change up to top even when being driven solo. However, a useful technique is to use 'sport' when you need to get moving or on twisty or hilly roads and to flick the switch to 'normal' to cruise, or on less demanding roads.

Increasingly, many automatics now have a manual touch-change override (like Tiptronic or Steptronic) where the driver selects gears manually by tapping the lever back and forth. These systems effectively create a clutchless manual, though their electronics stop you abusing the engine by holding too low or too high a gear. These gearboxes mean that you can tow on the

This modern automatic gearbox (right-hand lever) has a manual touch change for more control.

easy parts of the journey in automatic but make smooth manual changes in difficult or unusual conditions. This gearbox option is not the same as the manual 'hold down' positions on all automatic gearboxes, which allow you to lock the box out of the gears above that position with the box still behaving as an automatic to that point.

Whatever gearbox you choose, it must be suitable for the different driving requirements of towing. You need a gearbox in which there are no big gaps between the gear ratios, so you do not find that at a given speed, say, third gear sounds too busy but the vehicle is struggling in fourth. It is particularly important to avoid gaps like this at commonly held speeds, like around 30 mph. If you notice such gaps when test driving the car solo, they will be exaggerated by a trailer.

With a manual system, you want a gearbox that shifts easily with a precise movement through each position's 'gate' because, when you are trying to drive smoothly for your horses, you do not want to be fighting the gearbox. Also, especially on older off-roaders, make sure that the clutch is not too heavy for you.

You want automatics to change up fairly easily on part throttle, but not so readily that, when towing, they may do it too enthusiastically. This can lead to them 'hunting' up and down the ratios which, apart from being annoying, can make them overheat. But when test-driving an automatic, make sure you try all the gearbox settings. All automatics should change down quickly at least one gear when you use 'kick down', which is a switch activated by flooring the throttle for overtaking – but you also want it done reasonably smoothly.

Towing Equipment

Cars registered after 1 August 1998 can only be fitted with an EC type approved towbar. These use all and only the fixing points specified by the car manufacturer, must have a loop to attach the trailer's breakaway cable to and must carry an EC type approval sticker or plate giving details like the type approval E-number and the car it is approved for. In practice, the plate may not be easily visible, especially on bars designed to hide behind the bumper.

You cannot put an old, non-approved towbar onto a post-August 1998 car even if it looks the same. Ironically, many car manufacturers have long tested their towbars to higher standards than the EC type approval requires, and still do so. Vauxhall engineers say that when they put a bar to type approval standards through their own test, part of it sheared off! So,

while manufacturer approved towbars are often more expensive than those from independent towbar manufacturers, they may be worth the extra. However, car manufacturers usually buy-in towbars from specialist companies, so the same bar may be available wearing either the car manufacturer's or the specialist firm's badges.

Towbars may be adjustable and/or detachable. Adjustable ones are useful if you tow more than one trailer because, while most have a standard towball height of about 46 cm, some more specialist, non-horsy trailers may not. Detachable towbars allow you to remove the towball when not in use. On some off-roaders this is done with a standard bolt-on towball attached to a removable plate, but most detachable bars have a swan-neck towball on which the ball is moulded to a long, curving neck.

Detachable bars have the advantage that, because the ball can be removed when not in use, it is less likely to get damaged and will not get in the way when

Cars registered since 1998 have to have towbars with a type approval plate.

you are loading luggage. Some are so well concealed that, when the ball is removed, there is no sign the car has a towbar fitted. But you must follow the fitting instructions carefully to ensure that the ball is locked on, and keep the mechanism clean and lubricated. As the removed towball is extremely heavy it must be stowed safely if it is carried in the car, or it can become a lethal missile in an accident, which is why many cars have purpose-made stowage for it under the boot floor.

A drawback with both fixed and detachable swan-neck towballs is that it can be difficult to fit stabilizers between the towcar and trailer. A stabilizer is a device the main job of which is to lessen the side-to-side movement of the trailer, but blade stabilizers, which have a blade or bar between a bracket on the car and another on the trailer's A-frame, also greatly reduce the see-saw movement called pitching. They are well worth having on a horse trailer because they improve the ride for both horses and people while enhancing the handling of the outfit. Make sure any stabilizer fitted is designed for use with large trailers.

There are three types of towing electrical socket. In Britain we normally use different seven-pin plugs known as a 12N and a 12S. The simplest towing electrical system has only the 12N plug, which connects the car's indicators and tail lights to the trailer. The 12S socket is usually added for towing caravans because it runs their interior lights, battery charging and fridge, though it also includes a connector for a reversing light, which might be a useful addition to a

Many detachable towbars are completely invisible when the ball is removed. (left above **ball in place;** left below **removed.)**

below **Detachable towballs must be stowed safely when not in use.**

orse trailer. The 12S plug and socket are usually colour-coded with white or pale grey collars and covers.

In Europe, and on car manufacturer towbars for many European-made cars sold in the UK, they use a single 13-pin plug and socket that does the jobs of both the 12N and 12S. Don't worry if your car comes with one of these and you don't want to change your trailer's plug. You can get two types of adaptor: a neat little one that converts the 13-pin to a 12N or a 13-pin plug with Y-shaped cabling going to 12S and 12N sockets. If you change your trailer's plug to 13-pin you can add a reversing light to it, but this means that you may not be able to tow it with a different car if you need to in an emergency.

Fitting towbars and electrical systems are jobs best left to experts and, if the car is under warranty, these should only be done by the franchised dealer, to retain warranty cover. Towballs and towbars are

under a great deal of stress, so all the nuts and bolts must be of high tensile steel, ideally with some sort of locking facility that prevents them coming undone, like sprung washers or Nylock nuts, which have a built-in nylon washer to grip the bolt thread. *If you replace a towball, use only the nuts and bolts sold for the purpose of securing them.*

While wiring-in towing electrics is something a competent DIY car electrician could manage on older cars, with modern cars it could do expensive damage. Many cars now use Multiplex wiring, which links everything electrical via a power wire and a message wire, instead of having separate wires running between each component and its switch. When you flick a switch it sends a signal along the message wire, which is picked up by a receiver which turns on the relevant component. This

This twin blade stabilizer from Bulldog is designed for large trailers.

reduces the amount of wire in a car literally by a mile or more but if the message wire is cut and rejoined, the change in resistance can interfere with the signals. It is said that even changing the plug provided for connecting trailer electrics to the system could cause problems.

When haggling over the price of a car, use the towbar and electrics as a bargaining point. A dealer may be more willing to throw in a towbar, or to do the job at a discount, than to reduce the price of the car, especially if he has been told by the car manufacturer that discounts may not be offered on that model. After all, if a towbar secures the sale of an expensive off-roader he may make far more profit than supplying and fitting the towbar cost him – though check the price of the bar before you push too hard because some lightweight, integrated towbars, like the detachable one offered by BMW, cost several hundred pounds.

Buying Used Towcars

The checks you make when buying a used towcar are basically the same as for buying any other used vehicle but it is worth remembering the extra stress towing can place on a car and its major components.

The essential checks on a used car are mechanical and general condition, mileage and status. Magazines like *Used Car Buyer* and *What Car?* and monthly used car price guides like *Parker's* have sections giving buying advice and lay down in detail things you should check about cars and vendors.

You may not know enough to make a full mechanical inspection of a car, but a good look round could save you the expense of getting further, professional checks made. Stand back and look at the car: is the general impression one of good order and cleanliness? If a private vendor couldn't be bothered to clean it up to sell it is unlikely they cared for it during the rest of its life. A dealer who cannot be bothered to tidy cars up before putting them on display may be equally slapdash about the rest of his preparation before sale.

Check the bodywork for signs of repairs and resprays. Good quality repairs should not be cause for concern, but then, neither should you be able to spot them. On off-roaders, have a look underneath for signs of damage from clumsy off-roading. Check that all the lights, indicators, washers and electric windows, mirrors and sunroof work and that the towing socket is in good condition.

Examine tyres for damage and uneven wear – don't forget the spare – and if they are worn demand either new ones or money off. Uneven wear along the edges of the front tyres suggests that the steering is out of alignment, which is cheap and easy to put right but, if the treads are worn to too much of an angle, tyres may still need replacing.

Inside the car, look for damage to the upholstery and trim, especially in the back of off-roaders and estate cars, which are often used for dogs and heavy loads. Wear to the gearknob and steering wheel should match the mileage – a gearlever polished by constant use would not be right on a car with modest mileage.

Under the bonnet, and under the car, look for oil and water leaks. Check the coolant for signs of oil and the oil for signs of water, which may show up as a deposit like mayonnaise where the water and oil have emulsified. That suggests a gasket has gone, allowing the two to mix, which means expensive work on the engine.

On a test drive, be aware of the feel of all the major controls. Steering on some off-roaders is more vague than on most cars, but there should not be excessive play or any odd noises.

Engine, clutch, gearbox and brakes all come under extra load when towing, so

you need to pay particular attention to checking them. But, so long as the owner has restricted towing to within the limits laid down by the car manufacturer, the car should not have suffered unduly. Find out what the owner has towed, and how often.

When you test-drive the car be aware of how much travel the clutch has before it engages – if everything happens at the end of its travel it will need replacing soon, which can be expensive – especially on off-roaders. Brakes should be effective and not too noisy, though it is normal for drum brakes on off-roaders used in dirty conditions to squeak a bit. The gearbox should feel normal, with no odd sighs and rattles, especially in the lower gears, and 4WD systems should not clank and shudder excessively. Off-roaders with worn gearboxes often jump out of second or third gear if you accelerate hard and then suddenly come off the throttle. Engines should sound normal and not smoke, though a little white smoke from cold diesels is usual. With off-roaders,

above **A badly perished tyre, which would be unsafe under load.**

right **The inside of the oil cap should show only oil, not 'mayonnaise'.**

don't forget to check that the 4WD and low-ratio gearbox engage and stay engaged, though remember that you normally have to stop, or be going very slowly, to move into low ratio. It is normal in some off-roaders for the low ratio selector lever to be stiff and for those with electronic selection to take a little while to make the shift fully (the warning light normally flashes for a few seconds before glowing steadily).

Check the towbar and its anchorage points for damage caused by clumsy reversing, off-road use or overweight towing. With ordinary cars, a lot of overweight towing can actually weaken the bodywork's spot welds and lead to the body creaking on uneven roads.

Check the mileage against MOT certificates and the service record. A service record is important, because it can help confirm mileage and shows that servicing has been carried out to the manufacturer's schedule. It can take the form of dealer stamps in a book, or a collection of receipts. If the owner is a DIY mechanic, or a company or farm vehicle has been serviced in their own workshop,

ask to see proof, like receipts for parts or a company service record. Turbodiesels, though longer-lived than petrol engines if cared for, do not do well if servicing is skipped or skimped.

Incidentally, never buy an off-roader that has belonged to a construction company, or shows signs of having been leased by one, because they are usually abused for the length of a site contract then sold off. In addition, constant exposure to wet concrete and cement dust stimulates under-body rust. Farm owned off-roaders can have been abused if they were a workers' runabout, but because farmers are usually self-employed they tend to look after the vehicles they have invested money in.

If anything about the car or the vendor does not seem right, walk away. You are spending a lot of money and it is not worth taking risks when there are plenty of other cars about.

The safest way of buying a used car is from a franchised dealer with a man-ufacturer approved used car warranty. The best warranties have few exclusions from cover and a very high standard of

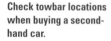

Check towbar locations when buying a second-hand car.

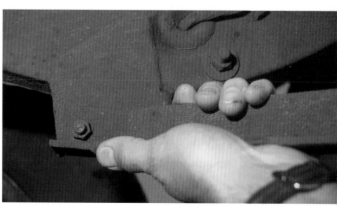

benefits, which include things like UK and European breakdown cover, MOT failure cover and exchange policies in case something goes seriously wrong. But, on top of that, the car manufacturer lays down strict preparation standards for the car, including a status check, and has systems in place to make sure dealers do as promised. Franchised dealers tend to cream off the best examples of used cars, putting any less desirable ones out to the trade, so the cars do tend to be more expensive. However, when car magazines run checks on these schemes they usually find that the cars are rarely far enough over the trade's 'book' guide prices for the difference to be more than the warranty benefits would cost if bought separately. You might also get a manufacturer's towbar fitted as part of the deal.

The next safest way to buy is through a used-car dealer. They are bound by all the trading laws so, if something is not as it seems, you have some redress through the courts (see Chapter 5). The dealer should also care about his local reputation enough not to sell dodgy cars, though it is worth asking around just in case. Many used-car dealers offer warranties, but if they cost extra, get a copy of the warranty handbook to make sure you are buying something that is worth more than the paper it is printed on. If you are buying an off-roader, there are many used-car dealers who specialize in them and they are generally a safer bet than the ordinary dealer who just has the occasional one, and may not know much about them.

Buying privately, through the small ads, can save you money, but just about your only legal protection is for misrepresentation of goods, which means if the vendor has lied about the car. That can be very difficult to prove unless you have written evidence, like the advert, and even then it could prove expensive to enforce. You must satisfy yourself that the vendor and the car are genuine. Never take the vendor's word for things, seek evidence. Walk away from any vendor who does not seem to know how various aspects of the car work, who is cagey about it or, most importantly, offers excuses instead of documentation. Be wary of anyone who only gives a mobile number or says they will meet you anywhere other than their home – they may be trying to prevent you from tracking them down later!

When you phone up about an advert always say you are phoning about 'the car you're selling', not 'the Discovery you advertised in the *Evening News*'. A genuine owner will immediately know what car you mean, whereas a dodgy trader trying to pass himself off as a private vendor will have to ask which car. The only reason a trader would pretend to be a private vendor is to prevent you from taking full advantage of the trading laws when something goes wrong. If you have any doubts about someone in this respect, call your local Trading Standards office because they know most of the people doing this in their area and, if your vendor is dodgy, they appreciate the 'intelligence'. (See Chapter 5 for what to do if a purchase proves bad.)

You can save even more money buying at auction, but you get little time to inspect cars and get little consumer law protection, so that is best left to experts.

Dealers should run status checks on cars they sell with the data handling firms HPI Equifax or Experian. These checks confirm the car's mileage and that it is not stolen, an insurance write off, or subject to a finance sceme (under certain finance schemes, like hire purchase, the vehicle belongs to the finance house, not the buyer, until the final payment is made). The dealer should be able to show you paperwork proving that the test has been done, while manufacturer-approved used warranties usually include a check certificate. But, if you buy privately, it is essential that you carry out this check yourself before you hand over any money. Both companies back up their checks with compensation if anything proves wrong. HPI are on 01722 422422 or contactable through the RAC on 0870 6061122, and Experian's services are available to the public through the AA Used Car Data Check on 0800 234999. To get a thorough check you will need the car's registration number, Vehicle Identification number (VIN) and, preferably, engine number.

Data checks are cheap, especially when you consider that if the vehicle you buy is stolen you could lose everything you paid for it. Getting that back though the courts could be costly and difficult, assuming you can find the vendor.

If you have little mechanical knowledge it is worth investing in a vehicle engineer's inspection, especially if you are buying something as complex as an off-roader. These inspections cost a few hundred pounds but could save you much more and

you may be able to use the engineer's report to negotiate the price down to cover any repairs needed. You may find vehicle engineers in your local *Yellow Pages* but the most common route is to use the vehicle inspection services of the AA (0800 7834610) or RAC (08705 333660), or the Automobile Buyers' Services (01625 576441). These examinations include a status check and, if the car fails that, that is all you pay for.

Choosing a Trailer

Once you have sorted out the weights involved you might think choosing a trailer is largely down to budget, but there are a lot of other things to consider and going for your second choice to save a few hundred pounds might be regretted later.

If your horse is exceptionally large, headroom becomes important and most manufacturers produce taller than average trailers for big horses. But don't get an extra roomy trailer if you don't need it because, apart from the extra cost of buying one, the increase in size means an increase in weight, which reduces towing safety margins and increases fuel consumption.

Research has shown that horses prefer travelling facing the rear because they can cope more easily with acceleration and braking. Rice Richardson were the first company to produce a trailer designed for the horses to travel facing backwards, and others may follow, but you must never travel horses that way in a trailer designed to have them facing forwards, not least because there will not be enough room for

eir heads between the breech bar and
e ramp. The biggest problem with horses
cing the rear in a trailer is that horses
ve about 60 per cent of their weight at
e front (forehand) and, if that weight is
o close to the rear of the trailer, it will
duce noseweight or, worse, create
egative noseweight. That can result in
rious instability and you should check
ith the manufacturers of such trailers
hat they have done to prevent this. The
ce Richardson trailer is longer than a
ormal front-facing trailer, so the horses'
ils are well forward, but this also makes
heavier than most two-horse trailers.

If you usually transport only one horse,
ll width breast and breech bars are a
ood investment, allowing you to use the
ailer without a centre partition. Never
se a trailer without bars. Given this much
ace, horses usually stand diagonally
cross the trailer, though those used to a
artition may move about more at first as
ey find the best way to stand. It is best to
e them with a rope to each side of the
ailer so they cannot turn round,
specially if they are small.

If your pony is small, check that breast
nd breech bars can be set low enough to
erve their purpose. In most trailers, these
ook into bolt-on brackets, so getting
em to fit lower than normal may only be
matter of drilling an extra set of holes.
owever, if you are buying a new trailer,
et the dealer or manufacturer to do this
avoid warranty problems and get lower
oles as well as, not instead of, the normal
nes, or you may have problems selling
e trailer when you want to replace it.
Indeed, many manufacturers make

trailers to order, rather than building
masses in the hope of selling them,
so adaptation to suit your needs or
preferences can often be added at the
factory. If not, the dealer may be able to
make them, so do not ignore a model just
because, say, you would like an extra
window in it.

Do not be tempted to make or adapt
fittings yourself. A breast bar, for example,
may look simple but it has to take the force
of half a tonne of horse thumping against
it on heavy braking.

Take time to look at trailers at shows
and dealers' premises. Look at fittings
and the way things are finished, but if
there is something you don't like on a
manufacturer's trailers check to find out
whether they have changed it on the
latest models before discounting them.
Ask other horse owners about their
trailers and the dealers they bought them
from. Have a look at older versions of the
trailer you intend to buy to see how they
take wear – though remember that manufacturers improve models all the time,
so the unsightly rusty chains holding a
latch pin on may nowadays be made of
stainless steel.

Do not assume that, because one
manufacturer's trailer is heavier than
another's, it is also stronger. Modern
lightweight materials can be as strong,
or stronger, than old, heavy ones. For
example, why have a steel roof when
lighter aluminium or glass fibre would be
as strong?

When comparing prices of new trailers,
make sure you are comparing like with
like. The days are gone when essentials

like spare wheels and galvanized chassis were 'extras' on some makes – but do both trailers come with, say, sealed-for-life wheel bearings, or full-width breast and breech bars?

From time to time, firms start importing trailers from foreign manufacturers. Some of these offer innovations not found on home-produced trailers and, especially if they are from European manufacturers, they should comply with British regulations. The drawback is that, if the importer stops bringing them, in or the marque (make) does not take off, you could have trouble selling it on in the future, or getting spares. It may be the BMW of horse trailers, but if nobody knows what it is, your advert will attract far fewer responses than the ones next to it for Ifor Williams and Rice trailers. For the same reason, it may also lose more money than a home-grown trailer because, in the second-hand market, it is the demand for the model that sets the price it fetches, whether you sell it privately or trade it in.

When you think you have decided what sort of trailer you want to buy, see if you can borrow or hire one to find out whether you and your horse get on with it. Many trailer dealers have hire services, or may allow a 'test drive' of a used one. But, if you hire or borrow, make sure that the trailer is insured for your use, because you do not want to spend your trailer budget on replacing someone else's!

Thinking Ahead

An important consideration when choosing a trailer (already mentioned in passing) is the availability of spares and servicing. If you are unable, or unwilling, to do the servicing yourself you have to consider how close the local dealer is – you don't want to spend a day just taking your trailer to be serviced! But you must also get matters into perspective.

Apart from warranty work, you do not have to have the work done by the manufacturer's franchised dealer, because any trailer or caravan dealer should be able to carry out standard servicing jobs like brake adjustment. In addition, unless you make unusually high use of your trailer, it is likely to need to visit the dealer only once a year. The only proviso is that a non horse trailer specialist might not realize the importance of things that could be more serious with a horse trailer than with other types of trailer, such as a deteriorating floor.

If you are capable of maintaining the trailer yourself, this is not such a problem. Most manufacturers and independent parts dealers have mail order services for spares, so getting them should not be a problem.

Fortunately, most mechanical parts are not unique to an individual make or model of trailer, because manufacturers buy them in. This applies to parts such as axles, hitches, brakes, wheels and jockey wheels – even items like door catches may also be used for something else. That means that many spares can be obtained from any trailer or caravan dealer, though you must make sure you get the right parts, because horse trailers may use the heavy-duty versions of look-alike parts found on lighter weight caravans.

Similarly, when buying a used trailer, do not let finding spares put you off good trailers from manufacturers no longer in business, because the parts manufacturers are almost certainly still supplying the industry. Many trailer or parts dealers know who used what part when, or can identify, say, a hitch, or suggest an alternative that will fit.

The only spares problem with trailers from manufacturers no longer around lies with parts unique to the trailer, principally bodywork. Even so, flat metal or composite panels, riveted or bolted to a frame, are easily replaced, and it should not be too difficult to find local metal-workers and body shops who could fashion a curved metal panel. Similarly, repairing minor damage to glass fibre should be within the scope of specialists more used to working with boats, caravans and vehicle bodies, but getting a uniquely shaped new glass fibre roof made could be too expensive to be practical. It is a good idea to bear this in mind when buying any new or used trailers.

Make sure that the trailer looks light and airy to assist easy loading.

Features to Look For

Anything used to transport horses needs to be light and inviting inside, or you will have trouble getting horses to enter it. Look at the trailer with the ramps down to see if it gives the impression of walking into a well-lit room, or a dark cave.

Most trailers at least have a window in the nose. It is handy if this is low enough for the driver to see through from the towcar, in order to keep an eye on what the horse is doing. Horses also seem to like looking out of side windows as you drive

Horses seem to like side windows on boxes and trailers.

along and you can often see through these from the car's door mirrors. Unfortunately, not many trailers have side windows as standard, though they can usually be added by the manufacturer or dealer.

Front unloading is safer and a lot easier than rear and, while not having this facility might save a few hundred pounds when buying a new trailer, you will probably lose that when you sell it on because used trailer buyers have a wide choice of front unloaders. I do not think it matters which side the front unload goes to. Those who make trailers with left-hand ramps in the UK argue that, if you need to unload the horse at the roadside, this is safer, but you rarely unload horses on the road and your chances of finding anywhere safe to do it are slim, regardless of what side you unload from.

Galvanized chassis greatly lengthen the trailer's useful life and you are unlikely to find a new trailer of any kind which is not galvanized. This was not always the case, and used trailers without galvanized chassis are now likely to be old enough for the rust to have got a serious hold, so avoid them.

One-piece rubber matting gives better protection to the floor, though it usually needs two people to take it out for cleaning. Granulastic flooring is rubber chips bonded in a rubber-like solution, which is spread on the floor and sets to look like tarmac. Done properly and thickly, it offers a good, hard-wearing flooring that is easily cleaned, but it makes it impossible to check the state of the floor beneath and, if moisture seeps in, it cannot easily get out. Matting needs to be thick because it helps to absorb impacts and spread loads, reducing the stress horses put on floors.

Most trailer floors are of wood. They are either a double-skinned floor of solid hardwood, with planks at 90 degrees to each other, or a heavy-duty plywood, often with fibre reinforcing between the layers, and resin sealed. More recently, Ifor Williams switched to aluminium floors, which have long been used in lorries. These require less maintenance and should be more resistant to deterioration than wooden floors, though they still need to be cleaned and regularly inspected for damage. Critics point out that aluminium can corrode, especially where it is in contact with bare steel, but this takes some time to create a weakness and is much more obvious than internal rot in a wooden floor. Anything that reduces the need for maintenance is a boon, so sealed-for-life wheel bearings, introduced in the mid 1990s by Ifor Williams, are worth having. If a trailer has these, the nut under the dust cap in the centre of the wheel will be a stake nut, which has a raised collar that is punched into a groove on the axle to stop the nut turning. If it has a castellated nut, locked with a pin through slots that make the nut look like battlements, then it has bearings that need regreasing every two years

Ramps with counterbalance springs or gas struts are far easier to lift than those without, and this includes even the smaller front-unload ramps. Catches that are simple to use and maintain can also save a lot of grief.

Inside, you want partitions and bars

that are easy to move and remove. Padding isn't that essential, because anything that feels soft to our touch is likely to be squashed flat by the weight of a horse leaning on it. But you do want rounded edges, no potentially damaging bolt heads or other projections, and all cut or welded edges smoothed off. Check that you are able to reach tying-up loops.

If you regularly transport only one horse, it is worth having full-width bars as well as the usual partition system, but most manufacturers only fit them as extras.

Good ventilation is a must. A good trailer has some permanently open ventilation, though this is not always easy to see. For example, many have a vent under the lip of the roof at the front of the trailer. You also want vents you can open when the weather is warm: these usually take the form of roof vents.

Prop stands are little legs that can be dropped down at the rear corners to steady the trailer when parked. They are usually an extra and can be useful if you have a horse who is worried by the trailer shaking as he steps onto it, or if you want to unhitch the car from the trailer at a show, but leave the horses in it.

Some manufacturers offer mesh grilles that fit to the partition between the horses' heads. These make unloading awkward, so are only worth having if you have a problem with two horses who squabble, which most don't.

Anything that helps security is worth having. Most trailers these days have locking hitches and some manufacturers automatically register the first owner with The Equipment Register.

There are many little conveniences manufacturers offer as extras, ranging from built-in feed bowls, through tack tidies to electrically pumped water hoses for hosing down horses at shows. If you really think these would be handy, by all means have them, but consider what weight they will add and where. A tack

When checking aluminium floors, pay attention to areas around steel fittings.

box in the nose may be useful, but if your towcar has a low maximum noseweight you could create stability problems by adding weight to the trailer's nose.

When you are buying a new trailer, buy all the extras you want with it, because you are able to negotiate an all-in price that will make the extras cheaper than if you order them separately later.

Running In

When you buy a new trailer, make sure you read the handbook and any warranty material you are given. Manufacturers and dealers say that many of the queries they get from new trailer owners would not be made if people read the documentation, and it is only by doing so that you will get the best from your investment.

Apart from telling you how its fittings work, the handbook explains how to look after it and, most importantly, whether there is anything that needs attention after a running in period. It is usual, for example, for the trailer brakes to need adjusting after the first 500 miles or so to compensate for the system bedding in – shoes wearing to match the drum walls, cables stretching and so on. For that reason, many dealers offer a free check and adjustment after a certain period or mileage and it is sensible to take up that offer, especially as it may even be a condition of the warranty. It also means that they can check everything was assembled properly and nothing has worked loose.

Treat your trailer as an investment, because it will only retain its value if it is looked after.

Buying Used Trailers

Before you buy a used trailer, make sure that you are going to save as much as you think. Well-kept trailers from well-known manufacturers hold their value, so you may find that once you have haggled with the local dealer the difference between new and used may not be that great – and the new one will come with a warranty.

Buying a well-worn trailer is also a false economy because of the cost of making it safe and legal. Many a horse owner has got a 'bargain' trailer home to find when they start taking it apart to make the 'minor' repairs that it needs a lot more work than they thought. For the same reason, never take the vendor's word on the likely cost of a repair – if you want to take the risk, find out how much the work would cost from the person who is going to do it.

Frankly, there are so many trailers out there that you would be far better off finding one that does not need the work. If a repair is simple or cheap, why hasn't the vendor done it and asked a higher price?

Before you go to look at a trailer, ask questions about its condition, age, how long the vendor has had it, how often it has been used, how it has been looked after, whether it has any damage and why it is being sold. If the vendor is vague, or appears not to have thought about important things like servicing, don't even bother looking at it. Someone who does not know the answers to such simple questions has either not looked after the trailer or it is not theirs to sell.

Read the trailer maintenance information in Chapter 11 to get a better

dea of what needs to be checked and how
t should all look.

If you have been looking at similar
railers and talking to their owners at
shows, you should have built up an idea of
what that type and age of trailer should
ook like. If you view one that appears to
pe in a bad state for its age, don't waste
your time making a closer inspection,
pecause it probably will be in a bad state.
Similarly, if someone could not be
pothered to clean out a trailer to sell it,
you have to question how well they have
looked after it when nobody was coming
to look at it.

If general appearance is good, the first
thing you should examine is the floor.
Horses suffer terrible injuries if they go
through trailer floors so, if you have any
doubt about the soundness of a floor, do
not buy the trailer unless you have
sufficient budget to replace it and the
trailer price is low. Lift the matting to
examine the floor from above and inspect
it from below. If the vendor is unwilling to

unscrew anything holding the matting
down, make it clear you are not buying it
without checking the floor. In particular,
check where moisture can get in around
the edges of the floor and around any
floor fittings, like the slots for partition
supports. Push a screwdriver at any
suspect area: if it is rotten, it will be soft.

If a trailer has had the floor replaced,
ask to see documentation that proves it
was done properly by someone with
experience of horse trailers. Non-horse
trailer repairers may consider the original
manufacturer's flooring to have been
unnecessarily strong, because they do not
realize the stress a horse puts on a trailer
floor. Do not touch a trailer with a patched
or DIY floor and be suspicious of one
which shows evidence of recent attempts
to make it more difficult to see faults, like
painting.

If the floor is sound, give the ramps the
same thorough going over for the same
reasons. Horses may only be on ramps for
short times, but not only do they face risk

**Checking a wooden
floor for rot.**

of injury themselves if one breaks, there is the additional risk of injuring whoever is leading them on. Ramps should also raise and lower easily and their catches should all be sound and easy to use.

Check the condition of the lights. Cracked lenses are cheap to replace and easy to get if they are common makes, but if someone could not be bothered to do that, what else have they neglected? Plug the lights into a car to see that they all work.

Inspect the tyres. They should all be in good condition and of the same size, weight rating and construction (it is illegal to mix radial and crossply construction on the same axle). They should have a reasonable amount of tread and they should be free from cuts and bulges. Make sure they are not perished by looking for telltale little cracks in the sidewalls. Have an idea of how much it costs to replace trailer tyres so that you can haggle the cost off the trailer's asking price if they need renewing.

Brakes should have been adjusted for wear regularly. Ideally you should get underneath and check the amount of friction material still on the brake shoes through the inspection holes in the brake back plates, but this may not be practical. With the handbrake off, you should be able to push the hitch back, though it needs a hard push, and it should then return to its original position. If it does not, it has either not been lubricated properly or the hitch damper (like a gas strut inside it) has seized.

Ideally, you should take the trailer for a test tow, or at least get the vendor to do so. The jockey wheel should wind up and down easily and the hitch should lock on smoothly. In a safe place, brake firmly and watch to see if the trailer pulls up straight. It should also tow straight and there should be no delay between the car braking and the trailer brakes coming on. When you get back, none of the wheel centres should feel excessively hot – if they do, a wheel bearing or brake is seizing.

Make sure that ramp catches are sound and easy to work.

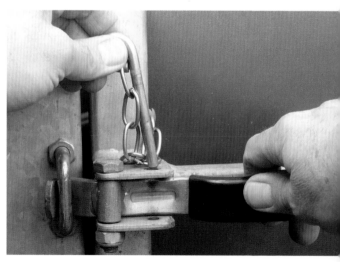

Before you hand over any money, seek vidence that the trailer belongs to the endor, because there are no registration ocuments for trailers, so theft is easy. he crime prevention group Trailerwatch stimates that around 300 horse trailers year are stolen in the UK and, at the ime of writing, their website (below) isted more than 750 stolen trailers, so here is a good chance of being offered a uspect one.

If you have viewed a trailer somewhere ther than the vendor's home, ask for vidence of their name and address. Be articularly wary of anyone who has no aperwork or handbook for a relatively ew trailer.

Never buy a trailer which has signs of aving had a chassis plate removed or hassis number (which may be anywhere n the chassis) filed off – there is only ne reason for doing that. A give away is hat, quite often, the thief will paint a alvanized chassis to hide such tampering nd there is no good reason for painting ver galvanization.

If the trailer is registered with an rganization like The Equipment Register t will bear a sticker carrying their phone umber, so call them with the trailer's hassis number or check it online at vww.ter-uk.com (TER charge a modest fee or this service). Some manufacturers also eep databases on which reported thefts re recorded and an online check can be nade on the www.trailerwatch.com vebsite, which receives theft notification rom several manufacturers and insurers. Jnfortunately, none of these checks are nfallible because there is nothing to compel trailer buyers to register their ownership with anyone, or to report theft to these organizations.

If you buy a stolen trailer you risk losing all the money you paid for it because it still belongs to the original owner, or their insurers. You also risk being prosecuted for receiving stolen goods if you could reasonably have known it was stolen. Don't think you are unlikely to be found out, because you have to give a chassis number to insure it and, at some time, you will need spares for which you have to quote the number to get the right part. Sadly, this is how many buyers find out that 'their' trailer is stolen.

The safest place to buy is from a franchised trailer dealer. Not only do you get the full protection of the trading laws, but they have their local reputation to worry about and tend to cream off the best of the trailers traded in to them. In addition, anyone who traded in a trailer to buy one of the same make must have been happy with it. A used trailer from a dealer may cost a little more than one sold privately, but the peace of mind and the fact that it should have been thoroughly checked and serviced, make it worth the extra.

If you buy a used trailer privately, it is wise to get it professionally checked, preferably by a horse trailer specialist.

Getting Acquainted

Whether your trailer is new or used, it is new to you, so take time to get to know it before you put horses in it. This applies even if it is the same make as your last trailer, because manufacturers change things all the time, either to improve the product or because a part previously used is no longer available. It is better to work out how a breech bar is adjusted in an empty trailer than while trying to stop an impatient horse backing out!

Practise opening and closing doors and ramps, moving partions to the loading positions and putting them back again, hitching up and unhitching and, simply, driving and reversing it.

While it is hitched up, practise loading and unloading the horses. It is better to solve any problems when you have plenty of time than when you are in a rush to go to a show.

This will also give you time to check the trailer over to make sure nothing is wrong and to put things right before you make full use of it. Before you take the horses anywhere, just check that the wheel nuts and the nuts and bolts holding in place vital parts like axles and hitches are all tight, especially on a new trailer which has never been on the road before. Sometimes, the initial use moves and stretches things, loosening nuts that previously seemed tight enough. Indeed, on any vehicle, wheel nuts should be checked about 30 miles after changing the wheel.

Finally, take a good drive with it to get used to the feel of towing it before you take horses out in it.

4

Buying a Lorry

The way lorries are made takes us back to our motoring past. Early in the twentieth century, most car companies built the chassis with the mechanical parts, then the bodywork was added by a specialist coachbuilder. So, until after World War II, your Rolls-Royce may have had bodywork by Mulliner, Labourdette, Hooper, Park Ward, Gurney Nutting (yes, really) or any of the hundreds of local craftsmen coachbuilders then around.

It is still the same with lorries, because there is no way one vehicle manufacturer could make all the different bodies required for the amazing variety of jobs lorries have to do. So, when someone tells you they have a 'Mercedes horsebox', they really have a horsebox built by a specialist coachbuilder onto a Mercedes-Benz chassis and the German truck maker had no part in building the horsy part. The lorry chassis comprises a steel 'ladder' with the cab on top and the engine, transmission, suspension and wheels attached below. Indeed, they are so mechanically complete that they are often driven from the chassis manufacturer's

factory or import centre to the coach-builder's workshops.

The so-called 'Transit-sized' boxes are usually built on what manufacturers call a chassis or custom cab, like a lorry chassis. Though most vans are built by the manufacturer as a complete vehicle, in the same way as a car, they also produce chassis cab versions, to which other people add bodies. However, a few are converted from the high-roof versions of the standard vans. Note that Transit is a Ford registered trade name and not a vehicle type, so calling a similar sized van from any other maker a Transit is like calling every hatchback a Golf. However, even people in the industry call equivalents from Citroën, Fiat, Iveco, Mercedes-Benz, Peugeot, Renault, Vauxhall or Volkswagen 'Transit-sized' because everyone knows what that means.

So, when you buy a horsebox lorry you have to choose the products of two manufacturers at the same time. Probably the best route is to choose the horsebox builder first and then take their advice on which chassis work best with their designs. Similarly, if you are buying a used vehicle, decide which coachbuilder's designs you like and look at those rather than the chassis manufacturers' names, because the biggest differences between boxes will be in the horsy part.

The great thing about this is that, if you are buying new, your lorry can be tailored exactly to your needs and it can be anything from simple horse transport – almost a self-propelled trailer – to a mobile stable yard with all the comforts and conveniences your budget allows.

However, as with a car, you must make sure the cab suits you: check that you are comfortable, can reach all the controls, see all the instruments and, if your mobility is restricted, that you can actually climb in and out of the cab. Find out what comes as standard on the chassis: one may be cheaper than another but, if the cost of the dearer one includes things you need that are extras on the other, it may work out cheaper.

Also, investigate the availability of spares and servicing in your area because lorry dealers may be less accessible than car dealers. You might like a Scania cab but, if the nearest dealer is 80 miles away, getting servicing and spares could become a chore.

If you have a big budget you can fund a completely new vehicle, which means a brand new chassis with a body designed to your specifications on top. This simplifies matters in that you know everything is new and in good order. However, most 'new horseboxes' are a new body built onto a second-hand chassis. If you follow this route, make sure you know how the builder is going to source the chassis, its age, mileage, how it will be prepared and what guarantees they will give on it.

Frankly, if you cannot afford a decent chassis, don't bother doing it this way. There is little point in getting an expensive new body fitted to a chassis that does not have a reasonable life ahead of it. True,

Make sure that you can get comfortable in the cab. This one has satellite navigation, a dual-ratio gearbox and hands-free phone.

The chassis of a Mercedes-Benz Sprinter, into which a horsebox could be built. It has a 5-tonne MAM.

you could fit the body to another chassis later, but that is expensive and it may not fit a more up-to-date and reliable chassis. You would be far better off buying a complete vehicle second-hand because you will probably get more for your money.

Remember, too, that if your budget is extremely limited, you may be better off buying a towcar and trailer. An unreliable lorry gives you nothing but grief and expense, while retrieving one after a roadside breakdown is time-consuming and expensive.

Whatever You Want

Carriage driver Sallie Walrond's unique horsebox is a fine example of how the coach-built nature of trucks means you can tailor one exactly to your needs, no matter how specialized. Sallie also went about it in a characteristically common-sense way.

She used to transport her carriage and ponies to events using a Rice trailer and specially adapted Land Rover pickup, with planks and a hand winch used to haul the carriage into the load bed. Apart from the inconvenience of this arrangement, it also meant little security for an expensive carriage and its fittings, and that the carriage often had to be cleaned before entering the show ring.

Her 10-metre long horsebox has a purpose-built carriage area with a power winch to pull the vehicle up the rear ramp, tie-down points in the floor, to which the carriage axles are lashed, and windows into the horse area through which the shafts project, protected by travelling boots. There is also a curtained-off chemical toilet in the corner of this section. Sallie stresses the importance of having an isolator on the winch as a fail-safe current cut-off in case the hand control jams on.

The ponies travel in the middle of the

truck – the most comfortable part – with a side unload ramp, so it is not necessary to unload the carriage to get them out in an emergency. Sallie was worried about urine rotting the marine ply floor, so she had it coated in thick Granulastic, which she insisted was curved up the sides. She wanted no drain holes for the same reason, insisting that shavings do the job of soaking it up well enough.

The living section is accessed through a door from the horses' section, allowing more usable wall space in the small section for tables and seats. Sallie only wanted somewhere comfortable to change and have refreshments, so it is simply

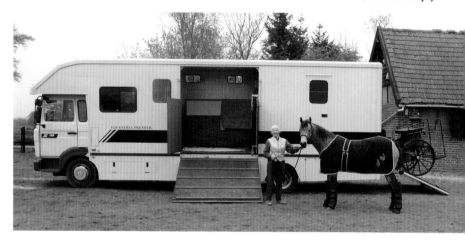

above **Sallie Walrond's unique box has a rear ramp for the carriage and a side ramp for the ponies.**

above **Sallie wanted a simple but comfortable living section.**

left **Sallie's carriage is simply winched up the ramp.**

equipped with a sink and small gas hob, but there is enough space above the cab to sleep two in sleeping bags.

Being quite small, Sallie spent a lot of time choosing a cab, finding several in which she could not reach the pedals. She went for a 7.5 tonne Renault Midliner, which also had the advantage of a lower than usual chassis, giving shallower ramp angles and making it easier for her to lift the ramps.

Before ordering the body from Equestria Horseboxes in Royston, Hertfordshire, she drew her exact requirements, including all the measurements and the positions of fittings, from the carriage tie-down rings to the toilet's curtain rail.

She says that the Land Rover and trailer's only benefits over the lorry were cheaper running costs, four-wheel drive and that the pickup could be used for shopping trips.

Weights and Payloads

As with trailers, weights are important when choosing a lorry, not least because overloading a commercial vehicle is an offence with hefty fines and the potential for extreme inconvenience.

As explained in Chapter 1, all vehicles have a maximum authorized mass (gross weight) laid down by the manufacturer – it is what we mean when we talk of a 3.5 tonne or 7.5 tonne truck. That is made up of the kerb weight of the lorry plus the payload, which is everything you put on board including you, your passengers, horses, tack, water and even your sandwiches. So, when choosing a vehicle, make sure that the payload will be big enough to take horse and human occupants with enough left over for all the odds and ends. Some 3.5 tonne 'two horse' boxes would actually be very close to their limits with two average-sized horses aboard.

A compact box, ideal for transporting two horse of modest size.

Remember, too, that when you are planning your dream horsebox, every item of fitted equipment you add to it takes the equivalent weight off the payload. So, if the cooker and microwave add 75 kg to the weight of the truck, the payload drops by 75 kg – about the weight of the average adult. In smaller boxes this can be crucial.

Many boxes have roof racks, which can be useful, but check the maximum roof loading if you think you are likely to make a lot of use of one.

Engines

While most manufacturers of medium goods vehicles do produce petrol versions, the vast majority of lorries sold in Europe are diesel, for the very good reason that large petrol vehicles are very thirsty. A neighbour of mine swapped the petrol engine in his box for a diesel because he said he could actually see the fuel gauge needle moving as he drove along! The pros and cons of diesel engines, and diesel terminology, were covered in Chapter 3.

Most large modern lorries are designed to have tilting cabs to allow easy access to the engine. Some horseboxes are now made so that this facility is still available but in most, the cab is fixed because of the bodywork around it. If the vehicle you are looking at has a fixed cab, make sure that provision has been made inside the cab to allow access to the top of the engine, or you could have problems if it requires major work. This access is often hidden under matting so, if you fit anything in the cab, make sure that you do not prevent the matting being removed.

Bodywork

To many people, the body of a lorry is just a metal box, but while that is so on removals vans, it is not on horseboxes. Indeed, this is one of the reasons why removals-style box vans converted to horseboxes are best avoided. Such a body may be able to carry cargo to the equivalent weight of the horses, but even something heavy like a piano does not put the same extreme stresses on the floor as a horse – and neither does it kick the walls! Reputable converters usually halve the distance between floor supports on a horsebox compared to a lorry used for conventional cargoes. Consider that half a tonne on a pallet is spreading its weight over more than 3 square metres whereas a half tonne horse is putting it down through an area about the same as a page of A4 paper. That alone represents considerable stress on the floor, but horses also stamp and kick. (This issue of stress on the floor has been dealt with in detail in Chapter 1.)

Aluminium is lighter and more rot-proof than wood but it can still corrode and, as it is a relatively new material for this purpose, nobody really knows how long such floors can last.

Horseboxes usually have some sort of drainage in the floor, especially if they are designed to carry several horses. Check that this is not just an unlined hole in the floor, especially in wood where it is likely to promote rot. Some manufacturers guard against this by having long pipes hanging down from drain holes so that the urine draining out is carried well away from the floor and its supports, but make sure these are not likely to spray it over the transmission or brakes.

Metal side panels are undesirable on a horsebox. They provide no insulation against heat and cold, which also promotes condensation and, in turn, the risk of fungal growths which are bad for horses. Horses are also perfectly capable of kicking through all but the thickest of sheet metals, leaving sharp edges which can cause serious injury.

Hardwood used to be a favourite material for horsebox bodies because it gave good insulation, took equine assault well and was easy to repair, but it is also extremely heavy, so it is rarely used nowadays. Most manufacturers now use composite sheeting, like Glasonite, which is light but strong and has good insulating properties. These materials usually take the form of reinforced layers of plastics and wood with a smooth, decorative outer layer bonded to the facing edges. Modern composites may be entirely of reinforced plastics or resins and are extremely strong.

Look carefully at the design of the interior. It should have no sharp corners with which horses or people might come into contact. Fittings should be robust and well finished but not so heavy and stiff that it takes all your strength to undo a catch.

A common option on larger boxes nowadays is an awning extending from one exterior side of the vehicle to provide a covered area at shows. Such awnings give useful cover in wet weather, saving you from trying to tack up inside the box, and can give welcome shade in summer. But check that they are high enough at the edges for horses to walk under safely, and that they are strong enough to withstand blustery conditions, when they can be subject to enormous stresses as they behave like sails. Powered ones need a manual emergency folding facility.

Showgrounds can get very muddy, so

A horsebox floor viewed from below shows more closely spaced supports than a cargo lorry's.

make sure that the lorry has recovery rings strong enough to take its own weight coupled with the resistance of deep mud. It is best to have recovery rings front and rear so that you have the option of pulling in either direction. Rear rings need to be low enough to allow a pull without the recovery rope or cable damaging the bodywork, though on trucks with long rear overhangs this may be difficult.

Paintwork is not just cosmetic, but protects the bodywork, though it is not strictly necessary on composite bodies. If you want your name or sponsors' logos added, the best option is vinyl artwork, or what is often called vehicle wrapping. Vinyl artwork can take the form of stick-on standard letters or of shapes cut from self-adhesive vinyl (a high-tech version of Blue Peter's sticky-backed plastic) using computer controlled cutters. Vehicle wrapping is where similar material is printed with designs and lettering, often using vinyl that matches the vehicle's

paintwork – this is the system used where you see trucks bearing pictures of the products they deliver. The advantage of these methods over painting is that they can be removed if your sponsors change or if you sell the vehicle. Some upmarket horsebox manufacturers offer artwork as part of their service, or you can go to a specialist company locally.

above **Vinyl artwork is an excellent way of personalizing your box; it can be removed if you change lorry or sponsor.**

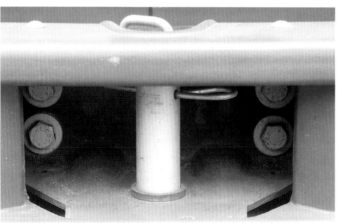

Attachment points for recovery ropes are essential, preferably front and rear.

Technology

Much of the electronic technology found on modern cars is also found on lorries and anything that improves your safety margins is worth having. The most obvious example is anti-lock brakes (ABS), which became compulsory on new lorries in 2002. If you are using an older chassis, it is worth seeking one with ABS because it greatly increases your safety and that of other road users around you. In addition, by 2010 it is likely to be compulsory for lorries used for taking driving tests to have ABS fitted. Since it is a feature that has to be factory-fitted, you cannot have it installed afterwards.

Top of the range truck chassis often have air sprung suspension whereby, instead of conventional metal springs, they have huge airbags inflated by a computer-controlled compressor. This gives an exceptionally good ride, not least because it compensates for loads, but in addition it can usually be lowered for unloading, which reduces the ramp angle.

Powered ramps are popular on larger vehicles but they must have a fail-safe, manual way of lowering them, too. The most common cause of vehicle fires is electrical and you do not want your horses stuck on a burning lorry because the electrical circuitry has burnt out and you cannot lower the ramp. Neither do you want to arrive home at the end of a long day to find you cannot unload the horses because a fuse has blown.

A battery isolator switch is worth having because it can be used to stop battery drain while the lorry is unused and it provides an instant way of disconnecting the power in an emergency, like a fire or crash.

A useful 'luxury' is a closed circuit television monitor in the back so that you can check on the horses as you go along and instantly see the cause of any odd noises or movements. However, it is illegal to have a television screen in the view of the driver on the move unless it conveys important information relating to the driving of the vehicle and nobody has yet tested in court whether keeping an eye on the horses is legally 'important'.

An increasingly popular option on new boxes is satellite navigation but, while it is getting cheaper all the time, I am not

These big rubber cylinders are air springs, giving the best ride possible.

convinced the technology justifies the outlay. These systems use signals from geo-positioning satellites to pinpoint your location and plan routes using digital maps on CD ROMs or DVDs. The best systems work with real-time traffic jam information and can plot routes around problems. Satellite navigation generally works well on main routes where it means you can concentrate on driving because it warns you of approaching junctions.

However, I have tried several systems in cars and they have all been flawed. In rural areas they often see unmade tracks as real roads and use them in their routes, which could be disastrous in a lorry. Some systems plan circuitous 'quickest' routes in rural areas to avoid going through villages or to make use of dual-carriageways. They all have 'points of interest' but these do not include even large permanent show grounds, like the East of England or Stoneleigh – though once you have found your way there, most systems allow you to 'mark' them for next time. On the plus side, if you have a problem, they will tell you where you are for calling breakdown and emergency services. Even so, some systems cannot cope with British rural addresses, so only say you are in 'High Street', or give the name of the road and postal town, not that of the village you are actually in.

Smartnav from Trafficmaster, best known for their traffic jam warning system, is a cheaper alternative to CD-based navigation systems. You press a button and it dials their control centre, who send your route to the in-vehicle system, so it is ideal for technophobes. The base model has no screen, giving only spoken directions, but works well apart from getting the route downloaded in poor cell phone reception areas. You pay an annual subscription but routes take account of real-time traffic information, the extras include an anti-theft tracking facility and they say that there is constant updating of their mapping data. Trafficmaster are at 08705 561712 and www.trafficmaster.co.uk.

A hands-free kit for your mobile phone is essential because you will have your hands full driving and, as using a hand-held phone on the move is illegal in any vehicle, passing police will take a dim view of someone driving a large one while on the phone. However, the cheaper option is one of the speaker and charger units that plug into the cigarette lighter, because you can also use that in your car. Make sure you have at least one 12-volt cigarette-lighter-style socket in the cab – preferably not inside an ashtray – because so many accessories plug into them these days.

Air conditioning is not as frivolous as it sounds. It has been proved that a driver who is too hot does not function properly and these systems also help to filter a lot of impurities out of the air. Air conditioning is even useful in winter when its ability to condense most of the moisture out of the incoming air means that the cab windows de-mist more quickly and stay clear. And no, you don't have to be cold: you simply use the heater to warm the conditioned air. If you have the budget, air conditioning to the horses' part of the body is ideal because they benefit from its filtration ability and are kept cool even f you are stuck in a jam. However, with both humans or horses, make sure that air conditioning vents are not playing directly onto the body, because that can chill muscles and cause cramp.

Horses' Accommodation

t is very important to get the horses' accommodation right and this should take precedence over everything else in the orry. Human occupants have a degree of choice and movement in the vehicle that he horses do not have, so it is up to you to ensure their safety and comfort.

Research suggests that horses travel best if facing backwards, because they are then better able to compensate for the effects of braking. This is difficult in a trailer because of the problems of balance, and it may not be a choice in some smaller boxes, but if you have front-to-rear stalls, consider arranging things so that the horses can face backwards. However, if you buy a truck designed to face the horses forwards, do not change them round without seeking expert advice, in case there are structural or axle loading implications.

The herring-bone arrangement, where the horses are diagonally across the vehicle, seems to be a good alternative,

The horses' accommodation should be light and designed for safety. Note the drop-down nets in front of the racks.

because the horses can brace against the partitions, but this does mean that the partitions have to be substantial and have to lock firmly in place. This arrangement is often used in multi-horse boxes because it is the most space-effective way of arranging them. However, the layout of the travelling stalls is often limited by the size of the vehicle, so whereas a herring-bone layout is possible on a large box, it is not on a smaller one.

In lorries, unlike trailers, head partitions are not such an inconvenience and they can prevent squabbling on long journeys or if horses get bored waiting in the box at shows.

As mentioned, good ventilation is essential in the horses' part of the box. If you cannot afford air conditioning, at least get roof vents with electric fans so that you can keep the air moving even when stuck in traffic. Even with air conditioning or fans, you still need roof vents and windows that open to maintain ventilation

when parked at shows. These also allow you to reduce condensation in the truck when it is parked at home.

Windows in the horses' section should have internal grilles to stop horses trying to chew them or put their noses through the glass. All edges to these and other fixtures must be properly finished and rounded off. If rug racks are fitted, make sure they have a drop-down net so that rugs cannot fall out onto the horses.

In larger vehicles, it is helpful to have access to the horses' area from the cab, because this allows someone to go and check on them in situations where it may not be easy to stop, like on a motorway or a country road with no lay-bys. It also means that you can get in there without lowering the ramp, so there is no risk of a loose horse getting out onto the road. On a large, multi-horse box, groom's access at each end is a good idea so that you do not have to get round four or five other horses to get to the one at the back.

This two-horse box has rear-facing stalls, which research suggests horses prefer.

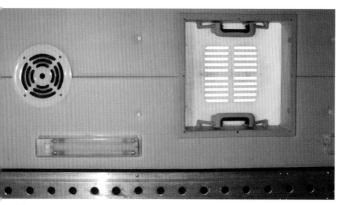

All horseboxes have roof vents (right), but electric fans (left) are far better for the horses because they work when the box is stuck in traffic.

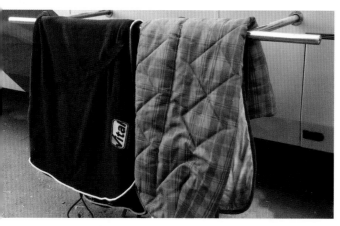

There are all sorts of useful options available, like these rug racks.

Having 'gates' to stop you falling off the sides of a high ramp is not a legal requirement, but it is sensible.

Stowage is essential, especially in multi-horse boxes – there is no point in being able to take seven horses to a show if there is only room for three horses' tack. Any space not turned into a cupboard, locker or bin is wasted. External tack lockers also make it much easier to get at and secure

tack and equipment on a showground. In addition, it is more than just handy to have enclosed storage for hay and feed for longer trips, as stops it getting wet or being contaminated by road grime.

Living Section

The first question about a living section is: do you need it? It is nice to be able to relax, make tea and have a hot lunch between classes but it adds cost, maintenance and weight to the lorry.

The secret is not to have everything you can afford that might be occasionally useful, but to think carefully about what you actually need. If all you want is somewhere to sit down and change clothes, do you need a living section when you can sit in the cab and change in the back, or put blinds over the cab windows? If you go to three-day events you may actually need an area you can live in but, even then, think carefully about what you install. If you can live for three days

above **External lockers make it easier to access and secure tack on the showground.**

Lockers for stowing feed are better than exposing it to rain and dirt on the roof rack, or hanging from the ramp.

without oven chips or pizza, why have an oven? If you never use the vehicle in winter, do you need heating? Having a lot of electrical equipment is going to mean the extra expense and weight of an auxiliary battery and a generator.

Gas appliances need careful maintenance because of the risk of carbon monoxide poisoning, so they add cost to caring for the vehicle. Gas cylinders are best stored in external lockers but, wherever they are stored, the locker must be vented to the outside so that any leaking gas goes harmlessly out of the lorry.

Water containers are best located internally so they are less likely to freeze, but you need easy access to the outside so that they can be cleaned, filled and drained, while on large lorries with big tanks there may be no alternative to hanging them under the chassis.

Beds with slatted bases are best because they stop condensation forming under the mattress. If you have a solid bed base, you

Only go for luxury living accommodation like this if you really need it, because it adds weight and increases maintenance requirements.

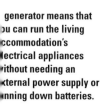

generator means that you can run the living accommodation's electrical appliances without needing an external power supply or running down batteries.

will have to let it air each morning or the moisture from your body will get trapped and turn the mattress mouldy. Similarly, cupboards for storing clothes and tack are best ventilated. Make sure that furnishings are filled with fire safety foam.

Most boxes have some sort of step up to the living section from outside. Fold-out steps can be risky because it is too easy to drive off forgetting they are out – which could prove expensive if you pass close to any parked cars! However, many boxes now have warning lights in the cab to show when these are out.

above **Gas cylinder stowage must be well ventilated, or positioned on the outside like this.**

above right **Fold-down steps can cause serious damage if you forget to raise them.**

right **This box has the luxury of hot water, central heating and a power hose, but these all add weight and need maintenance.**

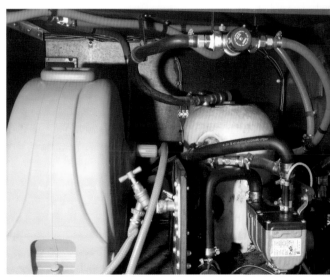

Security

Your transport and the animals and equipment you carry in it represent a substantial investment, so do not skimp on security measures. You are going to be leaving the vehicle unattended at shows, surrounded by people you do not know but who all know the value of your tack.

A good vehicle alarm can be installed either at the time of construction or afterwards. Discuss what you can have, and any special needs, with the installer. For example, it is usual in vehicle alarms to have sensors that detect if the vehicle is being tilted, moved or subjected to blows, all of which are things that bored horses may do to it, so you want to be able to turn those sensors off at a show. Similarly, most alarms have ultrasonic movement sensors which would be put in the cab and living accommodation and detect, say, someone breaking a window and reaching in. But if you want to leave dogs in the cab, you need to be able to turn those off, too. This still means that you can have an engine immobilizer and an active alarm on the doors and external lockers switched on.

All doors, including the one from the horses' section into the cab, should have good locks on them and it is useful if living section windows can be locked partially open. Roof vents offer safe ventilation without a security risk. However, ultrasonic movement sensors can detect air movement, too, resulting in false alarms if you leave windows or vents open.

You need at least one lockable cupboard for valuables, but the ideal is a vehicle safe. These are available from vehicle security specialists and some caravan dealers and range in size from those small enough to go under a car seat to something like a small house safe. This will give you somewhere secure to keep your cash, documents and trophies while you are riding.

External tack lockers are also a good security idea. Because you can turn conveniently from horse to locker, you are less likely to leave things strewn about or just thrown into the cab where potential thieves can see them. But they are no use if you leave them unlocked!

Though the actual theft of lorries is less of a problem than trailer theft, because there are registration documents, it is still fairly common. That is partly because thieves can steal a horsebox to put the body onto a cheap, legitimate chassis and scrap the 'hot' chassis, which has all the incriminating identification numbers. Alarms may only delay, not deter, the professional thief, so it is sensible to protect a horsebox, especially a new one, with a tracking device which can send out a signal if it is stolen.

There are two market leaders, Tracker (0500 090909, www.tracker-network.co.uk) and RAC Trackstar (0800 0961740, www.rac.co.uk) which both place transponders in the vehicle. Tracker uses proven technology whereby the activated transponder sends out a signal that specially equipped police cars can pick up. Its drawback is that a police car has to be within range, which may not happen in time in a rural area. However, it uses the same frequency in France and

Spain as in the UK, so vehicles stolen for export can be tracked on both sides of the Channel. The more expensive RAC Trackstar is newer and uses satellite technology so, when the unit is activated, the controllers should be able to see where it is right away, though that assumes the lorry is not somewhere that the satellite signal is masked, like under a concrete bridge. Trafficmaster's Smartnav navigation system (mentioned earlier in this Chapter under Technology) also has a stolen vehicle tracking facility like Trackstar.

While both companies charge an installation fee and an annual subscription, insurance companies usually give discounts on vehicles fitted with their systems. Tracker and Trackstar both offer the choice of two systems. With the basic system, you have to tell them that the vehicle has been stolen; with the more expensive keyring transponder system, if the vehicle is moved without the transponder (and thus without the key), it informs their control, who check with you before activating the tracking unit. The latter is well worth the extra money if your lorry is stored at a yard away from home. With either system, ask for the sender unit to be installed in the horsebox bodywork, not the chassis, so that if the chassis is detached and scrapped, the unit will remain active on its backup battery in the bodywork, at least for a while.

Do not ignore security just because the vehicle is insured. There are always uninsured losses when a vehicle is stolen and, unless the thieves are caught, there is nobody to claim those back from. In addition, it may not be just your lorry they steal – why should they leave the yard in an empty vehicle when they can fill it with tack, rugs or even horses?

Buying a Used Lorry

Buying a used lorry has many of the same pitfalls as buying a used car and it is up to you to lessen the risks by doing your homework and not assuming that everyone is as honest as you are. The safest way of buying a used lorry is from a dealer, because you then have greater protection under the trading laws. If you buy from a private individual you do not have the protection of the Sale of Goods Act, which requires that items have to be of merchantable quality and suitable for the use intended, including any special use made known by the purchaser to the vendor (like the need to carry unusually large horses). Private sales are only covered by the Misrepresentation of Goods Act, so if the vendor advertised the truck as five years old with 60,000 miles on the clock and you found it was ten years old with a 200,000 mileage, you would be entitled to sue – assuming you could still find them.

When you phone up about an apparently privately advertised lorry say only: 'I'm calling about the horsebox'. A private vendor will know what box you are talking about and where it was advertised. If they have to ask, it suggests they are trying to disguise the fact they are actually a dealer and the only reason for doing that is to deprive you of your rights under the trading laws.

However, there are some very dodgy traders about who do admit to being traders, so you must ask around locally to see who has a good reputation. It may also be worth calling your insurers to see if they are at least willing to say whether someone is known to them (it could save them grief later). For example, I know of a notorious dealer who has been investigated by insurers because he is believed to be involved in putting stolen bodies on legitimate but badly prepared chassis and he is known to make threatening and nuisance calls to customers who complain or start legal action. But there are also plenty of honest dealers who want to keep their good reputations and have good contacts for finding a lorry to suit you, if they do not already have one.

Lorries are complex vehicles so the best advice is to get them inspected by an expert. You should be able to find vehicle engineers who can carry out this sort of inspection through the *Yellow Pages*, but AA and RAC vehicle inspections do not cover those over 3.5 tonnes. The Organisation of Horsebox and Trailer Owners has a horsebox inspection service (01488 657651 www.horsebox-rescue.co.uk). A possible alternative is to ask the people you will use to service the vehicle to check it for you, but agree a fee for them doing it in advance.

Unlike trailers, you can check the provenance of a lorry using the same services as for used cars, HPI Equifax and the AA and RAC car data checking services (see Buying a Used Towcar in Chapter 3). This check will see whether the truck has been stolen, is an insurance write off, or is subject to a finance scheme (under certain finance schemes, like hire purchase, goods belong to the finance house, not the buyer). To get a thorough check you will need the lorry's registration number, Vehicle Identification Number (VIN) and, preferably, engine number. However, that only shows that the chassis is legitimate, and would not necessarily uncover a body switch. Though if someone who is not a coachbuilder is selling something that, until two weeks ago, was registered as a flatbed lorry, you know there is something odd about it. This is an essential check when you are buying privately.

Lorries are built for high mileage, so mileage is not as important as with a car. However, a low-mileage lorry is still worth more than a high-mileage one, so it pays to check this aspect. If the status check cannot reveal it, pay attention to it when you check the service record. Though lorries are built to last a high mileage, a service record is essential because they only live long if looked after. Diesel engines in particular do not thrive on neglect because they are so hard on their oil and, if too long is left between changes, it no longer does its job.

The service record may be nothing more than a book with garages' stamps to show when it was done, but, ideally, that should be backed up with bills to show more detail. You also want proof that the vehicle has a valid MOT or plating certificate, though these only indicate that it was roadworthy on the day of the test and are not a certificate of general condition or suitability for a particular use. You must see ownership documents and do not forget to check how much road tax is left.

Ask about the amount of use the vehicle has had. You are probably better off with a lorry that has had regular use than one that has spent months unused, because use keeps lubricants and coolants moving and reduces the risk of condensation causing corrosion in fuel tanks, engines and bodies. But one that has been all over the country every day of the week is likely to need things replacing.

Check general condition and tidiness. If someone could not be bothered to clean their vehicle up to sell it, it is unlikely they looked after it when nobody was going to see it. If it has living accommodation, ask when the gas appliances were last serviced – you do not want a bill for replacing a potentially dangerous heater, or to be gassed on your first outing.

Even if you know nothing about mechanical matters, check it over. There is no point paying for a vehicle inspection when a quick look under the bonnet

would have told you that the engine is leaking oil and water. Start on the outside looking for signs of damage or corrosion. Do not forget to look high up, where a clumsy driver might have hit an overhanging tree. Check that all doors and ramps open, close and lock properly and that all lights work. Examine the tyres, not just for tread but for damage and the cracks that indicate they are perishing, remembering the spare. Horseboxes usually do far less work than lorry tyres are made for, so it is common for them to perish before they wear out.

Examine the horsy part for damage and wear; check the condition of floor and ramp from above and below. While you are checking the floor from underneath, examine the main mechanical components for oil leaks. Look at the wheel ends of the driven axle and the differential housing (big hump) in the middle. Follow the prop shaft forward from the differential to the gearbox and have a look under the engine. Shiny looking oil and dirt deposits suggest

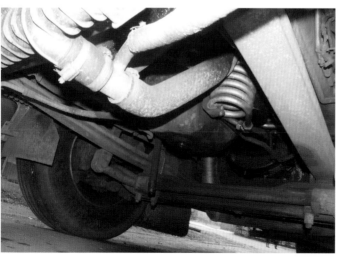

Have a good look under a used lorry for leaks and damage.

an active leak. Look at the ground while you are under there – are there any signs of fluids having dripped out from places you cannot see? Also check the brake lines and brakes for signs of fluid leaks, and the condition of the exhaust system – which should have no holes or signs of gasses having blown through joints.

The steering box is normally low down near the driver's side of the cab and may be visible from below, with heavy-duty shafts going into the cab and down to the front wheels. Check this for signs of fluid leaks.

If practical, lift the engine cover, which may be inside the cab, or even involve tilting the cab forwards, and again look for oil and coolant leaks, especially from the joints in the engine and anywhere where pipes join on. Check the oil level on the dipstick and remove the oil filler cap and look inside. If you see any mayonnaise-style deposits, coolant is leaking into the oil and being whipped to emulsification, just like the oil and egg in real mayonnaise, which means it needs major work or expensive replacements. Also check the coolant – but only remove the lid of the expansion bottle or radiator if the engine is cold. You are looking for signs of oil getting into it, rust, and that it is to the right level and has a colour you associate with anti freeze (usually blue or green, like in your car).

Check brake and clutch fluid levels, though the reservoirs for these are often on the truck's chassis rails rather than under the 'bonnet'. With air brakes, check that all the bleed valve taps work and, after running the engine to pressurize the system, check it for air leaks with the engine off.

Be suspicious of a warm engine because it suggests that the vendor has been running it to disguise poor or smoky starting.

In the cab, look for damage to trim and upholstery that suggests careless use. Ask yourself if the general wear is supported by the recorded mileage – a shiny gear knob, threadbare driver's seat and steering wheel worn smooth would be out of place on a low-mileage truck. Make sure that seats and mirrors adjust as they should without any looseness in the backs or the runners that the seat slides on. Check that all the switches function properly and that all the warning lights work. These should come on briefly with the ignition or when switches are turned on, depending on their function. If a warning light does not come on, is it because the bulb has blown, or because the vendor has disabled it because he knows it will come on as soon as you start the engine?

Start the engine and check the mirrors, or have a helper outside check, for exhaust smoke. It is normal for big older diesels to give a puff of smoke on starting, but it should not be excessive and should clear quickly. The engine should also settle down quickly to a rhythmic tickover, though expect more noise and vibration than you would get in a modern diesel car.

If insurance allows, take the lorry for a test drive. Be aware of how things feel. Does the clutch come in only at the end of the pedal travel? That suggests it is worn. Do the brakes feel right? Is there excessive play in the steering, remembering it will not be as precise as a car's, and does it make strange noises on tight turns? Is the gearbox arguing about engaging any gears, jumping out of lower gears if you suddenly come off the throttle, or sounding excessively noisy? All those suggest problems. Does the lorry feel lopsided or sway excessively? That may mean worn springs or dampers (shock absorbers). Listen out for unusual noises.

If you are not covered by insurance to drive, at least go for a drive with the vendor. You won't be able to check all the things mentioned here but will be able to see how the lorry goes, listen for odd noises and watch how easy it is for the driver to change gear and manoeuvre. You could still have a go at some low speed off the public highway, manoeuvring in an area of their yard or a field where there is nothing to hit. If controls are too heavy for you it will be most apparent at low speeds.

Above all, does it suit you? If you find it hard work or uncomfortable on a short drive, it may be too much on a long trip.

When you get back from the drive, leave the engine at tickover while you chat to the owner for a few minutes then, watching in the mirrors, blip the throttle. Worn diesels usually belch smoke if you do this. When you have turned the engine off,

have another look for fresh leaks – if someone had cleaned up a leak it may have reappeared.

You have now done all a layperson can do to check the vehicle's condition and it is time to call in an expert to check it over. It is reasonable to expect the vendor to want a deposit, but, as you would with a horse, get a receipt saying it is refundable if the lorry fails its 'vetting'. A vendor who refuses to allow an inspection or starts pressuring you into buying without one should not be trusted.

Do not discount a basically good lorry if the expert turns up certain faults. Ask him whether repair is viable and what it would cost, then haggle the asking price down accordingly, using the expert's report as evidence. Alternatively, insist on the owner having it put right and providing proof that the work has been done.

Always seek proof of the answers you are given. If someone says a new part has been fitted or a service carried out, ask politely if they can show you a receipt. If they take offence, just remind them that you are spending a lot of money and you do not know each other, so it is in both your interests. If they continue to object, be suspicious.

5

Preparing for the Worst

Things can go wrong no matter how careful you are, so it pays to be repared. If you know what to do eforehand and have the necessary quipment, you can significantly reduce he effects of a mishap and prevent it ecoming a disaster.

Buyer Beware

In the preceding chapters we have looked t buying trailers, towcars and lorries, but vhat should you do if that purchase does ot live up to its promise? Your rights if omething goes wrong are enshrined in he Sale of Goods Act. You can find details f those rights in pamphlets available from our local Trading Standards office or at he Trading Standards Institute's (TSI) vebsite at www.tradingstandards.gov.uk.

Your rights vary according to whom ou bought from and whether the item urchased was new or used, but vendors annot remove your legal rights, so hrases like 'sold as seen' are meaning-ess. Similarly, a warranty is in addition o your legal rights, not in place of them,

so vendors cannot force you to accept repair if the law entitles you to a refund.

When you buy from a trader the goods must be of satisfactory quality, as described and fit for purpose, including any special purpose you make known to the vendor (like the need to tow a heavy trailer). The law does not define 'satisfactory', though it lists factors courts take into account.

New vehicles must be just that: an unregistered car that has had a substantial repair because someone drove the transporter into a tree may not legally be new. With used vehicles age, price, mileage, description and 'all relevant circumstances' have to be taken into account when deciding satisfactory quality, because you would expect less from a high-mileage ten-year-old than from a low-mileage two-year-old. However, any used vehicle should be roadworthy, reasonably reliable and capable of passing an MOT or plating, unless sold as scrap.

Horseboxes with a new body on a used chassis are a bit of a grey area, which is why it is important to get in writing what preparation will be given to the chassis. If someone says its will be fully refurbished you have the right to expect it to be in top condition.

With private sales your rights are greatly reduced. It is up to you to check that the vehicle is of reasonable quality, but it must still be as described and the vendor's to sell. However, it can be very difficult to enforce your rights against an individual.

Keep all documentation relating to the purchase, including any adverts for the vehicle. It will be easier to fight your case if you already have this material, rather than, say, having to get hold of a back copy of the magazine it was advertised in.

Incidentally, if you buy a stolen vehicle you cannot keep it though, if you buy one that is subject to an HP agreement, the finance company cannot repossess it.

Auctions are not considered consumer sales, so here you are bound by the auction's written conditions.

Taking Action

If you buy a faulty or incorrectly described vehicle you have only a 'short time' after purchase to reject it and demand your money back, though nothing is laid down to say how much time you have. This appears to be because what might be considered a reasonable time to reject a vehicle could vary from case to case, depending upon the nature of the fault. The TSI recommends taking legal advice about individual cases and advises that if the vehicle is so bad you want to reject it, you must stop using it and contact the

vendor and, if necessary, the finance company as soon as possible. If a repair is then offered you can accept it without losing your right to reject the vehicle if it isn't sorted out.

If you are too late to get your money back you can demand a repair or replacement. In the latter case, the vendor may be entitled to an allowance for the use you have had of the vehicle, though you may be entitled to compensation for inconvenience. But you must give the vendor reasonable opportunity to put things right. Be firm but polite, back up verbal communication with letters by recorded delivery and keep electronic back-ups and hard copies of e-mails, though these are not good evidence in court. Try not to lose your temper.

Since March 2003, if a vehicle suffers a major failure within six months of purchase it is up to the trader to prove that the fault was not present when sold. But you have to provide evidence to support a claim, especially in court, so a vehicle inspector's report may be handy.

If things get nasty, take legal advice. Local Trading Standards and the Citizens' Advice Bureau (CAB) can give general consumer rights advice and the latter should know local solicitors who can give more specific advice. Your local CAB and Trading Standards office are in the phone book, though the latter may be under the county or metropolitan council. The TSI website has a facility for finding your local office from your postcode. Your motoring organization may be able to help, too, though you usually have to pay for this.

Court action is taken at the County

Court in England, Wales and Northern Ireland and the Sheriff's Court in Scotland. In County Courts, claims up to £5,000 are heard in a Small Claims Court without lawyers. The courts have a range of pamphlets available explaining how to proceed with claims.

Security

Take security seriously because insurance never completely covers the cost of replacement, nor can it recompense you for the hassle involved. In addition, thieves may not take the trailer or lorry alone when they can fill it with items from the yard, including horses.

We have covered lorry security devices in Chapter 4, Buying a Lorry because, if you are buying a new one, it is sensible to get these things included at the time of building, but if you already own a lorry please check that section for guidance. But there are additional security precautions you can take to protect your investment, which we will look at later in this section.

Trailer safety devices are more rudimentary, mainly because trailers have no battery to power alarms and tracking devices. However, there are a number of movement alarms available that run off their own batteries, usually the rectangular 9-volt type used in smoke alarms. Ask your local caravan dealers, but stress that you want it for a horse trailer without its own battery. These alarms make it harder for a thief to sneak the trailer past your window while you sleep and most would go off if they tried to jack it up to remove a wheel clamp.

Insurance companies usually favour a wheel clamp for trailer security and some clamps would also fit the wheels on smaller lorries. When you buy a wheel clamp avoid those that rely on padlocks because most padlocks can be cut with bolt croppers (like secateurs for cutting metal). Built-in locks should be well protected so that they cannot be knocked off with a heavy hammer, and they must be resistant to being drilled or pulled out. The clamp should wrap around the wheel in a way that makes it difficult to get off even if the tyre is deflated. A substantial wheel clamp is expensive, but it costs a lot less than your trailer.

Fit a wheel clamp to one of the back wheels. Thieves commonly get round wheel clamps fitted to the front wheels, or hitch locks, by hooking the hitch over the rear of a pickup until they get somewhere remote enough to work on it undisturbed.

Hitch locks usually take the form of a metal box that locks around the trailer hitch. They are a useful form of additional security, but should not be relied on alone

Many insurers require a wheel clamp for security.

because the trailer can still be moved with one fitted. The most useful can be locked on the hitch when the trailer is hitched up and parked, giving useful showground security. Remember that, if your insurers say a security device must be fitted when the trailer is parked, that means at shows, too. It is far too easy on a busy showground for someone to unhitch the trailer from your car and swing it round to theirs, telling passersby that they are helping a friend who has broken down. If your trailer has a locking hitch, always lock it when parked or hitched up.

If you park on hard standing, consider a locking security post. These are substantial steel posts that lock onto a bracket bolted to or set in the concrete, but they must be substantial if you expect them to stop someone driving a lorry away or reversing a hefty off-roader up to your trailer. A variation on security posts is one with a 50 mm ball on top that a hitch can

be locked to, but these are aimed at caravans, while a horse trailer, with its twin axles, is not so easy to manoeuvre precisely by hand. Be careful about using security posts in a way that would stop emergency vehicles getting to your yard or your home.

Think about making your lorry or trailer easily identifiable. This could take the form of unique artwork done professionally or just by you sticking pre-cut shapes to it. Equibrand (01327 262444) do rooftop postcodes which make vehicles instantly identifiable to policemen in helicopters or in cars on bridges and, for trailers, they do kits of the reflective material used on police cars, which also has a safety advantage. It is also a good idea to engrave or paint your postcode somewhere unobtrusive on a trailer or a lorry's bodywork so that, should the worst happen, you can identify it yourself and tell the police where the markings can be found.

Rooftop postcodes add security.

Never keep vehicle documents in the vehicle. Keep a note of identification numbers (registration, VIN and engine) somewhere separate from the paperwork in case someone breaks in to steal those, too. With trailers, always keep any proof of ownership, like the sales receipt, safe and keep a note of the chassis number as well as the make and model.

You can further improve vehicle security by keeping it somewhere sensible. The ideal is inside a locked building, though that is rarely possible. If you can, choose somewhere not easily seen from the road but overlooked by houses and let neighbours know that nobody has your permission to 'borrow' it. With lorries not fitted with alarms you can improve security by disconnecting the battery or having a battery isolator switch fitted, though this stops clocks and means that the radio security code has to be re-entered before you can use it. If you have an alarm or tracking device fitted do not

disconnect the battery because doing so eventually disables them.

Do not make thieves' work more rewarding by storing tack, rugs or riding clothes in a trailer or lorry. This also invites break-ins if anything worth taking is visible and the items may not be covered by household or vehicle insurance,

above **Some lorries have battery isolators which can be used to disconnect the battery in an emergency, or as a security measure if an alarm is not fitted.**

Equibrand's reflective stripes have safety and security benefits.

especially in trailers where you cannot usually lock the doors.

Finally, do not get lax on security at shows, especially big ones. Put things in the vehicle and lock it when you leave it, even if it is only for a few moments. Do not leave anything of value in a trailer because you cannot lock it. If you use a wheeled

tack bin, make sure it can be locked to the truck or trailer to stop thieves wheeling the lot away. You may find you can secure it with a bicycle cable lock.

Fire Risks

Vehicle fires are always a risk so, when transporting animals, it is a good idea to have an extinguisher because, if nothing else, it can give you more time to evacuate the horses.

In lorries with living accommodation, a fire extinguisher is essential because the risk of fire is so much greater – it only takes a forgotten gas ring or a cigarette lodged behind a cushion. Locate the extinguisher just inside a door so you do not have to enter the vehicle to get it.

If you have to drill holes to mount an extinguisher bracket in a car or lorry, make sure there are no wires or pipes behind it. With towcars, check the manufacturer's accessory catalogue

above **Make sure that tack bins can be locked to the trailer.**

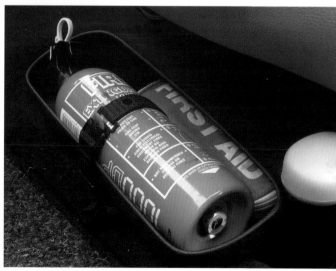

Many car manufacturers offer a purpose-made fire extinguisher and first aid stowage.

because some produce extinguisher brackets to fit their cars without drilling. The best extinguisher for a vehicle is a dry powder type because these are suitable for most types of fire. However, extinguishers should not be used on fat fires because they can blow burning fat out of the pan, instead, just cover the pan with a lid or damp cloth. Extinguishers should be at least 1kg in size, though in cars space restrictions may force you to have a smaller one.

Make sure everyone likely to travel in your vehicle has read the extinguisher's instructions and knows how to use it. Extinguishers must be used from as close to the flames as is safe, and be aimed at the seat of the fire. With fires inside vehicles, do not throw open doors and bonnets because the sudden inrush of air could make it flare up. Just open the door or bonnet enough to direct the extinguisher inside.

Above all, do not panic. Vehicles do not normally explode unless the fire gets a serious hold, because the fuel is enclosed and it is the petrol *vapour*, not the liquid, that ignites. Diesel is a much lower fire risk because it has to be heated to quite high temperatures to ignite. However, in lorries with living space, gas cylinders can explode violently if the fire gets them overheated, so always warn attending fire-fighters if a gas cylinder is aboard. Never go into a smoke-filled vehicle because the fumes from the plastics are poisonous.

If you have any queries about extinguishers or fire prevention, talk to your local fire brigade's fire prevention officer.

Tool Kits

It is foolish to get stuck at the side of the road for the want of a screwdriver, so put together a basic tool kit to keep in the vehicle. Check what your vehicle already has: in cars and small lorries there should at least be a jack and a wheel brace though in larger lorries it would be impractical to carry something big enough to use safely. With towcars, make sure that the wheel brace and jack can also be used on your trailer, because, for example, some Land Rovers have larger wheel nuts than those on trailers, and not all car jacks are suitable for lifting a trailer. If you have to buy a jack for the trailer, the wedge-shaped ones from Horseware stockists and Equibrand (01327 262444) are much safer than other patterns, because there is less chance of a horse rocking the trailer off them. You simply pull the good wheel on the same side as the punctured one onto the wedge, lifting the flat tyre off the road. These jacks are also useful for steadying ramps on uneven ground.

If you have a conventional jack, make sure it is capable of lifting the fully laden trailer's weight with a good safety margin, say, around 2 tonnes. Bottle and trolley jacks are best because they are hydraulic, which makes it easier for them to lift heavy weights.

Most car tool kits also include a double-ended screwdriver, with a cross head at one end and a flat head at the other: if there is not one in your kit, buy something similar, or a multi-shaft screwdriver. To that, add a set of ring spanners (for reasonably modern vehicles, these should be metric) and an adjustable spanner to use on nuts outside the range of the set, or where you need a spanner for each end of a nut and bolt. A pair of pliers is also useful and if you get square-nosed ones they can also be used for pulling those awkward short hairs from tails! Get a pair with built-in wire cutters.

To the tool kit add a complete set of vehicle fuses, a roll of insulating tape and a penknife.

A torch is a must in any vehicle used for transporting horses. Though trailers and lorries have interior lights, you never know when they might fail and, since they throw shadows, you may not be able to see, for example, if a travelling boot has come undone. In addition, the vehicle's own lights are no good if you have to delve under the bonnet or change a wheel. But do not put the torch in the tool kit, because you may need it to find the tools: keep it in the glovebox, preferably where it can be reached without moving

everything else. Use alkaline batteries because, unlike rechargables, they hardly run down when not in use.

A warning triangle and a high visibility vest are essential when towing or with a lorry because you are driving something that blocks a lot of road and can be difficult to move if it breaks down somewhere awkward. These items are also legal requirements in some European countries. Many cars have purpose-made stowage for triangles and many luxury models come with one tucked away somewhere, so check before you buy one.

First Aid Kits

Have separate first aid kits for people and horses for reasons of hygiene and convenience. It is best if they are in a case with a handle, so they can be easily grabbed and carried, and are kept in a dedicated place so you can go straight to them.

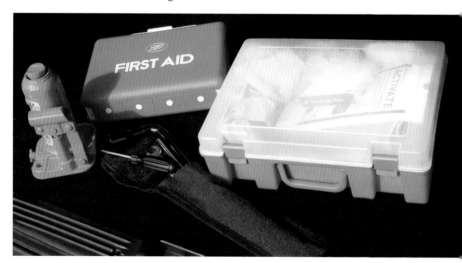

Make sure you carry first aid kits for people, horses – and the car.

Most car manufacturers include first aid kits for people in their accessory ranges, designed to fit the special stowage area which many cars have (the car's handbook may show where this is), because it is a legal requirement to carry one in some countries. Even if you do not buy a car manufacturer's kit, it is worth finding one that will fit this stowage area, because it will keep the kit safe and accessible.

In a lorry consider installing quick release straps (like bungee cords) to hold both kits, and the torch, in place somewhere accessible. Do not bury them under piles of tack and rugs.

Kits for Humans

While it is wise to carry a first aid kit in any vehicle (and a legal requirement in some European countries), this becomes essential in anything transporting horses because people riding and handling them tend to get hurt!

There are plenty of ready-made first aid kits for people available through chemists, car accessory shops and car dealers. The British Red Cross Society suggests the following for the contents of a motorists' first aid kit:

- A bottle of distilled water

- Adhesive dressings

- Large, small and medium sterile dressings

- Crepe and gauze roll bandages in various sizes

- Roll of surgical tape

- Triangular bandages

- Cotton wool

- Foil blanket

- Tweezers, scissors and safety pins

- Surgical gloves

Purchased first aid kits will contain most of these, but you may need to add missing items to cheaper kits. Horse owners should add insect bite cream and painkillers, such as paracetamol. Most kits include a basic first aid pamphlet, but a small first aid book would be a useful addition, for example *Pocket First Aid*, published by Dorling Kindersley.

Kits for Horses

An equine first aid kit tends to be bigger than a human one simply because you need large quantities of things to cover bigger limbs. For example, a small box of cotton wool may be fine for bathing human cuts and grazes but you need a decent sized roll to provide enough to clean up a wound then provide padding under a bandage on a horse's leg. Vet Karen Coumbe, author of *First Aid for Horses* (J. A. Allen), suggests the following for a travelling first aid kit:

- Digital thermometer (mercury ones can get 'cooked' in a car).

- Moist wound gel, which can be smothered on a wound to protect and cleanse it. Properly called hydrogel, brands include Robinson's Vetalintex and Equine America's Derma Gel.

- Roll of cotton wool for cleaning wounds and for padding under bandages. If pushed for space, Karen suggests substituting antiseptic wipes.

- **Dressings should include:**
  - Non-stick dressings to go over wounds, like Melonin or Rondopad, in a variety of sizes.
  - Stretchable conforming bandages like Vetrap or the cheaper gauze type that can be taped, like Kband.
  - Surgical, insulating or duct tape to hold bandages in place.
  - Animalintex as a poultice.
  - Cool bandages, which create a cooling action when wet to damp down inflamation, as with a tendon strain. There are many brands on the market.

- **Good antiseptic, like Hibiscrub or Pevadine.**

- **Curved scissors.**

- **Card with important phone numbers (vet, help services, friends with horse transport) and insurance details.**

- **Take as many bandages and dressings as you have space for.**

Breakdown Cover

Do not assume that, because you are a member of a breakdown organization, everything is already looked after. Ordinary breakdown cover usually only covers vehicles up to 3.5 tonnes, so they will not turn out to a larger horsebox. Though all the breakdown organizations say that if they cannot fix a towcar at the roadside they will recover it with its trailer or caravan, the RAC is the only one that will recover a horse trailer with horses aboard – and then only at the recovery driver's discretion. The others promise nothing more than getting your horse and trailer to a safe place, which may only mean to a motorway service area.

If your towcar is covered by the manufacturer's warranty breakdown cover, check the situation regarding the trailer with them, stressing that you are talking about recovery of a trailer with horses in it. Some of these breakdown warranties only agree to get the disabled car to the nearest dealer.

There are two dedicated horse owners' breakdown services offering various packages: The Organisation of Horsebox and Trailer Owners on 01408 657651 and at www.horsebox-rescue.co.uk and Equestrian Support Services (ESS) on 01300 348997 and at www.equestriansupport.co.uk (these websites contain lots of useful, regularly updated transport information). Lorry owners may find that their insurance company offers special deals for break-down recovery through one of these services. These organizations offer roadside breakdown assistance for lorries and trailers, plus recovery of vehicles, trailers and horses to the destination of your choice or overnight livery. They also offer back-up with emergency veterinary and farriery help anywhere in the UK.

While membership of these organizations is probably only necessary for trailer owners who travel long distances, it is an essential for lorry owners. Recovery of a lorry can be very expensive, especially from a motorway, and changing a wheel is not a DIY job, particularly with horses aboard. Lorry drivers who do not join one of these organizations should at least open an account with one of the nation-wide tyre-fitting companies, or getting a puncture fixed will mean lots of phone calls, a long wait and having to prove you can pay.

Since 1997, the RAC has also offered Horse Trailer Assist as an extra-cost addition to the usual breakdown services for members. It adds the ESS's horsy back-up services, like emergency information and getting the horses home or to overnight stabling. Details of the service and online purchase can be found at www.rac.co.uk.

Whatever breakdown cover you choose, programme the number into your mobile phone, remembering that 0800 numbers become 800. Also have your vet's number in the memory for local emergencies and, if you do not belong to an equestrian breakdown service, a business directory like Yellow Pages to help find a vet away from home. Keep a written note of these numbers, too, perhaps making use of the Important Phone Numbers sheet at the front of this book, in case your mobile stops working.

Horse Equipment

Even if you are not taking the horse somewhere to ride, take a bit and bridle with you. If you have to load or unload the horse in difficult circumstances, say after an accident, a bridle will give you far more control than a headcollar and lead rope.

However, it is not wise to transport a horse in a bridle in case the bit gets caught on something, because the horse's jaw is likely to break before the bit.

Even on warm days, take a lightweight rug with you in case it turns cool, or the horse gets wet. Remember, there is an inevitable wind-chill factor when the trailer or lorry is moving, which may be a blessing on hot days but could result in a cold horse and chilled muscles on a cool day.

Unless the journey is very short, take a bucket and container of water, so you can offer the horse a drink and have water to bathe injuries. Trailer owners should stow the water container well forward in the towcar, not in the trailer, because water is heavy and a 20 kg container in the trailer's nose or tail greatly affects its noseweight (see Chapter 3). Always stow heavy objects like water containers and saddles where they cannot cause injury to horses or people if they are thrown about in an accident, or by heavy braking.

Coping with Emergencies

Accidents and breakdowns are bad enough in a car, but are even more traumatic in a vehicle transporting livestock. Difficult though it may be if your horses are distressed, your priority must be towards ensuring human victims are safe and to minimizing the risk of further vehicles becoming involved.

Take care when entering the horses' part of the vehicle, because the animals may be frightened and no longer secure. In particular, do not do anything that might risk them charging out onto the road, like lowering a ramp. Do not unload horses onto the road unless it is unavoidable and then only do so with the police there to direct traffic. It is illegal to unload horses onto a motorway, including slip roads, and has proved fatal.

Before getting your vehicle off the road, check the surface you are driving onto. It will only make things worse if the vehicle sinks in or tips over in an unseen ditch or down a bank.

When calling the police or a breakdown service, make it clear that you have horses on board. Also make it clear that your vehicle or outfit is large and that if it represents a hazard to others.

Always use your hazard warning lights as soon as you have a problem. It is wise to carry a high visibility tabard with you and wear it if you have to get out on the road, not least because the size of your lorry or outfit may make it difficult to get right off the carriageway. Place your warning triangle 50 metres behind the vehicle on ordinary roads and 150 metres behind on fast dual-carriageways. Place it further back if you are on a bend. *The Highway Code* now says you should not use them on motorways because of the risk in walking along the hard shoulder. Hold the triangle in front of you as you walk from the vehicle to make sure people see you, especially at night, and keep an eye on the traffic as you return to your vehicle. Do not stand between the vehicle and the road, especially on motorways and fast roads.

If you do not know your location on non-motorway roads, your mobile phone service's recorded traffic information number should give a rough location (the information usually starts with something like 'You are on the A11 near Thetford...'). Many major A-roads now have motorway-style marker posts and emergency phones. These are used in the same way as on the motorway, though some phones have direct dial buttons to breakdown organizations.

In warm weather, make sure the horses have enough ventilation while you are stationary, but do not forget to check that all doors and windows are secure before driving off again.

Motorway Emergencies

Motorway hard shoulders may be a refuge but they are not safe, with more fatal accidents occurring there than on the carriageway itself. On a hard shoulder, pull as far to the left as you can without risking sinking into a verge or gravel drain. Use your hazard warning lights immediately and get out on the passenger side if you can.

Ideally, try to stop near one of the emergency phones. Most police forces prefer you to use these to tell them of breakdowns or accidents because the call goes straight through to a motorway control room and gives an instant location – you do not need money or to be a member of a breakdown organization to use one. If you cannot stop near a phone, which are at about 1-mile intervals, look for the nearest blue and white marker post to your vehicle. Each post carries a unique number, instantly giving your exact location to the police, and has an arrow

Emergency phones on motorways and some A-roads connect you to police control.

Motorway marker posts show the direction to the nearest phone.

showing the direction to the nearest phone. Do not hang up until told to do so, because the controller may not be able call you back. The police can call breakdown services for you.

If you feel you cannot leave the horses, are worried about walking along the road, or are unable to walk far, call the police on your mobile phone, telling them what motorway you are on, which direction you are going and the number on the nearest marker post, as well as the nature of the emergency.

Normal advice is to wait on the verge away from the vehicle because of the risk of tired drivers 'following you' onto the hard shoulder. However, with horses, you may have no alternative but to stay with them to keep them calm.

Once your problem has been solved, rejoin the carriageway by picking up speed on the hard shoulder while indicating to show that you are moving out. Remember that there will be a considerable difference in speed between your vehicle and those approaching you, so do not pull out assuming other drivers will pull into the next lane unless they are indicating that intention.

Accidents

If you are involved in an accident that involves damage to property, or injury to people or animals, you are required by law to stop and give your own and the vehicle owner's name and address, plus the registration number of the vehicle, to anyone having reasonable cause to require it. If you cannot do this, for example if you hit a parked car and cannot trace the owner, you have to report the accident to the police within 24 hours.

Carrying a copy of your insurance certificate may also save problems later, because you will be required to produce it to the police within seven days of an accident involving injury. You do not have to call the police to an accident where nobody has been injured party, though you may have to if the road is blocked or you cannot move your vehicle.

If vehicles are seriously damaged in an accident, ask everyone to turn their ignition off and ensure that nobody smokes. Call the police but, if you do so on a mobile phone, make sure you know where you are first. Keep calm and allow the police operator to lead you through the information they need – do not hang up before they tell you to do so. If your horses are injured or need sedation, tell them you need a vet, or alert your equestrian breakdown service, if you are a member.

Do not remove injured people from vehicles unless they are in immediate danger, but move uninjured people to safety away from the traffic. On a motorway or fast dual-carriageway, that means getting well onto the verge. Never sit on the crash barrier at the edge of the road in case anyone trying to avoid the accident crushes you against it. If necessary, get someone to direct the traffic around the scene.

Having secured human casualties, you may now attend to the horses. Your first priority must be to make sure they are secure. Check them for injuries and try to calm them, but do not put yourself at risk.

You must accept that you may be able to do nothing more for them until a vet arrives. If you need to evacuate the horses, tell the police as soon as they arrive and explain the problems. Make sure they understand that you may not have full control over them, especially if traffic is allowed to pass by. This is one reason why you should always carry a bridle when transporting horses.

Breakdowns

If possible, get the vehicle off the road or somewhere safe like a lay-by. If you break down on a motorway, let the police know you are there, even if it is something you can sort out quickly. If you have to attend to something on the traffic side of the vehicle on a motorway or fast dual-carriageway, ask the police to attend to create a safe working area, especially at night.

Before calling for help or setting out to find a phone, make sure you have your location, vehicle details, breakdown organization phone and membership numbers and know your own mobile phone number so they can call you back.

If you can make repairs yourself safely, do so, but do not try to botch repairs on major safety systems like brakes or steering, or risk pushing on when warning lights show problems with coolant, gear-boxes or oil pressure, because you could do serious damage.

Punctures

On all but the smallest lorries, a puncture needs specialist equipment to jack it up, remove the wheel and replace it safely, so ou will have to call your equestrian breakdown service or the tyre-fitting company you have arranged an account with.

With a towcar and trailer you can change the wheel, but need to take extreme care if the horses are on the trailer because of the risk of them shifting and pulling the car or trailer off the jack. If you use a car jack to lift the trailer, make sure it is up to the weight. (Most off-loader jacks have a 2-tonne maximum lift, so these should be fine.)

Wedge-shaped trailer jacks, like those marketed by Horseware and Equibrand, are by far the safest way of changing the wheel on a trailer because there is little or no risk of the horses jogging the trailer off. These take the form of a plastic wedge with a wheel-sized dip on top and you pull the good wheel on the same side of the trailer as the puncture into the dip, lifting the punctured one off the ground just far enough to change it.

But do not get carried away and start jacking up without preparation! Make sure the car and trailer handbrakes are on and that the car is in gear (especially if you are lifting a wheel that the handbrake operates on). Gather your tool kit together and get the spare out.

Before you jack anything up, loosen the wheel nuts. This means you can exert a lot of force without risking pulling the vehicle off the jack, and you have the ground holding the wheel still for you. Now jack it up. If you use a conventional jack on a trailer, use it against an axle or substantial part of the chassis, not the trailer floor. On your car, the handbook gives the safe, reinforced jacking points. In either case, check as the vehicle is lifted that the jack remains secure on the ground and against the vehicle. Jack it a little higher than you need to get the punctured wheel off, because the inflated tyre will be fatter.

Take care when removing the wheel,

A wedge jack like Equibrand's Trailer-Aid is safer than a conventional jack.

Wheel nuts must be tightened in diagonal pairs.

because it is heavy. When you put the spare on, do the nuts up enough to hold the wheel, but do not try to tighten them fully. Lower the wheel to the ground gently so as not to upset the horses – on hydraulic jacks, turn the pressure release nut very slowly, or the vehicle will crash down suddenly. Now tighten the nuts in opposite, diagonal pairs, to pull the wheel evenly onto the hub. Do not put excessive force on them or you may strip the threads or make it hard to remove them next time.

Check the tyre pressure against the manufacturer's recommended pressure (tyres are dealt with in more detail in Chapter 6). No matter how much of a hurry you are in, stow the damaged wheel and tools properly, because they can become lethal missiles in an accident. Check that the horses are happy and doors are secure, then make sure you release the trailer handbrake. After about 30 miles, check that the wheel nuts are still tight.

6

Pre-drive Checks

We all know there are certain checks we should carry out regularly on a car in everyday use, even if we do not do them as often as we should. The same basic checks apply to lorries and trailers but, because these vehicles may be used irregularly, some owners are tempted to assume that, because everything was fine when they checked it two months ago it will still be all right now, because it hasn't turned a wheel. This is not so.

Tyres can leak air slowly, and they continue to deteriorate when not in use. A pipe or gasket that was fine when the engine was hot may have started to leak as it cooled down, or vice versa. Brakes that got a good soaking last time out can seize as the moisture creates corrosion that sticks the shoes to the drums. That squirt you gave the windscreen before you got home may have been the last drop in the washer bottle.

Vehicle handbooks often give useful information about regular checks, picking out anything unusual on your model and letting you know where things that must be checked can be found. Many modern vehicles have things under the bonnet that need checking colour-coded (it's an old military idea) so, if you need a reminder on a vehicle that isn't colour-coded, you could put a dab of yellow or red paint on each item.

Tyres

Tyres are your only contact with the road and they only perform properly if they are well maintained. Tyres that are too hard or soft do not have their full tread in contact with the ground and under-inflated tyres flex more than they should, which makes them overheat and, eventually, break up. Tyre pressures are particularly crucial on trailers because uneven pressures affect their stability, especially when braking.

Trailer and lorry tyre pressures are much higher than those for a car – even a trailer's can be over 50 psi (pounds per square inch) – so you need a pressure gauge that can give accurate readings at high pressures. Types with digital or dial readouts are better for high pressures than the column type often used for cars, though such a gauge will still read the lower car pressures reasonably accurately.

Ideally, tyre pressures should be read when cold for accuracy.

An electric compressor makes life a lot easier when adding air to high-pressure tyres, or to the ten you may have to inflate on a car and trailer. For cars and trailers the type that plugs into a cigarette lighter is fine, though with lorries these may be slow, if they can manage at all. If you have to use a garage airline to inflate the tyres, take a pressure gauge with you, because those on airlines are not always accurate.

Since pressures are higher on warm tyres, allow for that and do not reduce their pressures. If you have to use a garage airline, check pressures at home first. If the cold tyres need an extra 4 psi, that is what you add at the garage to the warm tyres, regardless of the pressure shown there.

Optimum tyre pressures are shown in vehicle handbooks, though some vehicles, especially trailers, have a label stating the correct pressures inside a door. If you need a reminder, you could use stick-on

numbers over each wheel, like Post Office vans have.

For cars, a towing tyre pressure is sometimes given in the handbook. If not, use the pressure given for a full load. With cars where no towing or full load pressure is given you may find they feel better when towing with an extra 3 psi in the rear tyres, though do not exceed the maximum pressure given on the tyre's side wall.

While you are checking pressures, also check the condition of the tyres. You must have at least 1.6 mm of tread over 75 per

above **Correct tyre pressures are vital for safety, especially on trailers.**

Everything you need to check on this engine is colour-coded yellow as a reminder: you can do the same with paint.

ent of the tyre's width, and visible tread
on the rest for its whole circumference,
though once the tread is below 3–4 mm it
s unable to disperse water quickly enough
or reliable grip. All tyres have tread wear
indicators which show up as a bar across
the tread when the tyre is below the legal
minimum, but by then it is already illegal.
If you are in doubt, use a tyre tread depth
gauge.

However, horsebox and trailer tyres do
not generally get the sort of use these
heavy-duty tyres are designed for, so they
often develop other faults long before the
tread wears out. Look out for the myriad
of tiny cracks that show the rubber is
starting to perish, and replace the tyre
before they get too deep. It is illegal to use
tyres on which the reinforcing material is
showing through excessive wear, or with
cuts deep enough to show the reinforcing.
Bulges in the tread or tyre wall show that
the carcass is starting to break up, so air is
getting between the layers and the next
stage is a sudden blow out. On tubed tyres,
this sometimes shows as a barely visible
twist in the tyre that usually creates a

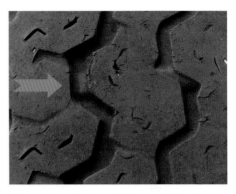

All tyres have tread wear indicators which show up as a bar across the tread when it is below the legal limit.

above **Using a tread depth gauge to check tyre wear.**

Regular checks should ensure that you do not drive on unsafe tyres like this badly perished one.

vibration which is constant, rather than being felt only at certain speeds, as is usually the case with an unbalanced wheel. If you find any of these faults, do not use the vehicle until they have been remedied.

Do not forget to check the spare wheel and, especially on lorries, make sure that the spare can be removed from its carrier.

Tread wear can give clues to problems that need attention. Tyres worn more up the central section of the tread have been run over-inflated, while those with wear up both sides of the tread have been under-inflated. Patches of worn tread indicate an unbalanced wheel, while tread taken off one side of the tyre, often accompanied by feathering of some tread blocks, usually means the wheels are out of alignment. Spotting these signs early can save having to replace tyres prematurely.

If you have to replace tyres, make sure you get ones of the correct speed rating and, most importantly, weight rating, the codes for which are printed on the tyre wall. For example, a typical trailer tyre size and rating would be shown as 165R13 89R, which means it is 165 mm wide, of radial construction and to fit a 13 inch wheel, while the 89 is the weight code for up to 580 kg (2,320 kg over four wheels) and the final R is the speed rating for up to 105 mph. Many trailers and small lorries take tyres that, like this example, are the same size as car tyres, but are heavy-duty items designed for the extra weight. Quote the vehicle's maximum weight and number of wheels when buying tyres.

If a tubeless tyre cannot be repaired correctly by plugging the puncture (for example, if the puncture is in or near the side wall) do not use an inner tube, especially on a trailer, because tubes deflate suddenly when punctured, which may result in loss of control. In such cases, the tyre must be replaced.

Under the Bonnet

The under-bonnet checks for cars and lorries are basically the same, though on lorries not all of the relevant items will actually be under the bonnet, but may be mounted along the chassis rails or behind special flaps, so check your handbook for their location. Also check for instructions specific to your model. For example, some lorry air brake systems have automatically draining water traps, but others may need to be bled manually and failure to do so can lead to problems, like condensation freezing in the pipes.

Oil levels should be checked with the dipstick. On older engines you may find a gradual drop in oil level, especially as a periodic service approaches, but any sudden drop may indicate a leak. If you have to top the oil up, check the handbook for the correct grade and specification; diesels are particularly hard on their oil so they must have the correct type. This is especially so of modern diesels, which often rely on special synthetic oils to enable long service intervals (diesels used to need more frequent servicing than petrol engines).

Towing puts extra strain on an engine, so coolant is even more important than usual. In most modern vehicles the oolant expansion tank is a translucent ottle with the levels marked on it. In lder vehicles it may be a metal or opaque plastic container, which you have to open o check, while older vehicles still, may not ave an expansion tank, so you have to heck the level of water in the radiator tself. If you have to open the system, only lo so with the engine off and cold, or you ould be sprayed with scalding water. Even then, open it carefully in case there is till any pressure in the system (there is usually a pressure release position as you urn the cap).

Any sudden drop in coolant levels ndicates either a leak, or that the seal on a radiator or expansion bottle cap has gone and the cap needs replacing. If replacing he cap fails to stop the loss, get the system hecked professionally. If you have to top up coolant it is better to use the correct antifreeze solution, because adding plain water gradually dilutes the antifreeze, which acts to prevent corrosion as well as freezing.

Oil in the coolant, or mayonnaise-like deposits in the oil, indicate a leak between the lubrication and cooling systems, probably because of a faulty gasket, which should be repaired immediately. Driving with a fault like this could do serious damage.

Check levels in the brake and the clutch fluid reservoirs (if applicable: not all cars have hydraulic clutches). These should remain steady and, while a small drop in clutch fluid levels is something you should

above **A typical brake fluid reservoir with max. and min. markings.**

On lorries, the essential checks are not always under the bonnet. This Renault's dipstick is just above the front bumper.

keep an eye on, any drop in brake fluid level is serious. It could mean fluid is leaking from a damaged seal into the brake drums, where it seriously affects their efficiency. The vehicle should not be driven until the leak is repaired.

The windscreen washer bottle may seem unimportant after that, but you are legally required to have working washers and not having them won't seem so minor on a mucky motorway in the fog. Plain water will not clear traffic film so use a proprietary washer additive, because these do not foam up like washing up liquid and have antifreeze properties. But never use coolant antifreeze in the washer, because it can damage paintwork and wiper blades.

While you check these things, cast an eye round the engine bay for leaks, damage and foreign objects. Oil leaves obvious traces and some diesel engines, like Land Rover's 200Tdi, are prone to nuts coming undone on parts of the fuel system, eventually spraying diesel all over the engine bay! Coolant may not leak out on a cool engine, because the system is no longer under pressure, but it still leaves white marks when it dries. Check any such spots when the engine is warm to see whether coolant is still leaking there when the system is under pressure.

Rural hazards include rodents chewing insulation, while mice and birds are fond of building nests in standing vehicles and cats like snoozing on warm engines. If your truck or towcar has been standing for any time, take a glance underneath for signs of leaks, or hidden animals.

With lorries, check that the lights are all in working order and clean, not forgetting the lights in the horses' section. Check out the horses' accommodation before you are ready to load, so you have time to sort out any problems.

Trailer Checks

Trailers are mechanically simple, but there are still things that must be checked before each journey. The most obvious is tyres, which we have already covered, but it must be stressed that their correct inflation is essential to ensure the trailer's stability, and a faulty tyre blowing out on a trailer is likely to have catastrophic results.

Just have a walk round the trailer, making sure everything is as it should be. Ensure that ramps and doors open, close and latch properly, that all the bodywork is secure and that lights are clean and undamaged.

Inside the trailer, make sure there are no loose or damaged fittings and check the floor for obvious signs of damage – a bump or dip in the rubber matting should be investigated before the horses get in.

As you hitch up, make sure that everything is working as it should. Anything that sticks or 'graunches' should be investigated: it may only need lubrication, but it is safer to ensure that everything is working before horses are loaded than to have something seize up on the road or at a showground. When you hitch up, which we will cover in the next chapter, you will be checking the lights after plugging them into the car.

Where Are You Going?

It is sensible to work out where you are going for any road journey, but with a trailer or lorry it is essential because you need to plan ahead to drive smoothly – no last-minute 'There it is!' turns – and turning round is not a simple matter. (I once had to do a 12-mile detour because of a badly signed show entrance.) It is also less stressful for horses and people if you can avoid frustrating tours of the countryside.

If you cannot find a location on the map, or follow the (frequently odd) directions that show organizers provide, give them a call to confirm details. If your vehicle has satellite navigation, programme the route the night before and check that it is not suggesting anything daft. Route-finding programmes for PCs like AA Milemaster and Microsoft's Autoroute Express, can be a boon, though none are completely foolproof, so be prepared to fine-tune routes before printing them out. Only Milemaster currently allows you to select a special lorry route option. You can, however, buy road atlases for lorry drivers which have weight and height restrictions marked.

When planning a route, think twice about nippy shortcuts you make in a car. Twisting lanes are not quick, or fun, in a truck or towcar, and are more stressful for the horses. You are also far more likely to have to slam the brakes on to avoid motorists who assume that nothing is coming the other way. Wide, straight roads are usually quicker in a large vehicle

than driving shorter distances on twisting, narrow ones. It may also be worth a detour to avoid steep hills and town centres, especially if there is a risk of stop-start traffic.

Finally, check your timing. Journeys in a lorry or towcar take a lot longer than the same trip by car because the vehicle cruises and corners more slowly, and you often to have to stop to allow for oncoming traffic in situations when a car would have been able to get through the gap. Even with a good towcar, on an all-motorway journey, you should still expect to take at least 30 per cent longer than when not towing. With a lorry, or on a more give-and-take route, allow even more time.

Issues relating to planning routes and driving large vehicles in demanding conditions are discussed further in Chapter 8.

Final Checks

When everything is loaded, pause before driving off. Take a walk round the vehicle and make sure that everything is in order – that tyres look all right with the weight of a horse over them, ramps and doors are shut, the lorry's fold-up steps are folded, trailers are properly hitched, with jockey wheels up and nobody has left the mobile phone on the bonnet. Run down your mental or written checklist of things you have to take, because there is nothing more annoying than remembering two miles down the road that you needed a girth. Oh, and don't forget to lock the house.

7

Basic Driving Skills

There are a number of basic driving skills that we take for granted when we drive an ordinary car solo, but which need extra attention or modification when we drive a towcar or lorry. This need to adapt arises, in the main, out of the fact that the vehicle is larger and you have a more restricted view of the world behind you than in most cars. But, in addition, such vehicles are also slower, and many drivers around you have no understanding of what is involved in driving a lorry or large car and trailer outfit with a live load. Indeed, many cannot even grasp that a large vehicle needs more space on the road than a car!

Before you consider your need to adjust your technical skills, you must first adjust your mental attitude. If you take professional training, this is something instructors try to instil in you, even if they do not lecture you about it directly. Large vehicles can be viewed by car drivers as intimidating, so you should try not to put pressure on others, which will only fluster them into making mistakes or make them aggressive. You should drive defensively, looking out for others' mistakes, even if

Learn to drive defensively when transporting horses, for example, by signalling and getting into lane early.

ou have right of way, because you do not have the agility to get out of the way readily, and you have a live load you do not want to stress. Think ahead and do not assume that people will react to your approach in the same way they would to a car – for example, they might pull out unwisely to avoid getting stuck behind ou. Do not retaliate to stupid driving, no matter how annoyed you are.

Remember, too, that even an average off-roader and trailer with one horse board weighs around three times more than a car like a Ford Focus, while lorries an weigh many times more than that. That massive weight difference means that our vehicle can do substantial structural damage to a car, potentially overcoming all the passenger protection engineered nto it. You owe it to other road users to remain alert to the dangers, even if it is their lack of observation and skill that puts their lives at risk.

Hitching and Unhitching

Since driving skill starts at home, we will begin with hitching up trailers. Hitching is something that comes with practise, though there are several little tricks that maker it easier. It is important to get into a routine for hitching so that you do not forget anything. The routine suggested here is based on the towing test, but you might want to adjust it to suit your circumstances or the way you remember things. For some people it is easier to do, say, everything to do with brakes, then everything to do with lights.

Caravanners may wonder what the fuss is about, but horse trailers are not so easy to manhandle, so the closer you can bring hitch and towball together, the easier the job becomes. You can get shields that bolt behind the towball to protect the car's bumper from clumsy hitching up, which are a particularly good idea on those with painted bumpers.

One device that makes hitching up a lot easier is the Equibrand Trailer Coupling Mirror, which is attached to the trailer's front and allows the driver to see the hitch and ball coming together from far enough off to adjust the vehicle's position. For those taking the towing test, the DSA says that there is nothing to stop you using fittings which aid coupling. Equibrand are on 01327 262444.

Equibrand's coupling mirror makes hitching up easy.

An alternative aid, not approved for the test, is a broomstick. If you lean one against the hitch, you get a good idea of where the latter is, long after it becomes invisible to you. At home, we have a variation on this in the form of a length of plastic pipe set in concrete in a flowerpot, which also serves as a bollard to make it easier to avoid walking or reversing into the hitch in the dark!

Even your rear window manufacturer can help you. Many glass manufacturers put their trademark in the centre of the lower edge of the screen, which you can use as a 'gun sight' to line the centre of the car up with the hitch. If your rear screen does not have such a mark, use a piece of tape or a sticker.

Cars with a lift-up tailgate may also allow you a better view of the hitch if you reverse with the hatch open and the rear seat back folded, but first check that there is no chance of the raised tailgate hitting the trailer.

A good assistant is also useful, but it must be someone who understands what is required. They must stand in your line of sight, so you are not trying to watch the trailer and someone off to the side, but not where they risk getting caught between hitch and towball. They will be safe if they stand alongside the trailer's A-frame, close to the trailer body, but they should never stand on or in the frame, where they may be injured if the car moves the trailer.

The assistant should give you clear signals, which you have agreed in advance. If they point left or right with a finger, wave you back with the whole hand and stop you with palm held towards you, there is no risk of confusion. Over the last 30 cm or so, it is more useful if the assistant uses both hands to mimic the closing distance.

The car's towball should always be lubricated with grease to prevent wear and stop it groaning. If the grease looks

If someone is guiding you when hitching up it helps if they demonstrate hitch to ball distance over the last 30 cm.

dirty, wipe it off and use clean grease, otherwise grit will turn it into grinding paste, wearing the ball and hitch (see also Chapter 11: Trailer Maintenance). Most hitches now have a wear indicator to show if the ball or hitch is worn, so check that after hitching up.

If your trailer has a locking hitch, start by unlocking it, then use the jockey wheel to raise the hitch to about 5 cm higher the towball. (Stand next to the ball and note where it comes to against your leg.) On the way to the driver's seat, remove any covers from the towball and electrical sockets.

Now reverse back until you are happy that the ball is under the hitch. If you are alone, step out and have a look. If you are close but not quite there, the easiest way to get the car a few centimetres back or forwards is to judge the distance between, say, a front mudflap or wheel and something on the ground. When you are as close as you can get, make sure the car's handbrake is on and turn off the engine (or you'll have to breathe exhaust fumes).

Lower the hitch onto the ball with the jockey wheel. On some hitches you must hold a handle up as you bring the hitch down; others are self-releasing, while some require only that a safety catch is pulled back. If the car is slightly too far forwards, a hitch will generally slide out the extra centimetre or two, but they do not usually slide backwards. If you need to push or pull the hitch to the side to line it up the last little bit, it may be easier to do it with the trailer brake off, but only do this on level ground and be ready to

above **Reverse up to the trailer, getting ball and hitch as close as possible, then apply the handbrake.**

Holding the hitch locking handle up, lower it onto the ball. Release the handle and try raising the hitch again.

reapply the brake if it starts to roll (do not risk this method on the towing test).

Check that the hitch has locked on by raising it with the jockey wheel, then fully raise and lock the wheel. Some jockey wheels have a specific position to return them to before they can be fully raised, so if yours looks low, check it is not because of this. It is essential that the wheel is raised fully because it could be damaged if you hit a hump.

Now attach the breakaway cable to a suitably strong point on the car. If the trailer becomes unhitched, this cable is designed to apply the brakes before it snaps, so it must be attached to something capable of taking that strain – not a plastic bumper. The approved towbars compulsory on cars registered since 1998 must have a purpose-made loop for attaching the cable. If your car does not have this, clip the wire to part of the towbar. Looping it round the towball neck should be a last resort because of the risk of it fouling the hitch cup, and because it gives no help if the towball breaks off.

If you use a stabilizer, fit it now. Then plug in the electrical connections. If the car has two electrical sockets, the trailer plugs into the one with a black spring flap cover. The one with the white or pale grey flap is for plugging in the auxiliary system on a caravan. Some European

above **Fully raise and secure the jockey whee**

Clip the breakaway cable to the towbar's ring or to a substantial part of the car.

manufacturers' towing kits use a single multi-pin plug for both these functions, for which you need either an adaptor, or to replace your trailer's UK plug with the continental type (see Chapter 1). Do not try replacing the car's socket, especially on the latest technology cars with aircraft-style Multiplex wiring, where cutting the wrong wire can mean replacing the whole wiring loom.

Now check that everything is properly fitted and stowed. Breakaway and electrical cables need enough slack to allow for tight turns, but not so much that they drag on the ground. You can usually allow for both by giving them a twist or two before connecting them. Also, make sure they will not foul the hitch, hand-brake or stabilizer on turns.

Finally, check the car's handbrake is on and release the trailer's handbrake. I usually pull the trailer forwards a short distance at this stage, just to check that there are no seized brakes, especially if it has not been used for a while.

Now check the lights with the car's ignition on. You need an assistant when checking brake lights and it is also easier to check the other lights with someone at the back. The assistant should shout out

Plug in the electrical connection.

Check that the car's handbrake is on and release the trailer's handbrake.

Check that the lights are working correctly.

what they are seeing, not just say 'yes', so you know they are seeing what you have just turned on. Test the indicators using the indicator stalk, not the hazard lights, because they are on different circuits and wiring faults can cause car and trailer to show opposite indicators. Check the car's lights at the same time.

To unhitch, stop on level ground and apply the car's and trailer's handbrakes. If you have to unhitch on a slope, with the trailer pointing uphill, you have to take steps to override the brakes' auto-reverse mechanism, which allows you to reverse the trailer without having to throw a lever

to disconnect the brakes (as on very old trailers). In this situation, after applying the trailer's handbrake, return to the car and release its handbrake. The outfit should roll back a few centimetres as the trailer's handbrake overrides the auto-reverse. On off-roaders you may need to actually reverse gently, because the resistance of a 4WD transmission means they will often not roll on gentle slopes. Reapply the car's handbrake and check that the trailer's is full on. On a hill it is best to chock the trailer wheels, too.

Next, drop and lock the jockey wheel, disconnect and stow the electrical plug and remove the stabilizer.

The DSA recommends disconnecting the breakaway cable now, but some trailer manufacturers suggest it is better to leave that until after you have unhitched, in case the handbrake is not fully on and the trailer rolls. With modern spring-assisted handbrakes, this is unlikely and by doing it the DSA way you reduce the risk of driving off with the cable still attached.

Now raise the hitch with the jockey wheel while holding up the hitch release handle. Occasionally, you may find the ball holds on to the hitch, raising the back of the car, but a push on the towbar with your foot usually frees it.

Drive the car away and refit any covers to the towball and electrical connectors. A towball cover not only protects your clothes from grease but also protects the ball from car-park knocks. Some people say covers on electrical sockets only trap moisture in them, but on mucky rural roads they protect the sockets from mud and worse.

Reversing

Reversing a lorry or car and trailer is a very different proposition from reversing a car, in which you are easily able to see around you and which behaves much the same going backwards as it does forwards.

The most important difference between a car and a lorry or trailer outfit is that, with the latter vehicles, your view behind is extremely restricted. Not only does this mean that much of the manoeuvre is carried out on mirrors alone, but it also means that you are reversing into a vast blind spot. Though you can assume the reversing area on the driving test is safe, in any other place always get out to check behind you. On busy showgrounds it is best to have someone see you back to ensure that nobody wanders into the area you are backing into – riders intent on their next class may not notice you are reversing.

Remember, especially on the road, that other drivers do not always realize how limited your view is, nor that it is possible for your vehicle to totally obscure theirs, so they may do nothing about you reversing towards them because they assume you know that they are there. Take care, after you have checked behind, that nobody drives up as you walk back to the driver's seat.

Some lorries have audible warnings for reversing (they are also available for cars) but it is still the driver's responsibility to make sure that the area is clear. The person behind you could be deaf, and young children and animals do not realize the significance of the bleeping sound. As with your horn, you are not allowed to use these devices on roads subject to a 30 mph speed limit between 11.30 p.m. and 7 a.m.

Reversing sensors are increasingly fitted to lorries and cars, and kits are becoming available for trailers. These are ultrasonic transceivers in the back bumper, which set off a bleeper in the car when they detect something. The bleep usually gets faster as you approach the object, becoming

Always check behind before reversing because lorries and trailers have huge blind spots.

constant at a distance of about 30 cm. They are a boon, but are not infallible and, again, it is the driver's responsibility to check that the area is clear. Incidentally, on towcars, once hitched up, a reversing sensor detects the trailer when you engage reverse gear and, on many cars, the off button only works until you select a forward gear, so it must be turned off every time you change from forward to reverse in difficult manoeuvres.

When reversing up to an obstruction, it may help to do so at a slight angle, with the back of the lorry or trailer angled slightly towards your side, giving you a clearer view of where the end of the vehicle is.

When reversing through gaps, like gateways, it pays to line up the truck or outfit as straight as you can then, once you are sure it will go through the gap, concentrate on keeping your side of the vehicle as close to the gatepost as is safe. That way, you are not trying to judge distances on both sides at once – but keep an eye on the far mirror for people, animals and other vehicles approaching on that side.

When practising reversing, choose a safe area into which people and animals are unlikely to wander. The more level it is, the better, especially with a trailer, which will turn around a wheel that has dropped into a hole regardless of how you are steering. Also keep an eye on the engine temperature gauge, because low-speed manoeuvres, especially in reverse, do not aid cooling.

Even if you are not taking the test, you may find it helpful to set up the driving test reversing area explained in Chapter 2, if you have the space. This combines elements of all the reversing manoeuvres and skills you are likely to need, but when learning how to reverse trailers, learn the basic methods first.

Reversing Lorries

A lorry in reverse behaves like a car, in that it goes the way you turn the wheel. However, you still have to master the art of steering and judging distances by the mirrors and practice makes perfect on that. Don't be afraid to get out and look (except on a driving test) if you are unsure of clearance and distance.

If you are making the change from a trailer to a lorry, beware the temptation to steer the wrong way when reversing using the mirrors, especially when reversing in a straight line. (The procedure for trailers is different from solo cars and lorries – see next section.)

Allow plenty of room for swinging the front of the vehicle round, and keep an eye

On lorries, having outrigger lights like these helps you to see where the end of the vehicle is for reversing.

on what the front is doing as you reverse, so you do not swing the cab into something. When reversing, the back is less manoeuvrable than the front and follows a tighter line, so you are likely to be seeing smaller movements in the mirror than the front is making.

If you practise at home, set out a course with gates to reverse through on turns and in straight lines, and 'barriers' to reverse up to help you judge distances.

Reversing Trailers

For reversing trailers, you have to learn a new set of rules. Most people realize that, to reverse a trailer, you have to steer the 'wrong way', at least to start the trailer going in the direction desired. It is easier to work out why if you imagine looking down on a car and trailer. If the back of the trailer is to go right, its nose must go left and, as its nose is attached to the back of the car, it follows that that must also go left.

The difficult bit is that the initial steering movement only starts the trailer turning and if it is not corrected in time, the trailer will turn more tightly than required. Ultimately, it jack-knifes, getting at such a sharp angle to the towcar that the car can no longer influence its direction in reverse and the driver must pull forwards to reduce the angle (for which you would fail the driving test reversing exercise). Seeing the point at which you must start steering the other way only comes with practice so, even if you are not taking the test, it is well worth doing reversing exercises and getting professional tuition if you have trouble.

Do not reverse aimlessly round a field, but start by learning to reverse to the right, which is easier, as if you were backing through a gate. Set out a 'gate' about one and a half times the width of the outfit with something easy to see that won't cause damage if you get it wrong, like plastic jump stands, cones or electric fence Polyposts. Pull up as straight as you can, about one trailer's length out from it and half a trailer's length beyond it.

As you start to reverse, turn the steering wheel left until the trailer starts to turn. Once it is turning towards the gate, you start winding off the steering, checking all the time that it is still going the way you want – if it isn't, steer back left. Eventually, you get to a position where you must steer the other way to bring the front of the car

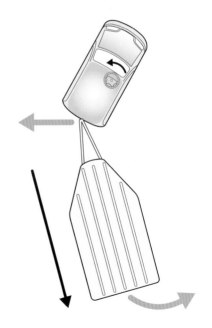

The reversing chain reaction: for the trailer to go right, the back of the car must go left.

round. Take care not to overdo this, or you may start the trailer going the other way. If you find you are 'fish-tailing' as you correct too much one way then the other, the best option is to pull forwards to straighten the outfit. Reverse back through the gate, then come out and try again, varying your starting position as you become more competent. Many drivers seem to find it easier to lean out of the window at first to judge the beginning of the turn, then switch to mirrors, but others find it easier to use mirrors alone.

Once you have lined up the outfit with the gate, it is easier to concentrate on keeping the distance between your side of the car and the 'post' constant. But do get into the habit when practising of glancing at the other mirror occasionally because, in real life situations, you need to check that people, animals and other vehicles are not approaching that on side.

When you have mastered that, try the gate exercise to the left, where you have to make far more use of the mirrors and, in some cars, have a very limited view out

Start straight and about a trailer's length ahead of the 'gate'.

To start the turn, steer the opposite way from the trailer's direction.

the back as the trailer turns. Also, try setting up a series of gates in a line to reverse through straight.

When reversing in a straight line it is easier to use the mirrors alone. When more of the trailer appears in one mirror than in the other, turn the wheel towards the mirror you can see more in. Make frequent small corrections until the outfit straightens, rather than trying instant correction with big steering movements. Some people find it easier to hold the bottom of the wheel so that their hands move in the same direction as the trailer.

When you are happy you can manage it, try the driving test reversing area in Chapter 2.

With an off-roader, it may be easier to do these manoeuvres in the low-ratio gearbox instead of constantly slipping the clutch, but check the handbook to make sure the 4WD system allows this. Off-road only systems have no centre differential to take up the differences in distances travelled by the wheels in tight turns which, on firm ground, may make the

As the trailer turns in, steer the other way to bring the car round.

Reverse in a straight line using the mirrors. If more of the trailer is visible in one mirror, steer towards that mirror.

Try to stop level with the back of your 'box'. (The towcar in this picture is a Hyundai Terracan.)

transmission 'wind up' under potentially damaging tension. Some full-time 4WD systems lock the centre differential automatically when low is engaged, which has the same effect.

Pulling Away

Pulling away in a towcar or laden lorry takes skill and care, even if you have practised without the horses on board. Their additional weight means you need more power to pull away. Because of the size of the vehicle or outfit you also need a lot of room and to be careful about checking mirrors and looking around you. The live load means you want to avoid having to turn out quickly or accelerate away hard.

Check your mirrors, look over your shoulder and use your indicators. Unless you are pulling onto a dual-carriageway from a lay-by, do not get a mirror fixation. Keep an eye on oncoming traffic, too, because the length of your vehicle may necessitate turning out close to or across the centre line. On a lorry with a long rear overhang, turning out too sharply may

also make the tail swing across the verge or pavement, with the risk of hitting a pedestrian or roadside object.

Look out for cyclists passing close to the side of your vehicle and, on a lorry, be aware that you may have a blind spot in front of the cab where you cannot see children, or even short adults, close to you.

Do not use more engine revs than you need to pull away, but be aware that, on a slope, you may need more than you expected. A useful technique to learn is using the rev counter to assist your clutch control. Find out the engine speed in revolutions per minute at which it develops peak torque (pulling power shown in lb ft or Nm). In first gear, with the clutch depressed, push the throttle pedal until the rev counter needle is around that point. Then, instead of juggling two pedals, hold the throttle steady and slowly raise the clutch pedal, using clutch adjustments alone to keep the needle around peak torque rpm as the vehicle moves off. As the clutch eventually comes all the way in, depress the throttle to accelerate away.

You should soon get a feel for pulling away on the flat without resorting to this method, but remember it for pulling away on steep hills. Hill starts can be difficult to judge on large vehicles, but it is essential that you do not roll back, because you cannot see how close the vehicles behind you are.

Use of Mirrors

You are much more reliant on mirrors in a lorry or towcar than in a solo car, because you either have no side windows, or a very restricted view through them. Make sure that mirrors are clean, undamaged and big enough. On some towcars you may need to add towing mirrors to see round the trailer.

In an unfamiliar vehicle, take time to check how far away things in the mirror really are, and where your blind spots are – those are the points at which overtaking cars are no longer visible in the mirrors but have not yet come into your line of sight. It may help to fit blind-spot mirrors, but only do so if it would not obstruct your general view. Even then, it pays to glance over your shoulder.

If the mirrors are big enough it can be helpful to adjust them so that, perhaps with a slight movement of your head, you can see the lorry's rear wheels or the trailer's wheels. This allows you to check their position on turns, when they follow a tighter line than the front of the outfit, or on narrow roads, where they are close to the edge.

What are you looking for in the mirrors? Anything that will affect what you are about to do. On the driver's side you are looking for overtaking vehicles, so you are not surprised by the effect of something big passing you and do not pull out into anyone's path. You are looking for people doing stupid things, like overtaking when you are about to turn right or following you too close. In towns, look out for cyclists who are unable to overtake quickly enough.

Towing mirrors help you to see round a trailer that is much wider than a car.

On the passenger side you are looking for cyclists and pedestrians, especially when turning left. On turns you are looking for obstructions that might catch the closer-turning back end. On motorways and dual-carriageways, check for cars coming down slip roads intending to overtake you before joining the main road. In country lanes and through roadworks with narrow lanes, check that you are far enough out from kerbs, hedges or cones.

Occasionally checking in the passenger-side mirror, to see how close you are to something you are passing, helps give you a better idea of your position on the road and the width of your vehicle. You can also use your mirrors to check how close you are to white lines dividing lanes or marking the road centre.

At angled junctions where you may not have a good view over your shoulder, you may be able to see down the road you wish to enter in the mirror, if you are positioned properly. However, look long enough to be sure nobody is close to you in a blind spot.

By constant observation, you will have a good idea of what is going on around you. You know that if the red car has disappeared from view it may either be in your blind spot or tucked in close behind. It will help you to avoid being taken by surprise and having to make a sudden manoeuvre, and it will help you avoid being a danger to others.

Changing Gear

Because the engine develops different levels of torque (pulling power) and horsepower at different engine speeds, you need gears to allow you to keep it in the optimum torque or power band for the job in hand. So, first gear allows relatively high engine speeds at low road speeds for pulling away, while fifth allows modest engine speeds at high road speeds for easy and economical cruising. Gearing is expressed as a ratio and the lower the number, the higher the gear, so 1:3 is fairly low while 1:0.75 would be a tall, cruising gear. Quite often, gears are also expressed as the easier to understand mph per 1,000 rpm (miles per hour per 1,000 revs per minute), which takes into account other factors such as the axle differential gearing and wheel size and means that, in

Some drivers need reminding that lorries and trailers are different from solo cars.

hat particular gear, the car will do, say, 25 mph for every 1,000 rpm of engine speed so, at 2,000 rpm it is doing 50 mph). mooth gear changing at the right time educes stress on the horses and vehicle, s well as reducing fuel consumption and ollution. It is also expected of you in the riving test.

There is no magic formula for predicting when you need to change gear ecause there are too many variables. It depends on gear ratios, engine torque, ow heavy the load is, and aerodynamics – ven a strong headwind can make a ifference with a lorry or horse trailer. It ll comes down to driver experience and here is nothing wrong with experimenting to see if the vehicle can take a higher gear in certain circumstances. Use the speed-ometer and rev counter to get an dea of when the vehicle can take a particular gear. For example, you might otice that your towcar can only take ourth gear when towing above 30 mph, or that your lorry is only happy in fifth bove a certain engine speed. Some lowpowered petrol engines only pull well a ew hundred revs either side of the peak orque point while others, notably urbodiesels, may show considerable lexibility over a wide rev range.

If the engine labours in a higher gear, specially if you get a shudder, you must hange down, even if the engine sounds usy in the lower gear. You do not save uel by labouring the engine in too high a gear, but you can increase wear on xpensive components.

You should also use lower gears to help low the vehicle down on hills, where repeatedly applying the brakes can make them fade, especially on heavy vehicles and outfits. This system effectively uses resistance from the engine to slow the vehicle down (engine braking).

Equally, a lower gear should be used when climbing hills. If you find that the engine starts to sound busy, but is labouring when you change up, go back to the lower gear and reduce your revs. Even if this means slowing the climb it will reduce stress on the engine, occupants and fuel bills. Delay changing up at the top of a hill until you have reduced engine speed on the flat because you have had the vehicle in a lower gear to increase the torque (twisting or pulling power) available and suddenly reducing this while changing gear makes a smooth change harder. With a towcar, that sudden reduction in torque, coupled with you being one- handed at the wheel, could be enough to upset the outfit's stability.

When changing up with a manual gearbox, you should get the clutch pedal fully up before returning to the throttle, but changes down will be smoother if you apply the throttle just ahead of bringing the clutch in. This allows for the fact that on a change up, the engine speed drops and on a change down it increases.

Never coast in neutral or with the clutch depressed, because you do not have full control of the vehicle nor do you have any engine braking. It is also important in both towcars and lorries to change down early enough for bends to ensure that the vehicle can be under power through the bend. If you go through a bend on a trailing throttle, or worse, in neutral, the vehicle or outfit's weight takes over and makes it drift out.

There are many types of automatic gearbox available in cars now. Even older, traditional automatics allow you to hold lower gears when required, for example when going up or down hills. You should always listen to what the engine is doing and be prepared to help an automatic if the engine starts to labour or if the gearbox starts to 'hunt' up and down the ratios. But, these days, most gearboxes offer a choice of 'power' or 'sport' settings in addition to a 'normal' one. The 'power' setting normally alters the change points so it holds gears longer, though on a few gearboxes it also locks it out of top. In some, this setting can be a little over-eager when towing and the system is often very reluctant to move into top, but the simple solution is to use 'sport' for the twisty or uphill bits, then flip to 'normal' when the road straightens out.

Many automatics now also offer a manual touch change override, whereby tapping the lever back and forth, or side to side, changes gear like a clutchless manual – though they always have a fail-safe to make or stop changes to avoid 'engine cruelty' if the driver makes an error. Most of these change smoothly without easing the throttle, but some fair better if you ease up. Do not get lazy when slowing for junctions and bends by allowing the fail-safe to change down for you, because it will simply move to the next acceptable gear, which may not be the optimum one for pulling away again. (Some lorries have a variation on this system called a semiautomatic, on which

the clutch is used only when stopping and starting.)

Some automatics 'learn' from the way the driver uses the throttle and vary their responses accordingly. Be aware that these may not respond after a period of slow traffic as they did on the open road before the hold up.

Off-roaders, and some larger lorries, have dual-ratio gearboxes, with a normal high set for ordinary road use and a low set for off-road use or for getting heavy loads moving and climbing hills. The shift can be either by a switch or, more usually in off-roaders, with a small gear lever. Check the handbook for details on how yours works and the circumstances in which you can use it and whether you have to stop to engage and disengage it. On very hilly, twisty roads, where speeds are low, you may find it easier in a vehicle with full-time 4WD which does not automatically lock the centre differential in low ratio to stay in low, using low fourth and fifth on the faster stretches. Lorry dual-ratio boxes are intended for road use, but there are maximum speeds at which you can make the switch.

Using 4WD

Off-roaders are becoming ever more complex so, if you use one for towing, read the handbook thoroughly. Not all 4WD systems are designed for road use, and improper use can do expensive damage, voiding the warranty.

Those vehicles with full-time road-going 4WD systems, like BMW X5s and post-1985 Land Rover vehicles, are

enerally the simplest to use because they
:ay in 4WD all the time. Those with
electable road-going systems that allow
ou to use 4WD or 2WD on the road, like
1itsubishi Shoguns and some Jeeps,
enerally feel more reassuring in 4WD but
ll have a maximum speed at which you
an make the change. Road-going 4WD
ystems sometimes have a manual method
f locking one or more differential to stop
pinning wheels immobilizing the car.
Differentials are systems of gears
esigned to take up the differences
etween distances travelled by driven
vheels as the vehicle turns, preventing the
ransmission from 'winding up' under
ension.) Part-time, off-road only systems,
ke in Isuzu Troopers, Nissan Terranos
nd most 4WD pickups, cannot be used on
rm surfaces because they have no centre
ifferential and rely on the wheels slipping

to take up the differences between front
and rear wheel travel.

On most 4WDs you have to stop to
engage low ratio but – useful when getting
a heavy trailer moving on a steep hill – you
can usually change up on the move at low
speeds, though you may have to double-
declutch, as drivers once had to do on all
changes. This means you pull away in low
first and, when you get to a reasonable
speed, you push the clutch pedal down,
slip the high-low lever into neutral, bring
the clutch pedal back up and raise the
engine revs briefly before dipping the
clutch to put the lever into the high
position. This takes skill to do smoothly
and, if you live in a hilly area, it is a good
idea to practise doing it.

However, some dual-ratio systems do
not allow this option. With part-time
systems with no centre differential, or a
full-time system on which selecting low
automatically locks the differential, you
should only use this pulling away method
in a straight line, or it may refuse to make
the change because of tension in the
transmission.

You may also find low ratio useful for
getting off muddy showgrounds, but take
care when changing gear in low ratio
because it is difficult to do so smoothly
and the loss of momentum it creates could
get you stuck. In such circumstances, low
also allows you to trickle the power in very
gently so you can creep forward without
losing traction. Once wheels start spinning
there is no point feeding more power
through, because the wheels haven't got
the grip to use it. (See the Snow and Ice
and Rough Ground sections in Chapter 8.)

his transfer lever in a Shogun is clearly marked to
how the 4WD positions.

Road-going 4WD generally gives more even engine braking and better stability when towing, but cannot defy the laws of physics. State-of-the-art systems give you very high levels of traction and handling security, but can also disguise how slippery a road has become and, when all four wheels start sliding, 4WD is not going to help you – especially with a trailer to push you along. So, on icy or muddy roads, drive as carefully as you would with a 2WD car, relying on the 4WD to give you higher safety margins.

An off-road driving course, preferably one that combines it with on-road tuition, will help you to understand the vehicle and get the best from it in difficult conditions.

Using Electronic Driving Aids

Electronic driving aids were explained in Chapter 3. All these driving aids are intended to widen your safety margin. If you have pushed it so far that warning lights come on, or ABS (anti-lock braking) activates, you have overstepped the limits in a way that would be foolish in a car, never mind a lorry or horse trailer outfit.

ABS is the most common of the electronic aids and is offered on almost all cars – at least as an option – and it is now compulsory on large lorries. In a solo vehicle, it does not normally stop it any quicker – though it preserves directional control and stability under heavy braking – but in towcars it has been shown to as much as halve emergency stopping distances. If ABS comes into play you feel

a pulsing through the brake pedal. If you feel this in what should have been a normal stop, it means you were going too fast or braking too hard for the road surface conditions but, if you feel it in an emergency stop, resist the temptation to ease up on the pedal. *Never pump the brake pedal on a vehicle equipped with ABS because it interferes with the system's programming and may even cause a wheel to lock up.*

Traction control uses the ABS sensors but works the opposite way, with the system gently braking wheels that are starting to spin. Systems either make a twanging noise or have a warning light to let you know they are activated. In some cases they work best if you assist them by easing up on the throttle a little, so that your heavy foot is not overriding their efforts; others need steady power to work with. However, on mud, with a few powerful, road-orientated 4WD vehicles, the margin between enough power for the system to work and enough to push the back sideways is slim. Some traction control systems may be briefly triggered when you hit large bumps or potholes, but if they are activated in normal driving it is a warning that the road is slippery and you should slow down. Traction control relies on detecting differences in wheel rotation speeds, so on sheet ice, when all wheels may spin at the same rate, it cannot work.

Electronic stability programmes (ESP) again use the ABS sensors and detect when the vehicle is drifting out on a bend, using the brakes to counter the movement It is something well worth having in large

ehicles and, especially, towcars, where
he trailer can push the car out on a bend
though with horses on board, you should
o everything you can to avoid cornering
hat fast). A warning light tells you that
ou have overdone it.

A trailer stability programme allied to
SP was first offered on the BMW X5.
lugging in the trailer's lights lets the ESP
now that the car is towing, and the
omputer starts monitoring for signs of
nstability in the trailer. Should the trailer
tart snaking, ESP brakes the car's wheels

in a way that maintains stability as you
slow down. It is said to be able to detect
the first signs of snaking earlier than a
driver would and warns you by showing
the ESP light, indicating that you should
ease your speed. Snaking is covered
further in the next chapter. ESP should
be turned off when off-road because it
mistakes natural sideways movements on
slippery surfaces for instability, braking
wheels when you least need it. This is
unhelpful on muddy showgrounds.

8

On the Road

When you venture onto the road with a large vehicle or trailer and a live load there are a lot of things that need even more careful consideration than when driving a car because you do not have the same manoeuvrability, you occupy a lot more space and you do not want to stress the animals. In addition, if you drive in a way that causes a horse to lose his balance, especially in a trailer or small horsebox, you could lose control of the vehicle as half a tonne shifts suddenly.

We are not going to cover here everything in *The Highway Code*, only those matters which affect transporting horses. If you have not read the code for some time it pays to read the latest edition because many new topics have been introduced in recent years. In addition, if you last read it for your car test you may not have paid full attention to aspects relating to towing or lorries. Similarly, the DSA's car and goods vehicle driving manuals (see Further Reading p. 208) give a lot of important and useful information on general driving matters, while also being part of the relevant driving test syllabuses (towing is covered briefly in the manual).

Vehicle Size

There are many circumstances on the road when it pays to know your vehicle's size. If you meet a weight, height or width restriction you may not have the time to work out if it applies to you. Towcar drivers are at particular risk because, in a solo car, none of these usually apply, but the trailer may be outside the safe width or height. This applies not just to obvious things like bridge heights: you may find width restrictions on motorway roadworks, village roads and car-park access.

It is a good idea to put this information clearly on a label you can refer to from the driver's seat, perhaps on the back of a sun visor. With an off-roader it pays to have the vehicle's height in the car anyway, because many car-park barriers are lower than the taller off-roaders.

Remember that other road users are not usually aware of the restrictions the size of your vehicle or outfit put on your vision and manoeuvrability. Many lorry companies now fit 'If you can't see my mirrors, I can't see you' notices to the backs of their trucks and drivers say this

Trailer ht: 2.6m (8ft 6in)

Trailer w: 2.12m (7ft)

LR ht: 1.96m (6ft 5in)

LR w: 1.79m (5ft 10in)

A label like this on the sun visor can save a lot of grief in a tall vehicle.

really does make motorists back off. But be prepared for other drivers getting into a position where you simply cannot see where they are, not allowing you the room you need for a manoeuvre, or expecting you to let them pass by pulling into a gap between parked cars that is little bigger than their Fiesta.

Speed Limits

Many car drivers are unaware that there are different speed limits for towcars and different sizes of lorry. They are as shown in the table below in miles per hour. (Urban roads are those with street lights, unless other limits are posted.)

Observation

Observation is the key to driving any vehicle well, and it becomes even more important with large vehicles and live loads. By looking ahead and using your mirrors you will be better prepared to meet the hazards around you and give yourself more time to prepare for bends, lane changes and junctions.

Get into the habit of looking well ahead while still remaining aware of what is happening close to you. Slow down early for bends and junctions to give yourself time to make gear changes smoothly. Also err on the side of caution when approaching other drivers pulling out, to

Vehicle	Urban	Rural single carriageway	Dual-carriageway	Motorways
Towcars	30	50	60	60
Lorries to 7.5 t	30	50	60	70*
Lorries over 7.5 t	30	40	50	60

*60 mph if towing.

Your mirrors can help you to see how far the trailer is from the road edge, as well as what is behind you.

give yourself time to react if they pull into your path – a remark that also applies when approaching potential bottlenecks. Many drivers simply do not recognize that you need more space than a car to get past obstructions or to pull in to get out of their way, while some will take silly risks just to avoid getting behind a slow vehicle.

In traffic queues, do not lock your vision on the vehicle in front, so that you have to *react* to what that does instead of *anticipating* it. By pulling back so that you can see a little more round the vehicle in front, you get more warning of what the queue is about to do and give yourself more time to respond. In stop-start traffic in towns, shop window reflections often give an idea of whether traffic ahead is about to move. In lorries and off-roaders you have the advantage of sitting up high, so use it. Look over lines of traffic so you can see that the car ahead is about to turn right, and look over hedges on twisting country roads to get an idea of what is coming.

Do not forget to look out for pedestrians and cyclists, who are often the most unpredictable of hazards since many have little idea of what it is like to drive a large vehicle, or of the way that its back turns tighter than its front. With towcars, they may not even notice the trailer behind you.

Steering

The steering on trucks and many off-roaders does not give as much road 'feel' as that of most cars, which is another reason why you must drive carefully. You should hold the wheel with both hands at a 'ten to two' or 'quarter to three' position and remember that a truck or towcar may not track straight if you drive one-handed while fiddling with a mobile phone or stereo. However, many newcomers worried about the new sensations of driving a lorry or towing react by gripping the wheel too hard. If you do this, you reduce your feel of what the steering is

oing and prevent the wheel from making
.s natural little feedback movements, so
ou have to physically correct the steering
or every bump and dip you drive over –
's like riding with too tight a rein. If you
eel you are having to correct the steering
ll the time, or that it is fighting against
ou, just try relaxing your grip a little – it
nay help you to relax, too.

In fact, you may find in certain
ircumstances, like when being hit by a
assing vehicle's slipstream, or if a trailer
s snaking (see later this chapter), that
asing your left hand grip totally will give
ou a better feel for what is happening.

Manoeuvres

Cornering

When driving with horses on board you
must try to corner smoothly and at sensible
speeds. Remember, your horses in the back
annot anticipate changes in direction as
ou can in the front – think what it is like
tanding in a bus when you can't see out.

Car drivers making the change to
orries, or those who are novices to
owing, must remember that these
ehicles have very different handling
haracteristics. Even if you are only
naking the switch from a car to an off-
oader, take time to get to know the
vehicle and the different way it behaves.
As they have a high centre of gravity, tall
vehicles tend to lean on bends, which
eventually makes them drift out early and
hey are less stable when they do run into
problems. Their weight, or the weight of
he trailer behind them, also means

recovery from over-eager cornering is
harder.

All vehicles, including solo cars, corner
better if they are 'driven' through a bend
instead of being allowed to drift through
on a slack throttle. However, this is even
more important with large vehicles and
especially when towing because, if it is not
under power, the vehicle's weight takes
over, showing the desire to go straight.
With a towcar, cornering on a slack
throttle often results in a feeling of the
trailer trying to push the car. Even more
importantly, never coast through a bend in
neutral, or with the clutch pedal down,
because you greatly reduce your control of
the vehicle.

But this does not mean that you have to
power through the bend like a rally driver.
The very lightest touch on the throttle is
usually enough to make a difference.

Make sure you have slowed and
changed down early enough in the
approach to a bend to be able to complete
the necessary gear change before turning
in. Mid-corner gear changes should be
avoided because they upset the vehicle's
balance. If you are in the right gear your
should be able to drive smoothly through
the bend and power out of it equally
smoothly. On fast, sweeping bends, keep
your entry speed down because sideways
forces build up as you continue through
the sweep. In a car this may only be
noticeable at high speeds, but in a truck or
towcar the effect can become worrying to
both driver and horses at fairly low speeds
and attempts to back off or, especially,
brake can seriously upset the vehicle's
stability.

Roundabouts

Horses do not like roundabouts. Many find the series of often shortly spaced changes in direction difficult to cope with, especially after a long straight stretch when they have got used to the lack of movement and may even have nodded off. You must therefore approach roundabouts carefully and do your best to reduce the horses' discomfort.

If the roundabout has a multi-lane approach, get into the correct lane for your exit as early as you can. This also saves you having to fight your way across lanes of traffic close to or on the roundabout, which is difficult with a long vehicle. If there are three lanes and you are going straight ahead, it is easier to do it from the left-hand lane rather than the centre one, but remember that some car drivers may take this as showing an intention to turn left, and you should not use that lane if it is marked for left turns only.

Before pulling onto the roundabout, make sure that you are allowing enough

Always corner carefully especially on roundabouts where horses do not like the changes in direction.

When approaching large roundabouts, get into the correct lane as soon as possible.

space for the length of your vehicle to be clear of the paths of vehicles already on the roundabout. If you are new to lorries and towing you must take particular care, remembering, with a towcar, that drivers on the roundabout may not have noticed, or been able to see, the trailer.

Make sure you use the correct signals so that everyone around you understands your intentions. If you are turning left, you should have the left turn indicator on during your approach and through the roundabout. For straight on, use no indicator on your approach and use the left on passing the exit before yours. To turn right, indicate right on approach and through the roundabout, switching to the left indicator on passing the exit before yours. On roundabouts with more than four exits it is usually best to use the straight on method for exits between first left and straight ahead and the right turn method for exits after straight ahead.

On mini roundabouts the advised signalling method is as if it were a crossroads without a blob in the middle. When negotiating mini roundabouts be aware of the humped blobs, which can worry horses with the way they suddenly tip the vehicle when they are already coping with a turn.

Observation is vital both on your approach and in the roundabout because other drivers may not judge correctly your low speed, length and course. A common experience is drivers entering the roundabout when you are already on it, and therefore have right of way, blasting their horn because you are across their intended line – keep an eye out for them

so they do not take you by surprise. Cyclists are also prone to this in towns because they often seem to focus on the towcar and not the trailer they are on a collision course with – a toot of the horn usually wakes them up!

Allow room for the trailer to follow a tighter line than the towcar, or for the lorry's rear wheels to turn tighter than the front ones. When turning left, or leaving the roundabout, you allow more room on the passenger side and, when turning right, you allow more between the driver's side and the island. But keep watch for people getting into that gap, especially cyclists when turning left. With lorries with a long rear overhang, position yourself far enough from the island so that the tail does not swing across it, risking damage to the vehicle or round-about signs, especially as you leave small roundabouts.

When turning right, look out for people accelerating round your left side trying to beat you to the exit. They are in the wrong, but you do not want them driving into your side.

Be particularly careful on multi-lane roundabouts where lanes are stopping and starting at different times. Make sure you are giving stationary cars a wide enough berth and that nobody has pulled into the turning space you have allowed while you were stopped.

Left and Right Turns

You barely think about left turns in a solo car, but they need much more care in a lorry or towcar. Again, this is because you need more space to turn since the back of the vehicle or outfit turns tighter than the front. Check your mirrors and signal earlier than you would in a car to give everyone a good chance of seeing your intentions. Remember, slowing down is part of the manoeuvre before which you should have mirrored and signalled!

When turning left, check your mirrors again as you reach the junction, looking for cyclists coming up on your inside who might try to overtake as you move out to allow turning space; also check your distance from the kerb. Take care to check your offside mirror, too, because other drivers may not expect you to move to the right when turning left and may be trying to squeeze past as you slow down.

Look out for street furniture and pedestrians close to the corner. If you can, it may be safer to let pedestrians cross rather than risk them failing to realize how much closer the back of the vehicle will be to them than the front. However, make sure that you also look into the street you are turning into to ensure you have enough room to swing round – oncoming drivers might not anticipate your need to go to their side of the road. It may be easier to let them out of the turning first, if it is safe to stop.

Right turns in large vehicles need good observation and positioning. Check your mirrors carefully and signal before moving out to just your side of the centre line. No matter how early or carefully you do this, beware of people still trying to overtake as you turn. Stop so that the front of your vehicle is just short of the centre line of the road you are turning into. If the road is narrow, and someone has stopped close to

the turning's centre line, you may have to wait for them to pull out. If anyone appears as you turn, be prepared for them not to anticipate how much space you will need and to carry on coming as your back end fills the part of the road they are heading for.

Do not try to hurry the turn across oncoming traffic. The drivers may not be able to judge the length of your lorry or outfit from straight ahead and be surprised at finding they are heading for its tail. There is also a serious risk of accident if, for any reason, you cannot complete the turn. It is also wise to let pedestrians cross so there is no risk of them doing so as you make the turn, leaving you stranded across oncoming traffic.

As you turn, aim the passenger side of your truck or towcar close to the kerb of the road you are turning into, to give yourself as much room as possible to get round without cutting across the centre line. If you get into this habit there is less chance of your clipping cars coming to the halt line as you turn in.

Passing Obstructions

In a solo car, you rarely have to pull out to the other side of the road to pass a parked car or other obstruction in the kerb, so it is rarely necessary to indicate your intention. However, with a lorry or trailer, your extra width and your need to allow for the back taking a tighter line mean that you need more road space to pass obstructions.

Check your mirrors, indicate that you are pulling out and look well ahead on your approach to the obstruction. Apart

rom making sure that nothing is coming
he other way, you are looking to make
ure there is enough room beyond it to be
ble to pull back in, and that there are no
ide turnings from which others may
merge, or into which they might think
ou are turning before or after the
bstruction. If there *are* turnings, be
repared for others to misinterpret your
ntention and pull out in front of you – it
nay be safer to let them go.

If your view beyond the obstruction is
estricted, perhaps by a bend, be prepared
o stop. Oncoming drivers may not realize
ow much time and space you need to get
ound things.

assing Animals

s a horse owner, you should not need
eminding to pass animals carefully but, if
ou are new to lorries and towing, it must
e stressed that horses in particular react
lifferently to these than to the way they
lo to a car. Your vehicle is noisier, bigger
nd causes more slipstream, so you need
o slow down well in advance and give as
nuch room as you can, remembering that
he horse you are passing may not be as
ensible as yours.

Many horses seem to react more
trongly to a vehicle with other horses
board, even if the travelling horses make
o sound. When passing a horse with a
railer, remember it is the distance you
ive with the trailer that matters because
t is wider than the car. Like people, horses
re often surprised by a car having a
railer behind it. The same applies in areas
vhere there are loose sheep, because they
ometimes stand patiently while the

towcar passes, then walk under the trailer.
They seem to understand lorries better.

Be patient if you meet someone herding
animals. They may be able to move them
over enough for a car to get past, but not
for a larger vehicle.

Overtaking

Overtaking needs caution in a lorry or
trailer, especially with a live load to
restrict your ability to accelerate hard, or
make sudden moves if you misjudge it.
Lorry and trailer acceleration can also be
seriously blunted by strong headwinds
and your length also makes it difficult to
pull back in if something comes the other
way. In short, you need a lot of room to
overtake safely so, even on a dual-
carriageway, you must plan ahead.

New towcar drivers, or those towing
with unfamiliar cars, need to have a good
idea of how much the trailer has affected
the car's acceleration before trying to
overtake. Even a heavier horse than the
one you are used to can make a significant
difference.

Check your mirrors carefully before
overtaking because powerful cars can put
on a great deal more speed than you can,
which presents a danger if they pull out
fractionally before you do. Indicate and, if
necessary change down, before pulling
out, remembering that some diesels
accelerate better in a higher gear because
their strength is their low rev flexibility.
Diesels may also hit maximum revs very
quickly when accelerating, so be ready to
change up before the manoeuvre is
completed.

Signal before pulling back in and watch

the nearside mirror to make sure you have pulled far enough in front of the overtaken vehicle.

On dual-carriageways, do not be tempted to overtake just before your junction because it is very easy to misjudge the amount of time you will need.

When following other lorries, remember that they may be sheltering you from headwinds, so you may not be able to go as fast as you think without their help.

Bridges

The obvious thing about bridges is to make sure they are wide enough and high enough for your vehicle. This is more of a problem with lorries, but you do occasionally find extremely low bridges where the clearance for a trailer is close, though these usually have extra warnings on them. Some arched bridges have markers showing the point at which they have maximum headroom, and if you have to pull into that part of the road you should signal before doing so because not all car drivers will appreciate your need to be there.

Also take care when going over bridges. Narrow ones may have width restrictions and, though the entrance may look wide enough for your vehicle, it may close up further on or have a bend in it. On narrow bridges without footpaths be prepared to stop to let pedestrians pass. Also look out for weight restrictions, which may apply to the vehicle's gross or actual weight.

If you have to cross a very narrow bridge, satisfy yourself that it is wide enough, then concentrate on keeping a suitable distance from the parapet on your side instead of trying to judge both sides at once. Either get a passenger to watch the other side, or give the occasional glance, to make sure there are no posts or pillars projecting further out than the rest of the parapet.

On windy days, be prepared for side winds to be stronger on the exposed road across a bridge, especially on motorways. Similarly, when going under a motorway bridge, you may be buffeted by side winds caused by the wind being deflected by the embankments on either side. There is also a greater risk of icing on bridges, especially on minor roads, because there is no earth beneath the road to act as insulation.

Town Driving

Busy town streets require careful observation and patience. You have to allow for people not giving you enough space or time to clear obstacles, or getting into the space you have allowed for turning.

With a trailer there is also the strong risk of people seeing the towcar and not the trailer behind it. This may be understandable when you are pulling out of a side turning, but you also experience it on straight roads. It is a particular danger when passing parked cars, because people getting out or pulling out are often relying on the restricted view in their mirror. It is sensible in these circum-stances to put your headlights on to draw people's attention to your vehicle, while the trailer sidelights will draw attention to its width.

Give parked cars as wide a berth as

Using lights in town helps to draw other drivers' attention to the fact that your vehicle is different.

ossible without blocking the other side of the road. Take care when pulling out from the kerb or to go round things, because you may have to pull over to the wrong side of the road, so you should look backwards as well as in your mirror before doing so. In a lorry with large rear overhang, allow enough room for it to swing over as you pull out or make turns.

In stop-start traffic, take care not to ride the clutch. If you stop for more than a few seconds, apply the handbrake and select neutral. It puts less strain on the transmission and on your left leg, and is safer. If you cannot see round or over traffic ahead, you may be able to see when a queue is starting to move by watching reflections in shop windows, but do not move off until you are sure the vehicle in front is moving. Be alert for pedestrians doing silly things while you are stopped, like crossing close in front of a lorry, where the high-up driver cannot see them, or even walking between the towcar and trailer.

Driving a large vehicle in town means planning ahead to make sure you know where you are going. Get into the correct exit lane as soon as you can, especially in one-way streets, not least because it can be very difficult to get across lanes of traffic in a large vehicle. Signal clearly and, in difficult situations, reinforce this with a hand signal – a driver close to your side may not be able to see even your side repeater indicator.

In multi-lane roads with stop-start traffic keep watch around you to make sure you give stationary vehicles enough room and be aware of how cars are filling the space around you when you are stopped. Look out for motorcyclists and cyclists tucking in close to you, especially in a towcar where being close to the car means they are on collision course with the trailer if you overtake them.

If you are stuck in traffic for a long time in warm weather, check that the horses do not need more ventilation. Also, keep an eye on the engine temperature, especially in a towcar coping with the weight of a trailer, because stop-starting without ever picking up speed to get air moving through the radiator is a recipe for overheating, especially if you have a slack fan belt or faulty electric fan.

Minor Roads

Lorry drivers avoid minor roads as much as possible, but horse owning tends to be a rural activity so you will have to negotiate narrow, winding roads to get to yards and events.

Apart from the difficulty of driving a lorry or outfit on these roads because of size and lack of manoeuvrability, you have to consider the risk to and from other drivers. We have all had a scare from coming round a country bend to find a lorry filling the road, especially if it was being driven faster than was sensible, or meeting the car driver using a single track road as if it was a closed-off rally special stage. You must drive in a way that reduces the risk to others and gives you time to react to others' stupidity.

Lorry and off-roader drivers have the advantage of being high up, so do look ahead. Do not concentrate on the bit of road you can see, but glance ahead over hedges and through trees. A flash of colour through the branches is enough to warn you that someone is coming, so you can be ready to stop or pull in. Keep your speed down so that you can stop quickly and with minimal distress to the horses.

You should also be driving slowly because minor roads are not as well maintained as main roads and may be twistier, giving the horses an uncomfortable ride at speed. You are also more likely to find road edge subsidence, which can unexpectedly sway a lorry or trailer sideways. In fact, it can seriously destabilize a trailer at speed and trigger snaking.

However, be considerate to others – if you have someone behind you and you can pull over or just stop on a straight section do so to let them past. But signal before doing so and do not be surprised if they merely stop behind you because they have got too used to following you and are not looking ahead. (I once had someone follow me into a lay-by before realizing I was no longer on the road!) By doing this you create less ill-feeling, you do not have to worry about someone following too close and you reduce the risk to yourself and others caused by them overtaking dangerously.

Be careful not to let the narrowness of the road make you hug the edge too closely. The edges of the road may go in and out and be broken, while rocks and branches stick out from banks and hedge. Also, if you get it wrong, there are soft verges and ditches to drop wheels into, with the risk of turning the vehicle over.

Don't forget to look up, too. Trees leaning out from the roadside may only clear the roof of a lorry or trailer if it is well out from the kerb. Be particularly careful after storms, when a tree on a familiar road may have damaged, hanging branches, or may even have been tilted over by the wind.

Overtaking may be impossible for you on narrow roads and even on wide, single carriageway roads, it should be done cautiously. You have the double handicap of driving a long, slow vehicle and having a live load you do not want to throw around. This means that overtaking can take a long time, with few options if you get it wrong, so only do it if you are absolutely sure you have enough clear, straight road. Towcar drivers should remember that even the most powerful car's acceleration will be greatly reduced by the weight and poor aerodynamics of the trailer. Do not swing out too quickly because, apart from being uncomfortable for the horses, the sudden change in camber can exaggerate the movement and destabilize the vehicle.

Motorway and Dual-carriageways

Motorways and dual-carriageways are the easiest roads to drive a lorry or trailer on, but don't let that lull you into a false sense of security. Speeds are higher than on other roads and it is very easy to let your own speed gradually creep up without you realizing it. You need to remain alert and observant because if things go wrong you will have little time to react.

Before setting out on a journey involving fast roads, make sure that the vehicle is in good order. Take account of the fact that the vehicle will use more fuel at higher speeds, in a situation where there may be long gaps between filling stations, particularly on motorways. With a towcar, reckon on it using about 30 per cent more fuel when towing.

Take care when joining the main road from a slip road, because vehicles on the carriageway may be going considerably faster than you. Indicate and gather speed as you come down the slip road, checking your mirrors constantly to get a picture of what is on the road you are joining. If it is crowded, be prepared to slow down or stop on the slip road. Do not force drivers on the carriageway to slow down or swerve and do not drive along the hard shoulder. Always glance over your shoulder to check for vehicles close to you before moving out. Allow for the length of your vehicle or outfit and for the fact that

Do not lose concentration on dual-carriageways just because the driving seems easy.

it can be difficult to judge your distance from cars behind you accurately.

Many car drivers are lax about lane discipline, but lorry and towcar drivers become a genuine obstruction to others if they do not stick to the rules. Vehicles that are towing, or weigh over 7.5 tonnes, are not allowed into the right-hand lane of a motorway of three or more lanes – though they are allowed there on dual-carriageways. However, other drivers may not expect you to move into that lane on a dual-carriageway, or for a truck weighing less than 7.5 tonnes to join them out there on a motorway.

Unless the left-hand lane is marked specifically as a turning-off lane you should stay in that lane except when overtaking (solo cars should do this, too). Remember, as lorries and towcars cannot move out to the right-hand lane on a motorway, you will be blocking their progress if you hog the centre lane, so move back left as soon as you safely can.

All lane changes must be preceded with mirrors and signals. A common failing among car drivers is the 'flash and flit' lane change, in which the driver indicates at the same time as moving over, which is even more dangerous in a long vehicle. Use your indicators for at least six seconds before changing lanes to give other drivers time to react and so that, if you have failed to spot someone, they have time to warn you of their presence.

Lorry drivers often flash other overtaking lorry drivers to let them know when they are safely past, and they commonly thank each other with a quick alternate flash of the indicators. There is no basis for this in law or in *The Highway Code*, it is just a courtesy. However, lorry drivers to whom you afford this assistance generally treat you with more respect and courtesy, often repaying the favour later. It also means that you must not flash your headlights if a lorry starts to pull out when you are alongside it (sound your horn) and you must, in turn, be careful not to misinterpret such a protest!

Keep a safe distance from the vehicle in front, obeying the two-second rule as explained in the latest edition of *The Highway Code* – though with towcars and lorries you should allow more than that, say three seconds. This rule works on the basis that the car in front won't stop dead so, if you maintain a two- or three-second gap between that car and you, you will have time to react. It saves having to judge what, say, 50 metres looks like at 50 mph and, of course, the gap automatically gets longer the faster you go, because you cover more ground in that time. The way it works is that as the car in front passes an object, like a patch in the tarmac, you start counting and if you pass the object before two seconds are up you are too close to the other vehicle. To make this easier, when speaking at normal speed, 'only a fool forgets the two-second rule' takes about two seconds to say, while 'only a fool forgets the three-second rule in a lorry' takes just over three.

Overtaking is easier if you keep your distance and easier still if you plan ahead so that you can pull out without having to first slow down behind the slower vehicle. If you plan ahead you can save fuel, frustration and gear changes by maintaining speed instead of having to constantly slow down and speed up. If you have to slow down, you will also be able to do it gently, with minimum wear on the brakes and discomfort for the horses.

Be constantly aware of what the engine is doing, because it may start to labour on long uphill sections which, particularly on motorways, may start with such a gentle slope that you do not notice how much steeper it has become. It is better for the engine and fuel economy in these circumstances to change down, even if it means slowing down to do so comfortably.

Towcar drivers should look out for sections of left-hand lane where constant use by lorries has worn ruts in the tarmac. These can cause the trailer, or even the whole outfit, to wander, which can feel alarming if it surprises you at speed. If you feel this, allow the outfit to slow down to reduce the risk of instability.

Keep an eye on your mirrors so that large vehicles overtaking you do not surprise you as their slipstream pushes at you, or when strong winds curling over a tall vehicle suck you towards it. This is particularly noticeable on trailers without stabilizers and the risk is that you overcorrect if it takes you unawares. The trick is to hold the vehicle gently against the sideways movement rather than steering over, which will make you wander into the next lane after the vehicle has passed. Resist the temptation to grip the wheel harder, because this reduces your feel for what your vehicle is doing and resists the natural feedback movements of the wheel. In fact, you may find it easier to compensate for the effects of an

overtaking vehicle's slipstream if you ease your left hand's grip on the wheel so that your right is better able to feel and react to what is happening. Tanker lorries, car transporters and some very large coaches create the worst slipstream. Also, take account of the fact that you are having the same effect on the smaller vehicles you pass, particularly motorcyclists and, on dual-carriageways, cyclists – so give them plenty of room, especially in blustery weather.

When you leave the carriageway by a slip road, move into the left lane at least by the half-mile sign and start indicating at the 300-metre board (three diagonal lines). Move into the slip road at the earliest opportunity and slow down. On uphill slip roads the gradient will help you to slow down, but take care on downhill ones that you are not going faster than you think.

After a long motorway or dual-carriageway stretch, always check the speedometer, because you may have a false impression of speed. This is especially important when entering a service area, where vehicles will be stopping and pulling out around you and pedestrians are about. You also want to avoid sudden braking or entering roundabouts quickly, because the horses will have got used to the gentle movement on the motorway and may even be asleep.

Incidentally, when you leave fast stretches of road to stop, for example at a service area, let the engine run for a short time before switching off. This is particularly important with turbocharged engines because the turbo runs extremely hot at motorway speeds, especially when towing, and if you let the engine tick over for a minute or so it allows the oil to dissipate some of the heat in the turbo bearings. If you do not do this you can damage the bearings.

Roadworks

Not only do roadworks affect larger vehicles more seriously than solo cars, but your vehicle represents more of a hazard to those working on the site.

When you see roadworks ahead, look out for signs giving weight or width restrictions. On multi-lane roads, roadworks may be accommodated by having more narrow lanes than normal, or by having one lane for wide vehicles with others restricted to smaller ones. Restricted lanes may have a width limit too narrow even for a horse trailer. If the lanes separate you could get stuck in one too narrow for your vehicle, which could be dangerous in a contra-flow system. Also look out for lanes with restricted access to certain exits, or which channel you towards an exit other than yours – with the difficulty of turning round in a lorry or towcar that could mean a long detour to get back on route.

Check your mirrors carefully, signal and get into the correct lane as soon as possible, especially if the road is busy. With large vehicles you do not have the agility or visibility to make sudden last-minute changes, and other drivers may not have the space to let you in if traffic is slow moving. Keep using your mirrors to check that you are giving cones and signs a wide enough berth.

Temporary speed limits posted on round red and white signs are legally enforceable. It is important to stick to them, especially in a lorry or towcar which creates a lot of turbulence as it passes and may thus put workers at risk by blowing objects at them. Restricted lanes also mean that you have little margin for error and, in contra-flow systems with even a 40 mph speed limit, the closing speed between you and vehicles coming the other way is 80 mph.

Take particular care where you have to swap lanes or carriageways. The lanes for these changes are laid out to angles set by the highways authorities as safe for most vehicles, which makes it important that you do not exceed suggested speeds. Even then, slow down, because the standards are not set for animal welfare. In particular, changing carriageways means crossing a roughly made up central strip with the road camber also changing which, apart from being unpleasant for the horses, can destabilize lorries and trailers. Again, you have little margin for error, with often only a few cones separating you from vehicles coming the other way.

You may also see signs warning of adverse camber, usually on bends. To understand this, think of a banked race circuit where the bends slope in the direction of the curve to counter the centrifugal forces on the racing cars. Most bends on fast roads are gently cambered in the same way, but adverse camber means it slopes the opposite way to the direction of the bend. Solo cars usually only feel worrying on adverse camber if going very ast, but it has a more serious handling effect at lower speeds on lorries and trailers and probably feels odd to the horses, who are leaning one way only to be tipped the other. It is particularly dangerous if a lane change throws you from the correct camber to the wrong one mid-bend.

Bad Weather

With lorries and trailers, the advice not to make a journey in poor weather unless it is absolutely necessary holds very true. When transporting horses you also have to consider the effects on them. If you get stuck in your car you might have to survive an uncomfortable few hours with nothing but old sweets to eat, but what would it be like for horses in a stranded lorry or trailer? And, in the worst conditions, the police might be able to evacuate you from a blizzard, but not your horses.

There is also the worry that a large vehicle hitting ice or being struck by a gust of wind could be very difficult to get back under control, while conditions may make it difficult for other drivers to avoid it. You also present a very dangerous obstacle to others in fog and do not have the agility to get out of the way if others drive unwisely in limited visibility.

So, your first question if the weather is bad, or is forecast to deteriorate, should be 'Do I need to go?' Strong winds, heavy rain, fog, snow and ice are all hazards you should try to avoid. If you have to go out in them, or are caught out, the number one rule is to take it steady. That gives you more time to react and reduces the effects of the hazard on your vehicle as well as the effect of your vehicle on anyone you hit! A sheet of ice or sudden push from strong wind may be nothing more than worrying at 25 mph, but at 50 mph you could leave the road before the problem even registers with you.

Driving in bad weather is very tiring, so take more frequent breaks because you need to concentrate. But only stop where you can get safely off the road. Even then, remember that in poor visibility there is a risk of drivers thinking the lights of a vehicle in a lay-by are those of something moving on the road, so use hazards unless you are totally away from the highway.

Wind

Strong winds are an unpredictable hazard because they can be deflected by roadside objects, terrain or other vehicles in odd ways. Gusty conditions are the most dangerous because you cannot predict how and when the gusts will affect you.

The problem with a lorry or trailer is that you present a far larger side area for winds to push against. Lorries at least have the weight of the chassis and heavy mechanical parts to aid stability, but a trailer, especially an unladen one, is easily upset, and even headwinds may cause stability problems. If you live in a sheltered place it may be wise to drive out to a more exposed area before deciding whether it is safe to venture out with a lorry or trailer. Also, think about changing your route: think twice about using exposed long bridges or roads on embankments.

On the road, keep an eye on what is happening to other vehicles and roadside trees to get warning of gusty areas. There can be sudden movement when you come out of a cutting or from under a bridge, but, equally, be aware that the side wind you have been taking account of will disappear when you enter a cutting or tunnel. On the approach to flyovers going over your road you may get air deflected by the embankments on either side. Bridges, especially those with superstructure, are prone to buffeting. Look out for overtaking lorries because, instead of them giving you a push, strong side winds curling over the top of them may suck you towards them.

You must also be aware that you may have the same effect on smaller vehicles you overtake, even with a towcar, and be especially careful when overtaking anyone towing or when passing cyclists and motorcyclists.

Try not to steer into the wind and, in particular, avoid jerking the steering to counter sudden gusts, though this is easier said than done. As when dealing with the effects of passing lorries, you should just try to hold the vehicle or outfit against the sideways movement. If it gets too blustery on motorways and main routes, consider more sheltered minor roads.

Rain

Rain reduces visibility by clouding your mirrors and creating spray. Many vehicles now have heated mirrors which helps clear the spray off them, or you can get liquids that you wipe on the mirrors to stop droplets forming (washing up liquid does that, too, but soon wears off). If you drive a vehicle which creates a lot of spray it may help you to see others, and others to see you, if you get spray suppression devices fitted. Since 1992, lorry spray suppression systems have had to comply with complex EU rules dictating what must be used, how far it is from the wheels and how much of the wheel it must cover, so talk to your lorry dealer or builder or a specialist supplier about systems suitable for your vehicle. If it does not comply with

Strong winds may curl over high-sided vehicles, sucking other vehicles towards them, so take care when passing.

EU regulations, your lorry can fail its plating test. The systems take the form of wheel arch linings and mudflaps covered in water-trapping plastic blades, like those on 'grass' doormats, and brush-like wheel arch valences. The blades and brushes capture the 'pulverized' water, causing droplets to gather together and run off instead of emerging as spray. On older and smaller vehicles you may be able to reduce spray by fitting mudflaps made of the plastic 'grass' but, again, talk to a specialist supplier (there are hundreds listed on the internet) to ensure that you do not break any laws. Also, remember that slowing down reduces spray.

You are required by law to have headlights on. If spray is reducing visibility below 100 metres you can justify the use of rear foglamps, but not in poor light or at night because in these conditions they cause even more glare for following drivers than on a clear night. This is because rain drops magnify and scatter the light. They may also make it difficult for other drivers to see when your brake lights come on.

Allow greater separation distances on wet roads because it takes longer to stop. In heavy rain, surface water can cause the vehicle to aquaplane, which happens when water builds up under the tyres faster than the treads can displace it. You feel this as a lightening of the steering, which is often accompanied by a sideways movement if only one tyre is affected. This is your early warning: slow down, but do not brake or the wheels may lock up. Areas where water is running across the road can cause this, normally creating a momentary twitch, but that can be enough to destabilize a trailer or send any vehicle skating towards the edge of the road.

In very heavy rain or hail, horses can become worried by the noise on the roof, so drive even more carefully to avoid worrying them more. With trailers, consider closing the rear doors to stop rain being sucked back onto the horses. If you are transporting one horse you can ensure ventilation by closing just the door on his side.

Fog

Fog is probably the most frightening weather condition to drive in. You must use your headlights, but rear foglamps should be used only when visibility is below 100 metres – they are not slightly

Fitting spray suppressors in the wheel arches and mudflaps improves visibility for you and other road users.

misty rear lights! Turn them off in traffic jams and, at night, think of them like beam headlights, turning them off when someone is close enough behind you to be dazzled. They can put you in danger if following drivers cannot see past them or fail notice your brake lights coming on because of them. It is important to make sure that all your lights work in fog: a lorry's side position lights, or a trailer's sidelights give other drivers warning that there is something long behind the headlights, or passing the junction they are approaching. (Towcar drivers need to be particularly careful at junctions because others may not be able to see the trailer in the fog.) Avoid beam headlights in fog at night because the fog droplets scatter the light back at you – check whether you can see further on dipped lights. Front fog-lamps, with the flat, fan-shaped beams, help pick out the edges of the road at night in fog.

In all foggy conditions, slow down to be sure you can stop within the distance you can see, and occasionally use your wipers to wipe condensed fog off the screen (you may not be aware it is there). Also, make sure your internal de-misting is working properly: air conditioning helps here by taking the moisture out of incoming air (you can use it in conjunction with the heater). At junctions, wind down the window to help visibility, and turn the radio off so that you can hear oncoming traffic.

Large vehicles tend to cut a hole through the fog, giving following drivers the impression that it is thinner than it is, so do not be surprised if people overtake you then slow down dramatically. Do not make the same mistake yourself.

When turning, signal early, remembering that drivers following cannot see the junction and may not know where it is. Even locals can become disorientated in fog.

Keep an eye on the horses because the high moisture levels in the air can create a lot of condensation in the back, which may result in them getting wet and chilled

Snow and Ice

Think very carefully before venturing out in snow and ice because lorries and trailer outfits have a lot of weight to carry you into trouble should they start sliding.

Some of the fog rules also apply to falling snow, because it has similar effects on visibility. You are required to have lights on in falling snow and can use front and rear foglamps if visibility is below 100 metres. But again, beam headlights are reflected back at you by snow at night, so check whether you can see further on dipped lights.

Fresh snow is deceptive because it gives a fairly 'grippy' surface to drive on, but it is a very poor one to stop on, especially if it has fallen over ice. This is particularly so with vehicles with sophisticated 4WD systems, where drive is distributed to the wheels with most grip. These sort things out so quickly that the driver may not be aware of lessening grip until it is too late, which is a particular risk when it may not be obvious that the road has iced up. 4WD makes driving in snow and ice easier by creating higher limits, but it still has limits set by how much grip the tyres have, so it

It is best to forget about taking a trailer out in weather like this.

cannot stop you any quicker on a sheet of ice than two-wheel-drive.

An outside temperature readout can give useful warning of the risk of ice. Most start flashing an ice warning at about four degrees above freezing because they indicate air temperature, which can be a few degrees above ground temperature.

Take care when pulling away on snow and ice, especially with a towcar, because you have a considerable weight to get moving and, if your wheels spin, you can make the surface more slippery or dig the wheels into deep snow. When wheels spin there is no point in giving more power because they are actually spinning through getting more power than the tyres have grip to transmit. In addition, on two-wheel-drive vehicles, a spinning wheel fools the differential, the job of which is to allow one wheel to turn faster then the other on corners. It 'thinks' the spinning wheel needs to go faster, so allows all the power to go that way. Some 4WD systems also do this if a wheel on each axle spins. Often, easing up on the

power, and slipping the clutch if necessary, is enough to get you moving. If not, you may be able to 'trick' the differential by gently applying the brakes with your left foot or the heel of your right. You can also do this by partially applying the handbrake, but only if you are sure it works on the driven wheels. Most Land Rovers and some lorries have handbrakes that lock the transmission, so these must never be applied with the car under power and, on most front-drive cars, the handbrake works on the back wheels.

In deep snow (or on soft ground), check that you are not trying to drive against a natural wheel chock, where the snow has created a wedge against the wheels. If this has happened, dig it clear and put sacking or branches in front of the relevant wheel. You may find rocking the vehicle between forwards and backwards may give it the momentum to lift it out of the trap, but this should be a last resort because of the discomfort it may cause the horses. With off-roaders, you may find low ratio helps and you should certainly have the centre differential locked on vehicles which have one – but don't forget to return to high ratio and unlock the differential if conditions improve. If you are having trouble pulling away with a trailer in snow or soft ground, one technique that might help is to reverse far enough to push back the drawbar to which the hitch is attached, so that, when you pull forwards, the car has a few centimetres of movement before the weight of the trailer comes into play.

If snow is heavy on low ground, avoid taking higher routes where it may be heavier still. If you get a horsebox or trailer stuck in snow in a remote place, rescuing the horses will be difficult, if not impossible. It might be cheaper and safer to find a livery yard for the night.

Ice is particularly dangerous to a lorry or towcar, because you have a lot of weight to speed up your slide. Exercise extreme caution on roads you think may be icy, or if you feel the characteristic light twitch of an icy patch. Vehicles without anti-lock brakes will not pull up straight where one wheel is on ice and the other not, while traction control, which depends on detecting differences in wheel rotation speeds, may not work where all four wheels are spinning at the same speed on sheet ice.

Trailers are at particular risk because their braking systems may not be activated by a sliding car and the trailer could try to overtake the car when you can do little about it. Also, there may be nothing you can do to stop a trailer sliding down the camber of an icy road.

In cold weather, make sure the horses do not get chilled. The draught from air vents could be enough to cause cramp and snow can swirl through vents and over trailer ramps. It is best to close trailer rear doors in snow. Also, check that snow does not block vents, including the car or truck's heater intake, which will result in windows steaming up. On trucks with living areas, check that heater flues and vents have not been blocked with ice before turning them on.

Rough Ground

Rough ground must always be traversed very slowly with horses aboard because they are standing up, with no comfy seat and seatbelt to help them cope with the movement. Even in a lorry they will feel far more of the bumps and body sway than you do. With a towcar and trailer it is very easy to misjudge how bad the surface is, because you are sitting in something with far more sophisticated suspension and with a lot more wheel travel than the trailer.

Even with an empty lorry or trailer you should take care, because the uneven surface can put a lot of stress on the bodywork as it tries to take up the unevenness the suspension cannot absorb. With trailers, you also increase the shocks passed through to the towcar's body and there is a risk if you go too fast of the trailer actually starting to bounce. On a series of humps, a bouncing trailer can set up a momentum that gradually gets worse and may become uncontrollable.

On muddy showgrounds take even

This is what modern off-roader's suspension can do, so you can be sure your horse feels more bumps than you do.

more care, especially when trying to climb slopes where the vehicle may slide sideways. Make sure you have enough room to clear a sloping or deeply muddy area, especially if it goes through a restricted opening, because restarting on may be difficult. Try not to drive in wheel ruts, because of the risk of grounding and the difficulty of getting out, even with 4WD. With off-roaders, you may find it easier to get started and tow across the muddy ground in low ratio, and in those with locking centre differentials is wise to put this in the locked position but don't forget to shift to high ratio and unlock the differential once on firm ground. The techniques described in the now and ice section may also help in deep mud.

Snaking

When you tow a trailer there will always be some side-to-side movement or 'yaw', but when this builds up to a momentum of

its own, affecting the outfit's stability, it is called snaking. When snaking starts it feels like an insistent side-to-side tugging from the back of the towcar. In your side mirrors, you will see the trailer's tail swaying from side to side. If you ignore it, the momentum will build up until it starts to affect the towcar, eventually throwing the outfit out of control, with a serious risk of it turning over. It may build up slowly or, especially at speed, it can start suddenly in response to a trigger, like braking or a gust of wind, and rapidly become more violent.

Snaking may be triggered by many other things, including uneven trailer tyre pressures, poorly adjusted trailer brakes, an uneven road (especially the parallel dips left by the constant flow of lorries), turbulence from passing lorries, accelerating down hill, sudden steering movements and simply going too fast. Speed, in fact, is always a factor: for example, if you were going slowly the passing lorry would have only given you a nudge, or the uneven brakes would have stopped you without drama.

As soon as you detect snaking, you must slow the outfit down smoothly. Do not snatch your foot off the throttle or brake hard, because these will make things worse. Ease off the throttle and do not try to counter the movement by swinging the steering around – just hold it steady. Land Rover towing expert Roger Crathorne suggests easing your left hand's grip on the wheel so that it is not countering the efforts of your right hand and makes it easier to feel what is happening, which makes sense. The outfit should stabilize as the speed drops. Ideally you should not brake, but if you are running out of road or going downhill you may need to brake to slow down, but do so gently and desist if it appears to be making things worse.

There is an old wives' tale that you should accelerate out of a snake to try to pull the trailer straight, but this is a recipe for having a more serious accident.

If the worst happens and the trailer starts to turn over, steer in the direction it is falling. This is easier said than done,

because your instant reaction is 'I don't want to go that way!' – but steering the opposite way tips the trailer faster.

If you suffer snaking always stop to check the condition of the trailer in case it was a warning that a tyre was deflating, or even a wheel coming off. If you are happy that it is safe to do so, continue on your journey at reduced speed. When you get home, the trailer should be thoroughly inspected and if you are unsure of anything you should seek professional help. If the snaking was triggered under braking, the brakes should be adjusted and you should also check the amount of friction material on the brake shoes and that the cables and linkages to the overrun mechanism in the hitch are moving freely. Then road-test the trailer to see if it pulls up straight under heavy braking and, if the problem persists, check that the components inside the brake drum that spread the shoes have not seized: this would result in one brake not coming on with the rest. These processes are explained further in Chapter 11: Trailer Maintenance.

9

Loading Horses

The reason why I have put this chapter after all those on safety matters and road skills is that you should not try transporting horses until you are sure you can cope with the lorry or outfit and are entirely familiar with it. You do not want to be coping with getting used to a vehicle which is new to you and worrying about your horse at the same time. However, you must be aware that carrying even one modest-sized horse will affect the feel of a small lorry or a trailer, so it may accelerate more slowly, handle differently and need longer to stop than when empty.

Loading the horse correctly is an important part of the transporting process because it sets him up for the rest of the journey. If loading is rushed or traumatic, you cannot expect him to start the journey relaxed. Many horses are cautious about getting into a vehicle, especially one with which they are not familiar, and need only gentle encouragement to reassure them. It is important not to make them associate loading with punishment, or you will create problems for the future.

Allow plenty of time for putting on travelling gear and loading so that you do not get flustered and impatient. As with hitching up a trailer, get into a routine to make it less likely that you will forget something.

Travelling Gear

The main purpose of travelling gear is to protect the horse from knocks and scrapes while loading, and in the close confines of a lorry or trailer. However, with foals and inexperienced youngstock it is usual to transport them without some, or even all, of the items usually worn by an older horse because the clothing may cause more problems than it saves. Their unfamiliarity with having things put on and seeing or feeling things moving about their body can lead to them getting frightened, especially if it starts coming undone (with or without their help). Indeed, with any horse it pays to get them used to travelling gear at home before using it on the move. It will be less worrying to them in their stable and you can do something about it if they have problems.

All travelling wear must be secure and

fit properly. Loose or damaged items can easily get snagged up, causing more injuries than they save, or simply worrying the horse. For example, a usually quiet traveller started crashing about in our trailer because a travelling boot came partially undone so that the top flopped over and started brushing his other leg. Removing something like that in a trailer at the roadside is difficult and risky.

Leather headcollars are far safer than nylon webbing ones for travelling because they are more likely to break if they get caught on something, so they should not strangle a horse or break his neck. For the same reason you should not travel a horse in a bridle because, if a bit gets hooked up, the horse's jaw will break before the bit.

If the horse is large, or likely to throw his head up when loading, a poll guard is a good idea. Traditional ones are like a leather cap backed with felt, with holes for the ears and for attachment to a headcollar, but there are modern foam and plastic versions and even ones that look like baseball caps. Whatever you choose, there should be no risk of it coming down over the horse's eyes.

A light rug is essential in winter and is something you should take with you in summer in case the horse gets wet or the weather changes. It keeps the muscles warm while the horse is standing still and protects him from the inevitable draughts. Remember, particularly with trailers where you usually have the rear top doors open, that moving air cools the body much more than the ambient temperature would suggest – as anyone who has ridden a motorbike in shirtsleeves knows.

Comfort Zone Equestrian (01476 585188) produce a Transit Rug which has cushioned panels on the shoulder, hips and on a flap over the tail to give protection when travelling without risking overheating. The tail flap means that you do not have to use a tail bandage or guard which saves time and a potential struggle if you have to put one on a young or awkward horse.

Tail protection, usually in the form of a guard or bandage, is essential, especially with large horses and in any situation where a horse has his back end against a rough surface, like a ramp. Horses can take the skin off their tails by rubbing them as they travel and large horses may not have the room to avoid doing this. Tail guards are easier and quicker to put on

A poll guard protects a tall horse's head.

han bandages, but more likely to slip down unless there is some means of tying them to a loop on the rug. Whatever you use should not be too tight, or you may affect the circulation in the tail.

To put on a tail bandage, start with about 20 cm unwound and lay that under the top of the tail with its end angled upwards on the outside. Wrap the bandage round once, fold the end over and put another turn of the bandage over that, then work down the to the end of the dock bones, overlapping the turns by about two-thirds of the width of the bandage. Then go back up so that the ties are about halfway up and tie them no

A pony ready for travelling with light rug, boots protecting much of his legs and a tail guard.

Comfort Zone Equestrian's Transit rug makes tail bandages unnecessary and has padding to protect the hips and shoulders of large horses.

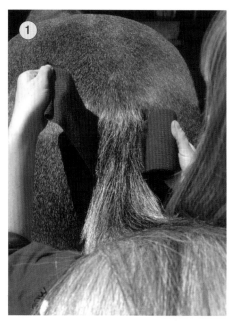

Fitting a tail bandage

1. Place the tail bandage under the top of the tail.
2. Take a turn over the end of the bandage.

3. Fold the end down and wrap the bandage over it before continuing down the tail.
4. Take the bandage back up the tail and tie the tapes before folding a turn over the bow.

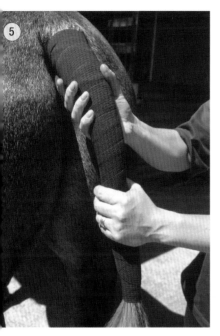

Gently bend the tail to its natural curve.

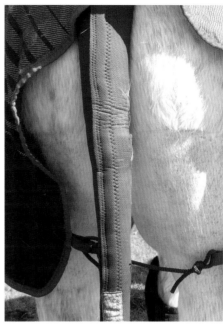

A tail guard is a good alternative to a bandage.

ghter than the bandage. Tuck the tape nds between the layers and fold the andage over the bow. Finally, bend the il gently to its natural angle. To remove e tail bandage, just undo the tapes, clasp e bandage at the top of the tail and slide all down.

Traditionalists feel that leg bandages fer more protection than boots, but odern boots often go further up the legs, rotecting the hocks and knees. Boots are so a lot easier to put on a young or vkward horse. Bandages should always e put on over some sort of padding, like amgee or purpose-made bandage pads, help spread the pressure and give more rotection. They must be tight enough to ay put, but not so tight as to create rculation problems.

Bandages are put on by overlapping the turns by about two-thirds of the width of the bandage. Most bandages these days have Velcro fastenings and should be put on so that the end of the Velcro faces the rear, as this means it is less likely to come undone if the horse brushes one leg against another. If your bandages have tie tapes, fasten them on the side of the leg, not on the front or back where they could press on bone or tendon.

Before putting boots on, separate the front ones from the back ones and work out which go on which side. Fastenings are always to the outside, with the tapes pointing backwards. On stretchy boots, make sure you do not pull the fastenings too tight.

Many horses, especially youngsters, find

the feel of boots or bandages strange at first – even if they have worn them previously – so walk them around a little to get used to the feeling and so that they have stopped auditioning for the Ministry of Silly Walks before you lead them up the ramp.

Preparing the Vehicle

Make sure that the vehicle is ready to receive the horse before you lead him to the ramp – you don't want to be hooking back partitions one-handed while holding a horse.

The more light and inviting you can make the interior appear, the more relaxed the horse will be about entering and the safer you will both be, because you can more easily see obstructions. If the vehicle has two ramps, lower both of them to allow more light and reduce the impression of walking into a dead end. However, close groom's doors and access to the front of a lorry, because horses occasionally try to exit through them!

Make sure that tying up loops are ready to use. Most people prefer to tie to a small loop of string attached to the securing ring

Travelling bandages must be fitted over padding.

After putting boots or bandages on horses' legs wait for them to finish their silly walks before loading them.

o that if the horse pulls back this will break before the horse's neck. However, if our vehicle has split-ring type tying loops, do not attach the string loops to these because it tends to slip out through the plit. If you are giving the horse a haynet, ie that up first and make sure that it is not o big that it gets in the horse's way – there s no point having a haynet if it prevents he horse turning his head to eat it.

Make sure that lowered ramps are table, because most horses are reluctant o step onto one that moves. Keep a wedge n the vehicle to slip under the ramp feet on uneven ground, or use a wedge-type railer jack. Never prop one with a brick, because they can suddenly split.

Partitions are usually swung to the sides o give a wider opening. If your trailer or orry has no means of holding them back, nvest in some bungee straps. When ravelling two horses in trailers and small orries where you can only swing the

partition over for the first horse, load the larger or more nervous horse first, while you have more room for manoeuvre. In trailers and lorries with front-to-rear bays you should always put a single horse or the larger of two horses on the driver's side to help counter the effects of the road camber.

However, if you are travelling one horse in a trailer, note that single horses are

above **Loading spotlights should shine into the vehicle to make it welcoming, not down the ramp to prevent the horse from seeing in.**

above **If there is no provision for holding partitions back, use bungee straps.**

left **Prepare your vehicle for loading by fixing partitions back and making it light and inviting.**

often happier if you have full width breast and breech bars with no partition, because this allows them the room to stand how they are comfortable, which is usually diagonally. Completely remove this sort of breech bar for loading and do not be tempted to drop it down on one side only to risk stepping over it.

Never travel a forward-facing horse without a breast bar both because it is illegal and because it means that the horse has nothing to brace himself against under braking. Breast and breech bars must be adjusted to suit the size of the horse. Breast bars must be low enough to come somewhere across the horse's chest, ideally just below where the neck joins, so the horse can brace against it without it pressing on his windpipe, but not so low that there is a risk of him trying to step over it. The breech bar should be at about the same height at the back – you do not want it so high that the horse can back under it, or so low that he can sit on it.

If you have a choice of fore-to-aft positions, try to get a small horse or pony standing slightly rear of centre, because horses have some 60 per cent of their weight at the front. However, you must achieve a balance between giving the horse something to brace against, and not restricting his movement so much that he cannot balance himself.

All partitions, ramp side guards, top doors and grooms' doors should be fastened in position before the horse steps onto the ramp, so there is no risk of them swinging round at the wrong moment. On trailers it is safer to completely remove breech bars, rather then leave them

hanging up, so there is no chance of them crashing down if you or the horse bump into them.

Make sure that the lorry's or towcar's handbrake is on before loading, and never try to load a horse in a trailer that is not hitched up, because the horse's weight will tip it on its tail. Some trailers have rear steady legs which are intended to stabilize the back as you load. but these are not usually intended to support the back of an unhitched trailer on their own while half a tonne of horse steps onto it.

Make sure you have sensible footwear to protect your feet and reduce the risk of you slipping or tripping. If the horse might be difficult, wear gloves and a hard hat.

Right Approach

The straighter you can make your approach to the ramp the easier it is for you and your horse. Turning in from the side, close to the ramp, means that the horse has little time to see where he is going, you are less likely to go up the ramp straight and you may end up stepping over the side of the ramp where its angle increases the chances of one or both of you tripping.

Approach at a steady walk to give you the forward momentum while remaining under control. Aim to be slightly ahead of the horse when you get to the ramp, especially with a trailer where there may not be enough room to go in side by side. Look ahead, encourage the horse forward and, in a trailer, walk straight under the breast bar (unless you are loading alone, in which case it may be better to tie up the orse from the same side of the breast bar, in case he moves back). If you have someone to help, they can put the breech bar in as soon as the horse is in place. In lorries with herring-bone partitions you must stop when the horse's head is in the right place and bring his back round by touching him where your leg would when leg-yielding. With young horses, you should practise this manoeuvre on the ground.

With many young horses, and some experienced travellers going into a new vehicle (or those who have not been out for some time), it is common for them to want to stop to look at the ramp before stepping on it. This is not unreasonable behaviour, because horses do not like stepping onto unusual surfaces. Usually, a little encouragement is all they need to reassure them and once they have 'tested' it with a foot they will move on.

A trick that sometimes makes young horses load more willingly is to take advantage of their natural tendency to follow you. Have someone who the horse knows make a fuss of him, then walk in as large a circle as they can just ahead of the horse as he is being led a short distance from the ramp. When you feel the horse is following his leader, give the word and the leader just walks straight off the circle and up the ramp with the horse being allowed to follow. If possible, the leader should walk straight through the vehicle, but if

above **Uncertain horses will often follow someone they know into a vehicle.**

Be ready for well-travelled horses to be eager to get aboard.

they cannot, they should stand to one side facing away from the horse. They must not turn to face him, which might be taken as a challenge or scolding, even if they are making encouraging noises – we know that horses read body language, and facing someone while looking them in the eye is horse language for 'How dare you do that!'

We will deal with more serious loading problems later in this chapter.

Securing the Horse

It is often better for someone to stand and hold the horse while partitions and bars are put in place, then tie him up. That way, someone can calm him and give and take with the lead rope if he tries to step back, rather than have him pull free and run back into whoever is moving the partition. If you are putting a bar or partition in behind a horse, talk to him to let him know you are there, especially if you have approached from an angle where the side of the vehicle would stop him seeing you. Always stand to one side as you fix the bar or partition so you are less likely to be kicked, or to get the partition kicked against you. Where you have a choice, pins used for fixing bars and partitions are best inserted in a direction that reduces the risk of a horse pushing them out.

When tying the horse up, use a sturdy lead rope tied to a string loop. Do not tie it so short that the horse cannot move his head, as this will impair his ability to balance himself on the move. If you are travelling a single horse in a trailer with full-width bars, or in a very roomy small lorry, it is best to tie with a rope to each side, which will allow some freedom of movement but will prevent him from turning round.

If your vehicle has multiple positions for partitions, give the horse as much room as you can. Many people think that putting the partition close to the horse will help him to balance, but it stops him being able to move his feet freely to counter movements of the vehicle. If their movement is restricted, horses are more likely to panic if they feel they are unbalanced. However all horses are different and there may be the odd one who likes something to lean on, so be prepared to experiment.

Once loaded, take a look round inside the vehicle to make sure that everything is in order. Check that partitions and bars are locked in place, vents are open, haynets properly tied and nothing has been left where it might roll about or provide something for a curious horse to try to reach.

When you raise the ramps, look out for noses being stuck round the sides, or tails swishing into the closing gaps. A common

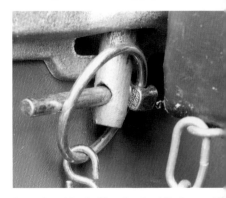

Bar and partition locking pins should be inserted so that the horses cannot push them out.

roblem on front unload trailers is for the
nd of the lead rope to get caught in the
imp. When raising and locking a rear
imp with forward-facing horses, always
o it from the side, so that you are out of
ie way if the horse kicks it back at you.
ry not to slam ramps shut because this
rill only upset the horses and cause
erious injury if any human or equine
ody parts are in the way.

**Where the horses are tails to the ramp, stand to one
ide to raise it.**

Unloading

Be particularly careful if you are
unloading an inexperienced horse at a
how, because he will be paying much
nore attention to all the interesting sights
han to where you are and where he is

putting his feet. In these circumstances, or
even with a more experienced horse who
has become excited, it is wise to put the
bridle on in the vehicle and lead the horse
off in that. You can always put a
headcollar over it to tie up outside.

The aim is to come down the ramp
steadily, because if you go too fast the
horse may pull you over, be tempted to
jump off the end or, simply, not stop at all.
As with loading, it is best to remove trailer
bars completely, so they cannot be
knocked down at the wrong moment, and
to fasten partitions back so that they
cannot swing round on you. On lorries,
ramp edge guards should be fixed in
position for safety. Make sure that the
ramp is stable and the ramp catches are
also safely out of the way, so they cannot
cause injury if you or the horse collide
with them. When unloading it is even
more important to make sure that grooms'
doors or access to the front of a lorry are
closed, so that the horse does not try to
exit through them. Also, check that rugs
and boots being worn by the horse are not
hooked up on anything.

In front unload trailers you have to
unload the horse nearest the ramp first so
that the partition can be swung aside to
give the other horse space to turn to the
ramp.

Keep the lead rope or reins short
enough for control but not so short that
the horse cannot move his head and neck.
With a trailer you may have to go through
the door slightly ahead of him, but try to
keep alongside him on the ramp and
steady his exit. If you have two horses to
unload, it is a good idea to keep the first

Always try to unload at a steady, controlled pace.

horse off in view so that the second one does not get over-eager about rejoining his friend.

Again, wear sensible shoes that will not lead to you slipping or tripping on the ramp and will protect your feet. Gloves are always a good idea and are essential if the horse is likely to be silly, as is a hard hat with difficult or unknown animals.

Loading and Unloading Dangers

The biggest source of danger when loading and unloading is that you and the horse have only a limited amount of space, especially in a trailer, so can get in each

other's way. That is why sensible footwear is so important and why you should not rush the process. Equally, pay attention to what is happening and don't take it for granted that a generally relaxed horse will not be spooked by something – it only takes the wind picking up a discarded sandwich bag!

You can also reduce the risk by making sure that catches and anything else that sticks out near the door are folded back. Certainly, do not leave breech bars, tack or grooming kits on the ramp while you are loading. Equally, do not leave anything close to the ramp, because if you or the horse come off the ramp you do not want to land on something hard or expensive.

On lorries with high ramps there is a very real risk of injury if you fall off, so if your vehicle is not fitted with some sort of safety screen to mark the edge of the ramp, like a folded out partition or purpose-made 'gate', get something fitted. The real danger is that if anything unexpected happens, you or the horse will not realize how close you are to the edge.

Ramps must also be sound. If a horse goes through an unsound ramp, someone will almost certainly be alongside him so there is a real danger of a person being crushed by a frightened horse. At the very best, the horse will suffer terrible injuries as the broken edges of the ramp lacerate his legs. But a ramp does not have to be weak to be dangerous: loose matting can be just as threatening because of the risk of horse or handler tripping or slipping.

Another big danger when unloading is the horse who is over-eager to get off, who may bash the handler against the door frame or drag them down the ramp. Always get control before you start forwards and, if things go very wrong, be prepared to let go before the horse smashes you into a metal door frame. True, you then have a loose horse, but you will still be in a fit state to catch him.

Problem Loaders

Horses with loading problems can be heartbreaking to own. All the hard work you put into schooling them and the anticipation of benefiting from it in competition can be soured by the frustration of the fight to get them to and from shows. But, with patience, you may be able to reduce the struggle if not entirely cure the problem.

If you have a horse who loaded happily then suddenly changed his mind, you must analyse why, or any remedial work will be wasted. If you have had a loading or road accident the reason will be entirely obvious, but many horse owners are baffled by the onset of loading problems because the cause may not be clear.

With a new horse, you should be exceptionally careful on the first few outings to get a feel for what he tolerates and what he does not put up with. Horses generally let you know with stamping and movement if they find something unacceptable, so don't ignore them, or you may end up with problems. For example, some horses used to herring-bone lorries get into the habit of leaning on the partition, but when they do that in a trailer or forward-facing lorry they find that bends in the road tip them off the partition or wall, and they then get annoyed. Horses who do this usually only stamp about on turns in one direction, so you have to take care to corner more carefully in that direction.

Apart from expressing such 'personal preferences', any horse who becomes difficult may be criticizing some other aspect of your vehicle, or your driving. In the first case, check that there is nothing about the vehicle that may be putting him off, like things flapping about inside or restricting his movement. Remember, it may be something your previous horse put up with, or that did not affect him because he was smaller, slimmer or better balanced. (Also, check that any old travelling clothes you are using fit your new horse properly.) If a horse you have had for some time starts showing problems, try to work out if you have changed anything and check that nothing about the vehicle has deteriorated – a broken spring or worn damper (shock absorber) could be affecting the ride in a way the horse dislikes.

Also, be self-critical about your style of driving. Your new horse may not be as tolerant of fast cornering as your last one, so slow down. He may be more upset by crossing rough ground, so drive carefully across showgrounds. (It's odd how many poor loaders at shows have been hurtled across the showground car-park on their arrival!) Ask yourself whether you have become slapdash about your driving as you have got more used to the vehicle or outfit. If you change your vehicle or trailer, including changing the towcar, it will ride and handle differently and your horse may need to get used to that, so give him time. For example, even if you buy the same make and model of trailer as your old one the newness of its suspension may mean that the ride is firmer than the horse is used to. If your new towcar is more powerful than your last, are you towing faster without realizing it? Are your gear changes still as smooth as they were?

If no other causes for problems are evident, have the horse checked by a vet to make sure that he is not suffering back, neck or leg problems. You may not have noticed them while riding, but they may be making it difficult for him to cope with the vehicle's movements. For example, a horse being hacked out is not going to have his head and neck thrown about in the way this could happen in a moving trailer. Indeed, horses with severe back problems can have serious difficulty standing up in a moving vehicle and may start crashing about or even fall down as soon as it moves.

If the horse's resistance to loading is minor, just sorting out little things may stop you heading for major problems – though it may take time for the horse to accept that you have removed his cause for worry. You can reinforce this acceptance by making him associate the trailer with pleasant experiences, like giving him his dinner in it. In fact, food often overcomes minor loading problems, with many a reluctant loader changing his mind at the sight of a carrot or the sound of pony nuts rattled in a bucket. Dinner in the trailer is also a good way of getting young horses used to it, especially if you follow it with just a short trip.

Similarly, practising loading when you have plenty of time can be a big help. But if you are going to do this, especially with a difficult loader, only do it when you do have *plenty* of time, because if you get into a battle you must be able to end it on a triumph for your side, no matter how small. You have the advantage, when you have time in hand, to take the attitude that if he wants to stand half on the ramp for the next half hour, that's his problem and you can wait for him to change his mind. When time is at a premium, this may not be possible. (The most relaxed handler of an awkward loader I have ever seen was a woman who, when her horse refused to go more than halfway up the trailer ramp at a show, simply tied him by a lunge line to the breast bar, so that the only way he could go was in. She then sat in the sun nearby with a book and a coffee. After ten minutes of standing stubbornly on the ramp, the horse walked into the trailer. This would only be safe if you knew the horse was unlikely to get silly, but it shows how patience will win – and I bet she did not have to do that many more times before he gave up.)

When practising, if you can walk through the vehicle, doing so reinforces the idea in the horse's mind that you can get out of this thing, and you also practise loading and unloading at the same time. With some young horses, their difficulty in going in is nothing more than working out where the ramp starts. This is because they are unable to see it when they get close to it and they may have been so interested in looking into the vehicle that they have not memorized the ramp's osition on the floor. Simply getting omeone to pick up a hoof and place it n the ramp gets them started. Recent esearch (still in its early stages) suggests hat this hesitancy may be because most amps are covered with black rubber. esearchers found that horses walked nore willingly onto other colours, notably reen and blue, perhaps because it is less ke stepping into a hole, or deep water. If our horse shows a serious reluctance to valk onto a ramp or into a trailer, covering : with bedding or a green tarpaulin may .elp, but make sure it is not likely to slip or low off at a crucial moment.

The big no-no when dealing with roblem loaders is anything that einforces fear. That includes the obvious nes like beating the horse, but it also neans you being aware of your body anguage and positioning as you load him. Many people with loading problems can e seen standing angrily at the top of the amp, in front of the horse, pulling on the ead rope. They are effectively asking the norse to enter the vehicle by walking over hem, which is something we all spend a ot of time training them to avoid. standing angrily tensed up in front of a norse, even if you are not scolding him, lso tells him he is in your bad books, because that is how a herd's senior mare hows her displeasure to yobbish oungsters. Looking a horse straight in the ye gives the same message for the same eason – try it when you are loose-chooling, or in the field, and see how you an even turn a horse by doing this! (Some norse-handling experts, when teaching lifficult loaders, can be seen standing

facing them, but they are always careful not to adopt a challenging stance or make eye contact.)

Generally, when loading, you should be alongside the horse, encouraging him forwards, but if restricted space means that you have to stand ahead of him, keep facing away from him as you encourage him forwards. Every step forwards should be encouraged and praised. But resistance should not be met with resistance because if you pull one way the horse is most likely to pull the other and he will always win a tug of war. I have heard of small ponies who have mastered the trick of flipping large men through the air on the end of a lead rope! So keep no more than an insistent tension in the right direction – enough to stop him going backwards. Using a lunge line gives you more room for give and take, but only if you can be sure not to get it looped around his or your limbs.

Dealing with a difficult loader will take time, but patiently encouraging him, meeting his stubbornness with your own (good-natured) stubbornness, encouraging him forwards, being careful not to be seen as a challenge or threat and, above all, not losing your temper will bring results. And it should bring far more permanent results than threats and ill treatment. There are times when you may need to be firm, but that does not mean ill tempered.

The classical way of getting a difficult horse into a vehicle requires two lunge lines and two helpers, but this is a get-you-home quick fix, not a solution to the problem. Everyone should wear hard hats and gloves, be familiar with what is expected of them and know that lots of people shouting and waving their arms will only confuse the horse. The two lunge lines are clipped either side of the ramp door frame and the two helpers hold them out to form a passage to the ramp. The horse handler walks steadily forwards and when the horse is far enough forward the two people holding lunge lines walk round behind the horse, crossing the lunge lines behind him. As he is walks forwards they keep a steady tension on the lines to encourage him onwards.

For some horses this is all the extra encouragement they need, but others get wise to this method and learn how to turn side-on to the lines. The handler may be able to counter this by using a schooling whip to touch the horse's side to move him over. I have seen people, as a last resort, try a similar method using a jump pole held by two helpers behind the horse to push him forwards. It may work but it is dangerous because, if the horse kicks at the pole, he can throw it back against the helpers with jaw-breaking force.

In fact, you must think carefully about potential dangers with bad loaders. Even a gentle horse may lash out or panic if he gets stressed, so never come round behind him to push or slap him, or get between him and something hard (such as a wall) that you might be crushed against if he surges towards you.

If things deteriorate to a dangerous stage, or if you do not have the patience to coax and encourage, it is time to get professional help. A professional horse transporter may be able to help you spot what is wrong or give the horse a few easy confidence-boosting journeys in a different vehicle.

Remedial handling experts whose methods start with forming a bond with the horse on the ground seem to have a lot of success with difficult loaders, but choose someone with a proven record and who can put you in touch with satisfied clients. There are far too many people setting themselves up as 'horse whisperers' who have little horse sense – indeed, it is probably wise to steer clear of people who call themselves 'whisperers', because you want common-sense help, not romantic ideas. Good professional help is not cheap but without it you or your horse may get hurt and you will not get the enjoyment you should out of horse ownership. Rather than struggle, you may feel it easier to resign yourself to not going to shows, but what happens if he needs to be transported to a veterinary centre for treatment?

10

Travelling Horses

The first rule about travelling horses is consideration for them. Think about what it is like to stand in a bus: keeping your balance is easy when it is going at a steady speed in a straight line but becomes more difficult on bends or if the driver brakes or accelerates sharply. It is also easier if you can see where you are going.

Even if your horse could see the road ahead he would not be able to prepare for the next bend or realize you were going to brake to avoid that cyclist who just pulled out. Unlike you in the driver's seat, he has no comfy cushion to help absorb bumps and no seatbelt.

So, you have to think ahead and concentrate on reading the road in order to corner smoothly and steadily, brake gently and well in advance and accelerate at a sensible rate, thereby minimizing the stresses you place upon the horse. Planning ahead will also make your gear changes smoother and means that you should spot potholes and overhanging trees sooner. These and other road skills were discussed in Chapters 7 and 8.

However considerate your driving, it remains a fact that horses are always under a certain amount of stress when travelling and it is your job not to add to it. If you have to undertake a long journey with a horse who is not a good traveller, talk to your vet about getting something to calm him. This can only be something mild because, if he is too dopey, he will not be able to balance himself and there is a risk of him falling, which will only add to his stress and reinforce his dislike of travelling.

Driving Breaks

Professional horse transporters are bound by the laws relating to tachographs to break their journeys and take reasonable rests. Similarly, those transporting farm animals are bound by various regulations concerning journey times and how they must be cared for. Unfortunately, private horse owners are not covered by laws enforcing rest times and horses are not legally farm animals in the EU, hence the awful live export pictures you see. The EU has been consulting on regulations regarding the extreme long distance transport of all livestock, including horses, so changes are on the way.

However, regulations aside, common sense should tell you that long, unbroken journeys are neither safe nor kind to your horses. Be prepared to allow for longer journey times and take more breaks than you would for the same trip in a solo car. Even a motorway journey with a car and trailer is likely to take about a third longer than it would with the same car on its own. Driving a large vehicle or towing, especially with a live load, also takes much more concentration than driving a solo car, and can thus be more tiring.

Ideally, take a break every couple of hours to give you and your horses a rest. If it is a very long round trip to be made on one day it is usually better to swap drivers during both the 'out' and 'back' journeys rather than to have one person drive all the way there and another drive all the way back – especially if one of them is riding at a show. By doing this you make sure that no one is arriving too exhausted to compete or driving straight after competing, and that no one is driving when they are fatigued because they feel they owe it to the person who is driving home. A tired driver cannot drive in a way that reduces the horses' stress.

When you take a break, check the horses and if you want to leave the vehicle, say to use the toilets at a motorway service area, take turns so that you leave someone with the horses. This is not just to make sure they do not do anything untoward, but also to make sure that passers-by do not do anything to upset them. People

may not mean any harm, but someone lifting a child to peer through a window o undoing a groom's door to look in could cause problems. You also do not want to risk someone feeding them something inappropriate – especially with competition horses who might be drug tested

In busy motorway service areas it is bes to park somewhere at the back where it is quiet. Towcar drivers should look out for parking areas set aside for caravans, or consider using the lorry park which will b set up for large vehicles.

With youngstock, take more frequent breaks because it is all new to them and they do not always have the stamina to cope with the demands of travelling. Mares and foals may need time for the foal to suckle (a difficult task to master on the move), so watch them when you stop to see if that is what they want to do and so that you do not interrupt 'lunch' by driving off just as the foal decides the world has stopped moving long enough to attempt it.

What to Check

The first thing to do is to have a look round inside the horse compartment. Make sure that everything is as it should be, with partitions and bars still in place, travelling wear still done up and lead rope and haynet knots still fast.

How humid is it in there? How hot is it? Has rain come in anywhere? Are the horses being showered with condensation off the roof? These things should tell you i you need to open or close vents or, in a railer, shut one or both rear doors (only do that in very bad weather). When you stop in warm weather, consider opening doors and ramps to increase the airflow if you can do so without risking horses getting out. But don't do it where people might drive into them and don't forget to close them before you drive on.

Run a hand under each horse's rug to check that he has not sweated up, or does not feel too cold. Bear in mind that individual horses may react differently to the same environmental conditions. Some sweating may be unavoidable in very hot weather, but at other times it needs action. Consider removing the rug or putting a lighter one on but also consider whether the difficulty of removing or changing rugs in the confines of a vehicle is likely to cause more problems. If the horse is not seriously overheating and the journey is not too long, is it necessary? If he is too cold, consider closing vents and windows or putting a rug over him if this is practical within the confines of the vehicle.

This horse looks relaxed and ready for the journey home.

If the horse is showing serious signs of distress, like sweating badly on a cool day, this needs investigation. He may simply be too hot because of a thick winter coat, but he could be stressed for another reason: maybe something in the vehicle is worrying him or, worst of all, he has colic. If it appears to be straightforward travelling stress, give him time to rest and drive more cautiously on the rest of the journey, stopping more often to check him. If you feel there is a medical condition, seek veterinary help immediately – you do not want to be stuck on a motorway with a sick horse. Always err on the side of caution because it will be far easier to get veterinary help in a decent-sized town than from a lay-by in the middle of nowhere. Remember, if you are in this situation and are not sure of your location you may be able to find out by dialling your mobile phone's traffic information service, because these usually start by stating your location.

On long journeys you should take water with you and offer it to the horses when you stop.

Very Long Trips

Very long journeys need military-style planning. You have to be able to care for the horses on the road so you must plan ahead for all contingencies, including delays (especially on cross-border trips outside the EU). You can accept that you will be able to fill water containers at service areas, but will you be able to if you haven't got a hose? Take sufficient food for the horses and, if you are on a trip likely to take days, take more than you think you will need in case of delays. Incidentally, never hang haynets on the back of the vehicle where they get covered in road grime and exhaust fallout.

If the journey is going to take longer than a day, consider booking in to a horsy bed and breakfast or getting the horses put up in a livery yard along the way (see the adverts in horse magazines, get British Horse Society listings, contact tourist information services and regional horse clubs, or search the Internet). Even in large lorries, you are asking a lot of the horses to expect them to stand in the same stalls day and night. Taking a break off the lorry gives you and the horses a good rest and means that you can give the vehicle a mucking out before the next leg of the journey.

If you are held up for long periods in warm weather, consider opening doors and ramps to increase the airflow when stationary – but not if you risk the horses getting out. If you think weather conditions in the area you are going to are likely to be very different from our own, take veterinary advice. You may need to take electrolyte drinks to stop the horses dehydrating and your vet should also be able to advise on any extra vaccinations that may be mandatory or sensible.

If you are crossing borders, make sure that you have all the correct paperwork, including vaccination certificates, for all the countries you are going through.

Above all, do not consider a very long journey with a horse who is anything other than fit.

Consideration for Others

When travelling your own horses, you must also show consideration for other people's horses. Think twice about stopping in a lay-by next to a field full of horses because, once they realize there are horses in your vehicle, they may start charging around risking injury and winding yours up.

When passing other horses on the road, take special care because they may be worried when they sense or hear your horses in the vehicle.

When you stop, make sure you do not block anyone in or lower ramps in places where other drivers may not see them. If there are other horse transport vehicles about, give them plenty of space so that there is no risk of the horses winding each other up.

Above all, not everyone appreciates the value of manure so if you decide to shovel the piles out, dump them where they will not cause offence or nuisance.

11

Trailer Maintenance

An important factor in favour of using a horse trailer instead of a lorry is the low maintenance cost. But that does not mean to say that trailers are maintenance free if they are to function properly and, most importantly, safely. For example, if a trailer's brakes or wheel bearings seized the wheel would lock up, slewing the trailer to one side. At speed, with the horses thrown out of balance, you would be very lucky if the outfit stayed upright.

In Britain, a trailer may never be seen by an expert after the dealer has prepared it for the first owner because, unlike everywhere else in Europe, we have no equivalent of the MOT for trailers. But using an unsafe one is still an offence and it is up to you to make sure yours remains safe for the sake of your horses, yourself and other road users.

We have covered the everyday maintenance matters, like checking tyres, in the pre-drive checks in Chapter 6. Here, we are looking at the tasks that must be carried out to keep the trailer in good order – like having your car serviced. Everything explained in this chapter

should be read in conjunction with a trailer handbook, because components vary even on trailers made at different times by the same manufacturer. If you do not have a handbook and find that something on your trailer differs from what you see here, do not guess but seek expert advice from the manufacturer or dealer. However, most trailer manufacturers buy in components like brakes, axles and hitches so, even if your trailer manufacturer has gone bust, the chances are that the parts were used by someone else, or that their manufacturer is still around.

If you have any doubt about your competence to carry out a task, or are worried by anything you find, go to the experts. If you do not have a trailer dealer in your area, a caravan dealer may be able to supply parts and advice, though explain that you have a horse trailer in case a more heavy-duty item is required than for a caravan. If you are not mechanically minded or do not have the correct tools it may be better to get the trailer serviced once or twice a year by a trailer dealer.

When you do decide to do a job ourself, if it entails jacking up the trailer, se an axle or a substantial part of the hassis as a jacking point, never use the oor. Also, never work under a trailer aised on a jack alone, because jacks often ollapse, so use axle stands. Always ensure hat the ground under a jack or stand is rm enough to take the weight. If you ave to put something under the stand or ack, use blocks of wood. Never use house ricks, which split too easily and without varning.

When working under any vehicle, wear ye protection, because you can easily islodge potentially damaging dirt. For reasy jobs, at least use a barrier cream n your hands and clean them using a uitable hand cleaner, like Swarfega or

nly work under a trailer if it is supported by axle tands.

Manista. If you have sensitive skin, thin latex gloves like surgeons use are essential when handling lubricants.

Storage

Where you keep your trailer can make a difference to its longevity and reliability. Ideally, you would store it in a building, but few of us have buildings big enough. Try to park it on hard standing so that it is not subject to dampness coming up from the ground. Hard standing also makes maintenance easier because it gives a firm surface for jacking the trailer up and getting underneath.

Always chock the wheels, or use a wheel clamp, and release the handbrake so that the brake shoes are not in contact with the drums, which thus stops the shoes sticking to the drums while parked. If that does happen, and the shoes do not free themselves immediately you try to move the trailer, you will need to refer to the section further on in this chapter about adjusting brakes. In the first instance, you will have to slacken off the adjuster nut or star wheel, then insert a screwdriver in through the brake shoe inspection holes to lever, or tap, the shoes free of the drums (with care). Once the wheel is free to turn, you will have to adjust *all* the brakes in the manner set out in the brake adjustment section. Now you see why it is better to leave the hand-brake off.

It is probably best to lower the trailer on the jockey wheel while it is unused because this makes it more stable in high winds, reduces stress on the wheel's column and helps keep the thread inside lubricated. It also means that a potential thief has to spend just that little longer winding it up to hitch up.

Most horse trailers have good enough ventilation to prevent condensation, but when it is not in use, especially in cold, wet weather, check yours is not getting damp inside and if it does, open it up on a sunny day to dry.

Cleaning

Never leave bedding in the trailer because it goes mouldy, which is bad for both trailer and horses. Disinfecting after every trip, as professional transporters must, may be excessive for private owners who are always transporting the same horses, but washing the trailer out keeps germs and moulds at bay. At least twice a year, and preferably much more often, give it a good clean out, power washing everything and then spraying a good, low-odour disinfectant, like Virkon, over all surfaces and letting it dry. Leave it open to dry out.

Externally, try to prevent mud building up in nooks and crannies because it absorbs road salt and becomes a corrosive poultice, as well as making it harder to see if rot sets in. Use a car shampoo for cleaning bodywork because is properly formulated for cleaning road grime off paint and usually has a protective wax content. Avoid household cleaners, which are harsh, and washing-up liquid, which is bulked out with salt and so does not do paintwork or metal any good.

A power washer is useful for cleaning trailers inside and out but even domestic

After cleaning a trailer or lorry, leave it open to dry.

ones can produce a 1,500 psi jet of water, so be careful not to force water into places you do not want it, like lights.

Wheels

If you do not use your trailer for very long periods (like all winter) it is sensible to remove the wheels and store them under cover to protect the tyres from the effects of weather and ultraviolet light. You can leave the trailer on blocks or axle stands, or buy 'winter wheels' from a caravan dealer; these are stands bolted on in place of the wheels, often with locking devices.

If you store your trailer with the wheels

n, you should move it about once a
nonth so that the tyres do not get flat
pots – just moving the trailer a 30 cm or
o is enough. Keep the tyres properly
nflated so that the side walls are not
tressed or, even pinched between the rim
nd the ground. This will also save a lot of
nflation time when you want to use the
railer.

General Maintenance

Bodywork

The materials used in trailer bodies vary
rom make to make and most handbooks
xplain the care required. Modern
omposites need little attention. Wood
hould be kept as dry as possible and
hecked for rot, though beware of using
wood preservatives on plywood in case it
ffects the glue bonding the layers
ogether.

Steel needs attention if minor damage is
ot to become a major rust problem. A dab
f paint on a small scratch as soon as it
appens prevents a rust spot forming,
which will eventually spread under
urrounding paint. If the steel is already
usty, you must remove the rust with
mery paper or a wire brush before
epainting, though anticorrosion paints,
ke Hammerite, only need loose rust
akes removed.

Galvanizing is self-healing over small
reas of damage because the zinc coating
eacts to cover the gap, but larger scrapes
hould be painted over with a zinc-rich
aint, like Holts Zinc Plate.

Bolts

Nowadays, bolts at crucial points are
usually self-locking, but their security –
particularly of those locating axles, springs
and hitch – should still be checked every
2,000 miles.

Brakes

Brakes are essential to road safety so, if
you have any doubts about your ability to
work on them, or about anything you find
on them, seek your trailer dealer's advice.

On some trailers, we are now starting to
see hydraulic and electronically activated
brakes which need specialist care and may
be self-adjusting for wear (see the
handbook). Most trailers, however, still
have overrun brakes, whereby the hitch
pushing against the slowing towcar
operates the drum brakes at each wheel
via rods and cables. These brakes are not
usually self-adjusting, so they need to be
adjusted for wear according to
manufacturer's recommendations.
Adjustment is normally done after about
500 miles on a new trailer, or after fitting
new brake shoes, and then at 2,500–3,000
mile intervals. Before adjusting the brakes,
check that the operating cables are
undamaged – kinked or broken ones
should be replaced.

To adjust cable operated brakes:

1. Jack the trailer up and put it on axle
   stands so that all four wheels are off the
   ground.

2. Ensure that the handbrake is off and
   the hitch is pulled fully forwards.

3. Rotate the wheel in the direction of

forward travel while adjusting the adjuster nut on the back plate of the drum until the brakes are applied. Do not rotate the wheel in the reverse direction, or the auto-reverse mechanism releases the brakes. (Note: The auto-reverse mechanism allows you to reverse the trailer without the brakes coming on. Many pre-1989 trailers have, instead, a lever which effectively disconnects the brakes for reversing.)

4. Now turn the nut gradually the other way until the wheel just rotates again. The nut does not have to be turned far.

5. Older trailers may have a star wheel adjuster inside the drum. This is accessed by removing a plastic bung in the back plate and is turned with a screwdriver blade, but adjustment is otherwise the same as with a nut adjuster.

6. Apply the handbrake a couple of times to centre the shoes, then recheck the wheel and make any final adjustments. Then do all the other wheels.

7. To check for correct adjustment, take hold of a brake cable where it comes out of its outer sheath at the compensator bar. With your thumbnail against the end of the sheath, you should be able to pull the cable out by 3–5mm.

Some brakes are adjusted using a star wheel accessed through a hole in the back plate.

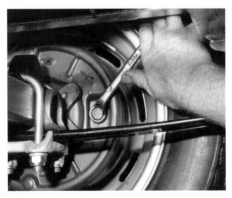

Modern trailers have an adjuster nut for the brakes.

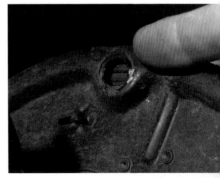

Most brakes have holes plugged with plastic bungs through which shoes can be checked for wear.

The cables themselves do not normally need adjustment, but should be checked. There should be no more than about 1mm of play between the hitch draw tube (see Hitches, this chapter) and the main brake operating lever it pushes against. With all the brakes adjusted at the drums, you can check cable adjustment by applying the handbrake and turning each wheel in the reverse direction: each should click and lock. If there is too much slack in the cables, the handbrake will come all the way up and the last wheel will not lock.

Adjustment to the cable is done by turning adjuster nuts on the main rod or cable connecting the lever to the compensating bar under the trailer, to which the individual wheel cables attach.

The brake cables to the wheels should all be the same length. This can be checked by measuring the distance between the compensator bar and a chassis cross-member. If a cable appears to have stretched, it should be replaced and

the others checked – a job best done by a dealer.

Once you are sure that you have adjusted the brakes properly, do a road test on a safe road. When you brake firmly, the trailer should pull up evenly and straight. When you reverse, the brakes should come off but, if they do not, you have adjusted the shoes and/or the rod too tightly and they should be readjusted.

Floors

Lift rubber matting regularly to clean underneath it and allow any dampness to dry out. Worn rubber matting must be replaced to protect the floor and to ensure that the horses have a safe, slip-resistant footing. This matting also helps to absorb some of the impact of stamping hooves.

Granular rubber compounds that look like tarmac are occasionally used on trailer floors instead of rubber sheeting. These provide a permanent slip-resistant surface but any moisture seeping in around the

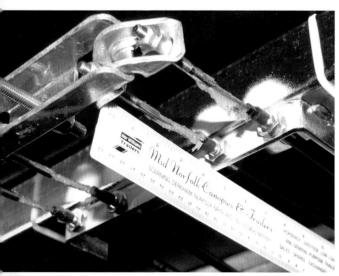

Check that cables are evenly adjusted by measuring to the compensator bar.

trailer sides or floor-mounted fittings cannot get out again and you cannot inspect the wood beneath for damage

It is, however, important to examine the floor periodically from above and below for any signs of rot or damage. Floors must be repaired by a horse trailer dealer who knows the correct materials to use – a horse trailer floor takes a lot of weight and stress and getting it wrong could be disastrous. Many non-horse trailer dealers do not realize the extreme stresses horses put on floors and a floor that would be fine with half a tonne spread out over a pallet may not be strong enough for a horse who puts the same weight down over a total area about the size of an A4 sheet of paper.

Some manufacturers are switching to aluminium floors. Though considerably more rot-resistant than wood, they are not maintenance free. Eventually the aluminium will corrode, most likely around points where it comes into contact with steel. As with any floor there is also the risk that horses putting extreme force on it may damage it. Therefore, you still need to clean and check it occasionally. It is particularly important not to let salty dirt build up underneath, since this will encourage corrosion from that side.

Hinges and Catches

Occasionally oil hinges and catches to prevent wear and ensure that they work smoothly and quietly – a nervous horse will not appreciate a ramp that squeals. If you find ordinary oil makes dust stick, try WD40. A smear of grease on the lugs onto which the ramp counterbalance springs hook stops them 'twanging' as it rises.

Ramps

Most trailers have some form of lifting assistance on at least the large rear ramp. This is usually a spring, which can sometimes be adjusted to compensate for wear by turning a nut or bolt, but in some cases the only answer may be to replace the spring. Only adjust the spring until you can lift the ramp easily, and not so much that it refuses to stay down.

Some trailers have gas struts on ramps, like bigger versions of those that hold up car hatchbacks. If these fail, or get bent, they cannot be repaired and must be replaced. Never take a gas strut apart, or puncture one, because they contain gas at high pressure, which can injure you.

Check the condition of the ramp itself because a horse going through a rotten one can suffer serious injury and may injure the handler. Some ramps 'give' a little as the horse walks on, but if a ramp flexes more than usual, or excessively, it should be investigated.

Hitches and Towballs

The hitch does more than just hold the trailer onto the car: it is part of the braking system. The hitch cup is bolted to a sliding tube, called the draw tube, which applies the brakes when it is pushed back by the trailer coming forwards as the towcar brakes. All trailers have at least one grease nipple on top of the housing for this tube, and most have two. A few also have one underneath to lubricate the pivot of the lever that the tube pushes against. Most manufacturers recommend using a grease gun to push grease through these nipples at intervals of between 2,000 and 3,000 miles. At the same time, push the hitch backwards: it should slide steadily back under firm pressure and, when released, it should slide steadily out again. If it offers little resistance to being pushed back, or comes back out quickly, the damper inside (like a gas strut) has failed. If it stays back, and a dose of grease through the grease nipples does not cure it, the damper has stuck or the draw tube is damaged. In both cases it should be corrected as soon as possible, because this affects braking efficiency, and the work is best carried out by an expert who is able to asses damage properly.

At the same time as this greasing is carried out (more often if you tow on dirt tracks), grease and dirt in the hitch cup itself should be cleaned out with white spirit on a paintbrush, otherwise the combination of grit and grease will act like grinding paste on the hitch and towball.

Using a grease gun to lubricate the draw tube.

Cutaway diagram of
hitch mechanism.

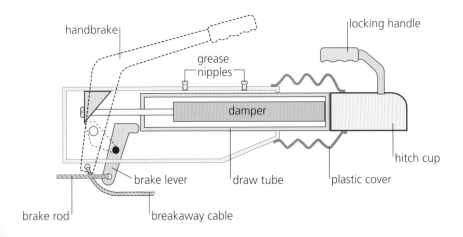

Once dry, wipe a smear of grease inside the cup. All moving hitch parts should also be kept oiled.

Worn hitches and towballs can be dangerous, so get them checked – garages can measure towballs when the car is serviced. Most modern hitches also have a wear indicator built in, so keep an eye on that and remember you only need half a millimetre of wear on each side and your 50 mm ball becomes an unsafe 49 mm oval. Putting a new trailer onto an old towball accelerates hitch wear so, if you buy a new trailer or hitch, spend a few pounds on a new towball and bolts too. (The bolts must be high tensile steel ones suitable for the job, preferably with locking nuts of some kind.)

With removable swan-neck towballs, the handbook normally shows which moving parts on the towbar's locking mechanism need lubricating. Make sure that you fit the plastic covers supplied for the lock and the hole in the towbar into which the ball fits. This prevents dirt from fouling the mechanisms and making it difficult, or impossible, to lock the towball in place.

Lights

The electrical systems in trailers are simple but they are subject to a great deal of spray thrown up by the towcar's wheels, so investigate any malfunctions immediately. Stopping a lamp leaking as soon as you notice it may save having to replace it later, or having it fail. But before working on the trailer lights make sure that they are disconnected from the car and, when cleaning the car's towing

socket, turn off the ignition and lights and remove the key.

A problem with more than one light suggests a wiring fault in the car or trailer. You can check which by plugging the trailer into another car's socket so if the problem disappears you know your car is at fault. The trailer plug and car socket are the most likely places for faults, so start your check there. Be very careful about tampering with modern cars' electrical systems because some have aircraft-style Multiplex wiring in which cutting the wrong wire can do permanent damage to the system.

Common, and simply corrected faults, are pins that have become compressed and loose wires in the socket or plug. The former is easiest to cure, so check that first. You will notice that the pins in the plug and socket are divided in halves or quarters to create enough 'spring' to make a good connection yet be easy to disconnect. Sometimes the gaps become closed up, causing erratic connections, so wiggling the plug makes lights go on and off, but gently pushing a screwdriver into the split in the pin should open it up enough to make a good connection again.

If this does not work, there may be a loose or corroded connection in the plug or socket. Simply open up the plug or socket (they may screw or clip together) and, using a thin screwdriver or pliers, gently pull each wire, remaking any loose connections. If a connection is corroded, take the wire out, clean it and remake it. If you have to replace a plug or socket, all the connections are numbered, so either swap the wires one at a time from new to old or write down what colour wire goes into what number connection (some car and trailer handbooks have lists or diagrams for this). Squirt WD40 over the metalwork before reassembling the plug or socket and check that the lights all work. Every 2,000 miles, or six months, examine the contacts in the trailer's electrical plug and the car socket and clean off corrosion and dirt (insects often get squashed deep between the pins). A Hella Kleenaplug, available from caravan dealers, makes the job easier and a squirt of WD40 helps prevent corrosion.

At the same time, remove the lamp lenses and check the contacts and bulb holders for corrosion. Some lamps have drain holes in them which must be kept clear. Also, wipe out any dirt on the inside of the lenses and give the contacts (but not the bulb glass) a squirt of WD40. Damaged lenses or badly corroded fittings should be replaced.

Finally, check the cable runs for damage to the insulation caused by vermin or abrasion. The cable between the plug and the trailer is most vulnerable.

Wheel Nuts

On a new trailer, or if you have to remove a wheel, you should check the tightness of the wheel nuts after the first 25 miles (you should also do this on cars). After that their tightness should be checked every 500 miles or so.

Some trailer manufacturers give a torque wrench setting for wheel nuts which, if you have the tool, is more sensible than using brute force. Never exert excessive force on a wheel brace because you may not be able to undo the nuts later and you can damage the threads. A smear of anti-seize grease (like Comma Copper Ease) on the threads prevents nuts locking on.

Wheel nuts on cars and trailers should be tightened in diagonal pairs to pull the wheel evenly onto the hub.

above **Tightening wheel nuts in diagonal pairs ensures that the wheel is pulled evenly onto the hub.**

left **Hella's Kleenaplug makes cleaning plug and socket contacts easy.**

Servicing Axles

By axle I mean everything on it, not just the bar between the wheels. The items in this section are vital for road safety so if you have any doubts about your ability to do the work properly, get your trailer dealer to do it.

In the mid-1990s Ifor Williams started using wheel bearings that are sealed for life, like those on modern cars, and so need no adjustment or regreasing. Others have since adopted these, so check what the trailer has on it before starting work. Instead of a slotted (castle) nut and split pin behind the hub cap most of these bearings have a stake nut, which has a collar projecting from it for locking the nut by tapping the metal into a groove on the axle (staking). Each time the drum is removed, the stake nut usually has to be replaced and tightened to a specific and very high torque setting (350 Nm on an Ifor Williams) for which a large torque wrench is essential. Any work on drums and hubs on these trailers is best left to a dealer.

A stake nut shows that your trailer has bearings lubricated for life.

REMOVING THE DRUM

This applies only to axles with a slotted nut and split pin – not those with hubs sealed for life.

1. Loosen the wheel nuts to finger-tightness then either put the trailer on axle stands, so that all four wheels are off the ground, or lift one wheel at a time and chock the others. Release the handbrake and check that the hitch is pulled fully forwards.

2. Remove the hub cap. You are supposed to be able to lever them off with a screwdriver, but metal ones often need tapping off with a hammer and large screwdriver or small cold chisel used evenly around the flange. Clean the grease out of the cap and put the part somewhere safe and clean.

3. Clean the grease away to reveal the slotted nut and split pin. Straighten out the ends of the split pin and pull or tap it out – this will be replaced, so discard the old one after checking that your new one is the same diameter and length.

4. Turn the nut anticlockwise to undo it and put it somewhere safe and clean.

5. Slacken the brake adjuster nut or star wheel right off (see the earlier section on adjusting brakes). You should now be able to remove the drum by pulling it towards you, though you may need to tap it gently around its back edge with a mallet or a piece of wood and hammer. The outer wheel bearing often falls out as the drum is pulled off, so be ready to catch it!

Servicing axles: removing the drum.

left **Remove the hub cap.**

above left **Remove the nut locking pin.**

above right **Undo the nut.**

left **Remove the drum.**

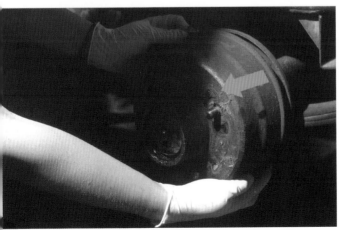

You are now ready to work on the wheel bearings or brakes.

Warning: *Do not inhale brake dust because it may contain asbestos and even asbestos-free dust is an irritant. Never blow it away by mouth or air line, but use a proprietary liquid brake cleaner or a damp cloth to remove it.*

GREASING WHEEL BEARINGS

The wheel bearings are two sets of roller bearings which prevent friction between the wheel hub (which is in the centre of the brake drum) and the axle on which it turns. They should be checked at least annually and regreased every two years – more often if mileage is high or you drive in dusty conditions.

1. Note how the bearings and grease seal are fitted. The outer bearing normally falls out as you slide the drum off – be ready to catch it! Place the hub outer side down and lever the grease seal out – it is sensible to replace this, but not essential unless damaged or worn.

2. Lift the inner bearing out of the hub and wipe the grease off both bearings and the hub. If the grease appears contaminated – or if you drop a bearing in the dirt – clean it off using white spirit, petrol or paraffin. Check for wear and replace if necessary.

3. Push grease down into the gap between the inner and outer rings of the bearing, but do not pack it too tightly. Use a heat-resistant grease suitable for wheel bearings, like LM grease.

4. Refit the inner bearing to the hub, taking care not to get grease on the inside of the drum, or it will ruin the brake linings. Fit the grease seal by putting a flat piece of wood over it (in the photo a purpose-made tool is being used) and tapping it with a hammer, ensuring that it is pushed in evenly to its original position. Turn it over and fit the outer bearing.

Now go on to the section on refitting and adjusting the hub.

Greasing wheel bearings.
top **Lever out grease seal.** above **Remove the bearing.**

BRAKE SHOE REPLACEMENT

Warning: *Brake dust may contain asbestos. If you get grease onto the friction surfaces of the shoes or inside the brake drum, clean it off thoroughly with a solvent. Shoes must always be replaced on both wheels on an axle or the trailer will pull to one side when braking.*

On most brakes you can check the amount of friction material left on the shoes through a hole in the back plate covered by a plastic bung. Manufacturers usually suggest replacement when the material is down to 1.5 mm.

Before you start taking the brake components apart, familiarize yourself with how they are fitted, drawing a diagram if necessary. Note whether the shoes are an asymmetric shape, if one spring is longer than the other and which way the hooks on the spring ends face. Compare your new parts with those fitted and set up the new shoes and springs to one side, using the originals as a pattern. Brake shoes can usually only be fitted the correct way round, but do not rely on that!

As you work on the brakes look for signs of wear or corrosion – replacing a rusty spring now will save work later.
You replace the shoes with the brake adjuster fully slackened off, so check that the shoe ends are resting on the adjuster's housing.

top **Grease the bearing.**
above **Replace the bearing and refit the grease seal.**

1. Release the shoe retaining spring, or springs, by compressing it/them from inside the brake and unhooking it/them from behind the drum's back plate. Some have tiny metal inserts to retain the spring.

2. Lift the upper and lower shoes and their springs out together by spreading the ends over the adjuster. If there are two springs between the shoes, you may need to lever the shoes apart with a screwdriver or spanner to lift them off the adjuster. If your new shoes do not come with new springs, transfer the old ones to them now while you can see the existing positions.

3. Remove the expander mechanism to which the brake cable is attached and check it for wear and freedom of movement.

4. Take hold of the end of the cable in a pair of pliers and check that it moves easily and smoothly. If it does not, it should be replaced.

5. Remove and clean the brake adjuster nut or star wheel, unscrewing it to make sure it is not stuck or corroded.

6. Ensure that the other adjuster parts move freely. They often stick.

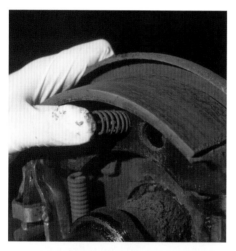

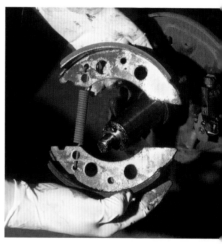

above left **Remove shoe retaining spring.**

above right **Lift off the shoes.**

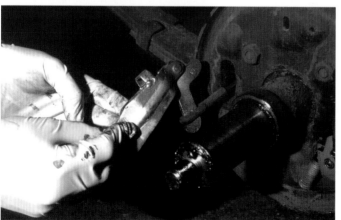

left **Remove expander.**

left **Check the cable for wear and free movement.**

Remove and clean the adjuster.

Ensure that the adjuster parts move freely.

7. Carefully clean any rust and grime off the back plate with a wire brush – *do not be tempted to blow it away!*

8. Clean the back plate and inside the drum with a proprietary brake cleaner and leave them to dry.

9. Check the drum's braking surface for any deep scoring. If it is scored, the drum should be replaced – unlike car drums, those on trailers are not usually thick enough for 'skimming'.

10. Carefully put a smear of heat-resistant copperized grease (like Comma Copper Ease) onto the points on the back plate, levers and adjuster touched by the shoe, but make sure that none gets onto the friction surfaces.

11. Reassemble the brake in the reverse order, ensuring that the expander mechanism lever to which the cable is attached sits in the position shown in the accompanying photo so that it is not applying the brake.

Clean off back plate rust

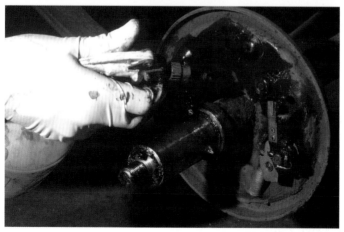

Wash with brake cleaner.

Check the drum for scoring.

Grease the contact points.

Reassemble and check that the expander fits in this position.

You are now ready to refit the hub and adjust it and should then adjust the brakes as explained in the earlier section in this chapter.

REFITTING THE HUB

Once you are satisfied that your work inside the brake's drum and hub is finished, carefully refit the drum over the end of the axle, being careful not to push the bearings out of place. Some people find it easier to slip the outer bearing in after the drum has been put onto the axle, but, if you can hold it there with your thumbs, it is easier to get correct alignment by having it in place.

You may need to tap the drum gently with a mallet or piece of wood and hammer to get it fully home, while checking that the brake shoes are properly aligned – do not force it! Replace the slotted nut finger-tight then put the wheel onto the hub, doing the wheel nuts up finger-tight.

HUB ADJUSTMENT

Some manufacturers require the adjustment of the hub nuts to be checked after the new trailer's first 500 to 1,200 miles. It must also be done if the hub is removed to work on the brakes or bearings. Note that rocking the wheel is not a check of whether bearings need adjustment because, on a trailer, the bearing needs some play to allow for heat expansion.

Some details of the hub adjustment process that follow may vary from trailer to trailer, so check with the manufacturer. For example, in step 1 the hub nut may need turning back anything from 30 to 90 degrees.

1. While turning the wheel, tighten the nut until resistance is felt, then turn the nut back until the wheel turns freely. Over-tightening the nut damages the bearings.

2. Insert a new split pin by aligning the nearest nut slot to the hole in the axle. You may need to tap it gently home.

3. Bend the ends of the pin apart with a screwdriver blade or pliers then tap the outer one back flat over the end of the axle and the inner one down against the side of the nut.

4. Check that the pin ends are not sticking out or interfering with moving parts. Put a little clean grease into the hub cap and tap it back into place with a mallet, or wood and hammer.

When you have finished all the work and lowered the trailer, tighten all the wheel nuts in diagonal pairs on each wheel. Road test the trailer, making sure it brakes evenly and straight. Also, feel the hub centres and examine any that feel warmer than the others. Don't forget to check the tightness of the wheel nuts after 25 miles.

12

Lorry Maintenance

Unlike trailers, lorries are far too complex to cover all the maintenance issues fully in this book. However, it is also unlikely that most owners would have the skill or facilities to handle all their lorry maintenance at home. Too many tasks which the home mechanic can easily carry out on a car involve heavy-duty equipment on a lorry. Even the simple task of removing a wheel requires a heavy-duty jack and a wheel brace that is long and substantial enough to allow you to exert the necessary force. On larger vehicles, you usually also need a hefty torque wrench to make sure that the wheel nuts are all correctly tightened when you put the wheel back on. This also rules out DIY work on brakes, suspension and axles.

Indeed, the only people I know who service their own horseboxes are farmers who have all the necessary equipment for maintaining their tractors. However, there are still plenty of lesser tasks the horsebox owner can carry out to keep the vehicle in good order. The regular checks explained in Chapter 6 should be seen as part of the maintenance you do and should not be neglected when the lorry is not used.

Storage

It is best to keep your vehicle on a hard standing where it will not be subject to moisture rising from the ground, where leaks can be spotted easily and where it can easily be worked on. If you have to park it on unprepared ground, like a corner of your field, remember that what might be a firm parking spot in summer could turn soft in winter, with your truck gradually sinking in under its own weight – so keep an eye on it and move it if it starts to disappear!

Even if you are not using the lorry, keep its tyres pumped up and fluid levels topped up to prevent deterioration. Before it turns cold each winter, check the anti-freeze concentration in the cooling system, especially if it has been topped up during the summer. You can either ask a garage to do this or buy a tester in a motor spares shop. These usually take the form of a large pipette containing coloured balls, which float according to the concentration (make sure you buy an anti-freeze one – not the similar looking device for testing battery acid).

If the lorry is not being used, it makes sense to run the engine occasionally, to keep the battery charged and to make sure oil and coolant are moved around the engine. Ideally, take the truck for a 15-minute drive, rather than leave it ticking over, because this gets everything warmed up and the higher revs help expel gases from the engine and exhaust that might otherwise condense there. If the lorry has a living section, remember that constantly using the lights in there will run the battery down if the lorry is not run to charge it up. This does not matter so much if you have a separate battery for the living section, except that the charging system may give priority to the vehicle's main battery.

Condensation can be a serious problem in horseboxes (because we put horses in them) with the risk that it may damage the vehicle and cause moulds to grow, which are unhealthy for both horses and people. Do not encourage it by leaving damp clothing in the living section, or damp rugs in the horses' section. If the living section has beds with solid, rather than slatted bases, lift the mattresses on their sides when not in use to allow trapped moisture to escape. While you sleep, your body produces a lot of moisture, which can become trapped between the mattress and a solid bed base, which is why many caravanners replace such beds with slats.

Check cupboards and tack lockers for condensation, too. If you have cupboards where it tends to collect, leave the doors open when the lorry is unused and consider getting vents added to the cupboard. It also pays to open the whole vehicle up on warm days to let the air blow through. If you still find mould growing, wash it off and treat the surface with an anti-fungal solution.

You can get meters from caravan dealers for checking interior panels for dampness. These give a more reliable indication of problems and may help to trace hidden water leaks by showing where the wettest areas are.

Condensation can also put water into the lorry's fuel system, which is why many hauliers insist that their drivers fill the fuel tanks before parking overnight. This is because, as the fuel is used, air is drawn into the tank and when it cools at night any water vapour in it condenses. It is not much of a problem in a car, but because lorries have such large fuel tanks it can put a substantial amount of water into the fuel system. All diesel systems have water traps which are either self-draining or need draining at intervals as laid down in the handbook, but it pays to avoid over-working them because, if water gets as far as the engine, it cannot be compressed like the fuel-air mixture and thus does substantial damage to a high-compression diesel. Diesel vehicles have a warning light for the water trap and, if it comes on, you should immediately drain the trap because it is abnormally full.

If your vehicle has gas appliances, turn the supply off at the cylinder when not in use. This prevents the risk of leaks from appliances, or if pipes become damaged. Gas cylinder lockers should have grilles, often in the floor, to allow leaking gas to leave the vehicle, so make sure that they are kept clear. It is best to leave oven and fridge doors ajar when not in use.

If the living section has a water system, it is essential to drain it in the winter or it will be damaged if it freezes. It is also sensible to drain it in the summer, unless you will be using the vehicle again soon, to reduce the risk of contamination. If the vehicle has a toilet don't forget it has a flushing tank, as well as a waste tank, that should be drained. (See the next section for details about cleaning these systems.)

Also remember to bleed water out of air brake systems so that it cannot freeze inside them.

Some lorries have battery isolator switches which disconnect the battery to stop it being accidentally run down when not in use. However, if you have an alarm fitted, make sure that this is wired so that it is not turned off by the isolator.

Cleaning

Professional horse transporters have to disinfect their vehicles after every trip, which is probably excessive for private

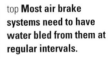

top **Most air brake systems need to have water bled from them at regular intervals.**

above **Some lorries have battery isolators to stop battery drain when not in use.**

Drain the water system when not in use, especially in winter.

owners, not least because we transport the same horses all the time. However, cleaning should not be neglected because it protects the health of your vehicle, your horses and you.

A power washer is a sensible investment because it enables you to blast dirt off the chassis and from inside the horses' section, though take care because even domestic ones can create a 1,500 psi jet which can force water into places you do not want it, like into lights or round door seals. Some power washer ranges also include power brushes on extending poles, which allow you to clean lorries without using a ladder. You can also get spray bottle attachments, which are handy for spraying disinfectant.

Car cleaning products are fine for the outside, though you'll need a lot of them. Giving a lorry an all-over polish is probably out of the question and is unlikely to be necessary with modern composite body panels. However, the occasional waxing of painted metal surfaces, like the cab, helps protect the paint and makes it easier to keep clean. Car shampoo is properly formulated for cleaning road grime off paint and usually has a protective wax content, while household cleaners are harsh and washing-up liquid is bulked out with salt which does not do paintwork or metal any good.

But the important thing is not to let mud and dirt build up underneath where it combines with road salt and horses' urine to make a corrosive poultice. Many horseboxes have drain holes in the floor so make sure you clean around those and keep them unblocked. You are required by law to keep lights and numberplates clean.

In the horses' section, clean out manure and used bedding every time you use it. At least twice a year, and preferably much

Don't forget to clean the lorry's underside: note how bedding has built up on the chassis rails here.

opposite page **Keep the horses' part of the box clean to prevent the build up of corrosion, harmful moulds and germs.**

more often, give it a good clean out, power washing everything and then spraying a good, low-odour disinfectant, like Virkon, over all surfaces and letting it dry. Check that you have not washed anything into drain holes or partition location holes that might block them – it will be easier to remove it now instead of when it has dried hard. Always leave the lorry open until it is thoroughly dry.

Clean the living section in exactly the way you would clean your own home. Never leave food in the cupboards or crumbs on the floor because they will encourage mice, with the danger of them chewing through pipes and wiring. If you find signs of mice, set traps rather than use poisons which will leave a corpse to rot where you cannot get at it.

If the living section has running water it will have two tanks: one for clean water and one for waste water. The clean water

one should be thoroughly rinsed after use and allowed to drain and dry – though cover its opening loosely with the lid to stop things crawling in. It, and the plumbing system, can be sterilized with a caravan product, like Puriclean, especially if they have not been used for some time. The waste system should also be drained after use and rinsed, but can be sterilized with household bleach. On luxury boxes with their own toilets, use caravan products, like Aquachem, to keep the waste tank hygienic. The instructions for cleaning products explain how and when they should be used.

Floors and Ramps

The condition of floors and ramps is vital for the safety of you and your horse. If a horse goes through a floor or ramp it will suffer terrible injuries, especially in a lorry

where there are an awful lot of mechanical parts underneath for legs to get tangled in.

Check the floor often for signs of damage or rot. In lorries you cannot usually lift the floor covering so look for any odd dips or creases in it. Crawling underneath with a light and eye protection is the only sure way of checking its condition, poking any suspect areas with a screwdriver. Don't forget to check the supporting structure, too – it is not a good floor if there are only rusty struts holding it up.

Aluminium floors are much more rot-resistant than wood but they still corrode and they can still be damaged by horses stamping and kicking. When you check an aluminium floor pay particular attention to the areas around steel fixings where electrolytic reaction can promote corrosion. If you suspect damage or corrosion on any floor, it must be properly repaired. Horses put an immense amount of stress on the floor which ordinary lorry repairers and builders may not fully understand, so make sure that the work is done by a reputable horsebox specialist. DIY repair is foolish because the materials used have to be exactly right for the stresses involved.

Lorry ramps barely give, if at all, when horses are on them and they should certainly not bend excessively. If your ramp starts bending more than usual, check it thoroughly. Also look for loose screws or screws projecting above the woodwork. Worn matting and damaged grip slats should be replaced before they trip someone up or give way as a horse needs grip. Ramp accidents are particularly dangerous because there is usually a handler alongside the horse, and on many trucks the ramps are quite high.

Bodywork

Modern composite materials need little maintenance and are corrosion resistant. Steel must be kept painted to prevent rust, so touch in any scratches before rust sets in. If the metal is rusty you must clean the rust off before repainting unless you are using an anti-rust paint like Hammerite.

Galvanized parts are protected by a layer of zinc which will 'heal' over small scratches, but if large areas of the underlying steel are exposed they should be repainted with a zinc-rich paint like Holts Zinc Plate.

Aluminium bodywork is resistant to corrosion, but it will corrode eventually and once it starts, it is difficult to stop. This is particularly a problem where bare aluminium and steel come together because it sets up an electrolytic reaction. Painting can slow this down but these days a plastic insert is often used to separate the metals. Take this into consideration if you attach anything to an aluminium-bodied vehicle.

Damaged body panels and doors that do not latch properly are illegal if they represent a risk to other road users. A tack locker swinging open on the road could easily kill a motorcyclist or pedestrian.

Body Lubrication

Moving parts always move more easily if they are lubricated, which also prevents wear and corrosion. Wandering round with an oil can or WD40 spray will save problems later and it is far easier to oil a catch than it is to free a seized one. (WD40 works best in door hinges and catches while squirting it into door locks helps stop them freezing as well as lubricating them.)

Heavier oil or grease usually works best on sliding bolts, ramp catches and door 'straps', which are the metal bars near the hinges which stop the cab doors swinging open too far. Greasing the points at which ramp springs hook on stops them 'twanging' as the ramp is moved. On a lorry you may find grease nipples to allow the lubrication of heavier components, for which you will need a grease gun. However, on mechanical parts of the chassis the type of grease to be used (it may need to have a high melting point) and the frequency of lubrication will be laid down by the vehicle manufacturer.

Servicing

Your vehicle's chassis manufacturer lays down service intervals for your vehicle and it is wise to stick to them. With the limited use horseboxes often get, you may have to get servicing carried out on a time rather than a mileage basis. On a very low-mileage vehicle there may be an argument for having it serviced once a year even if the manufacturer suggests every six months, but this means that you have to be even more careful about checking everything for deterioration between services. However, if the vehicle is under warranty, you have no option but to stick to the service schedule or you will void the warranty.

Choose your service mechanic carefully. You may save a lot of money going to a non-franchised person locally, but it is only a true saving if they do the job properly. Make sure you keep a service record, preferably with all the bills, to give you a record of when things needing periodic replacement, like drive belts and brake fluid, were last done and so you can show future buyers the vehicle has been cared for.

On lorries with a living section, electrical and, especially, gas appliances need servicing, too. If you get your box serviced at a horsebox specialist they will probably be able to do all that but if you go to a lorry person, get the appliances in the living section serviced by a caravan dealer or specialist in those fittings. This is particularly important with gas appliances because of the risk of carbon monoxide poisoning (for safety, have a CO detector in the living section).

Oil Changes

Many vehicles have an oil change 'small' service between the full services so one way that many horsebox owners reduce servicing costs is to do these intermediate oil changes themselves. Before contemplating doing this, there are several things to take into consideration.

First, check with the vehicle manufacturer, or in the handbook or workshop manual, to find out if there are any other things to be done along with the oil change. It will usually include changing the oil filter, but you may also need to drain water traps or change filters in the fuel and brake systems. You will certainly

The soot marks around this lorry fridge flue suggest that it needs urgent attention.

A carbon monoxide alarm in the lorry's living section could save your life.

Check gas systems for leaks and ensure that locker ventilation is clean.

have to check fluid levels and it may also be wise to check brake shoe wear.

You may need special tools to remove oil filter cartridges and you certainly need a container big enough to take all the old oil. Used engine oil has to be properly disposed of: it is illegal to pour it down drains or onto the land because of the environmental damage it may do (if you have a septic tank it also kills the bacteria that work on the effluent). Your local council can tell you which of its tips have oil disposal facilities, but you will need a uitable transport container and may have o leave the container at some sites that do ot have their own tanks. The impurities n used oil may also cause skin irritation nd can be carcinogenic, so wear gloves nd quickly wash off any that gets onto 'our skin with a suitable hand cleaner.

Replacement oil must be of the grade nd standard specified by the vehicle nanufacturer. We are all familiar with the 'iscosity grade, like 15W40, but the 'ehicle manufacturer will also state other tandards, the most common being SAE or)IN numbers. On modern diesel engines vith long service intervals the nanufacturers may also specify using ynthetic oils because only they can naintain their full lubricating qualities)ver a long mileage. The diesel version of n oil contains additives specifically lesigned to cope with the mechanical :haracteristics of diesels and the types of mpurities they put into the oil. The

correct oil is particularly important in diesels because their very high compression means immense forces and strains are put on the components, so good lubrication is vital.

When changing the oil, it is best to drain the engine while it is warm, because the oil flows more freely. However, this can mean that the oil is quite hot when it comes out, so take care. Always use the correct size of spanner or key to remove the sump drain plug. Old mechanics used to turn the engine over once when they thought all the oil had been drained out, but this is not wise with modern engines because manufacturing tolerances are so fine and compression ratios higher. If the oil filter has to be changed, remove it after all the oil has drained, but take care because it retains a substantial quantity of oil.

On some engines you may need to replace a washer round the drain plug to get a good seal, but on others the plug is

Always use the correct size and shape of oil sump plug key, or you may damage the plug.

tapered to make this unnecessary. Oil filter cartridges usually need their rubber seal lubricated with clean engine oil before they are put on and they are usually only put on hand tight, because they tighten up as they get warm. It is sensible to check they are still tight when the engine has warmed up.

Use a funnel to refill the engine with oil because it saves a lot of mess and wastage. On lorries with access to the engine through panels in the cab, you may need a funnel with a long, flexible spout and to cover carpets and upholstery. Only use the quantity of oil specified in the handbook and, towards the end of the filling, check the level on the dipstick frequently in case it takes less than expected because there was still oil in the engine. Check the level again after running the engine and letting it rest for 10 minutes. Never over fill the engine because too much oil can be almost as damaging as too little.

Keep a record of the date and mileage of the change and keep bills for oil and parts so that you can show prospective buyers in future that the changes have been carried out.

Brakes

Braking systems on small lorries may be hydraulic, like a car's, but larger ones are powered by compressed air. With hydraulic systems you need only check the levels in the reservoir, which may be in the engine compartment, on the chassis rail near the cab, or in its own compartment. If the level drops suddenly, the system should be checked for leaks. Leaks in the braking system must be repaired

immediately because they leak faster under pressure (when you use the brakes) and the fluid may contaminate other brake components.

Brake fluid is corrosive to paint and bodywork and absorbs water, so reservoir lids must be airtight and any topping up should be done from previously unopened bottles. Water absorbed into brake fluid vaporizes when the fluid becomes hot, creating bubbles that cause a spongy feel to the pedal and, eventually, brake failure. Similar fluid is used in hydraulic clutch systems and the same precautions apply.

Air brake systems must be checked according to the manufacturer's instructions. They all have water traps and filters but, while a few modern ones have self-draining traps (which still need checking) in most systems they need to be drained manually. The handbook will tell you when and how. Check that all the bleed valve taps work and, after running the engine to pressurize the system, check it for air leaks with the engine off. The bleed valves are under the large compressed air cylinders on the chassis and they may have to be bled separately, or each cylinder's valve may be linked to a single pull lever or cord. Mind your eyes when you release the valve.

Drum brakes usually have inspection holes in the back, with removable bungs, so that the thickness of the brake shoe friction material can be checked without removing the wheel and drum. If you are doing your own servicing, you need to check the shoes and replace them when the material is down to the limits set by the vehicle manufacturer.

Lights

Lights are important for your safety and the safety of others on the road around you. Your lorry will also fail MOT or plating tests if they are faulty.

Check them regularly for damage because replacing a cracked lens is cheaper than replacing the whole lamp once water has got in and corroded the contacts. Rear lights are particularly vulnerable because they are constantly in the vehicle's own spray.

As with trailers, it pays to remove the lenses annually and spray the contacts with WD40, though this is not possible, or sensible, on headlights which run at high temperatures. Most headlights now are quartz halogen: if you need to replace the bulbs in one of these, do not touch the bulb glass because the deposits your fingers leave shortens their life. For this reason, these bulbs are usually packaged with a card or plastic sleeve over the glass, but if it is missing, use a cloth or hold the bulb by the metal parts. If you accidentally touch it, clean it with white spirit. Keep lamp lenses clean at all times.

Checklists

What follows is a series of checklists which summarize the key points made in respect of buying, driving and maintaining horse transport. There is also a list of further sources of information which may be of value to those who transport horses. ➤

Buying a Trailer

The horse's/horses' weight

The trailer's unladen weight

Total trailer weight

Car's maximum towing weight

Car's 85 per cent weight

☐ Check that the weights above are safe.

☐ With large horses, check that the total trailer weight does not exceed its maximum authorized mass (gross weight)

☐ Is it high and wide enough for your horses?

☐ Can breast and breech bars be positioned high/low enough for them?

☐ Can you manage the ramps and partitions?

☐ Is it well finished inside and out?

☐ If you are not viewing the actual trailer you are buying, are there any items fitted to the 'showroom model' that are extras?

☐ Does it have a sensible warranty? (New trailers.)

☐ If it is an unusual make, or an import, what is the spares situation?

☐ Is the vendor prepared to haggle?

Used Trailers

☐ Can the vendor prove it is not stolen?

☐ Does it have a TER sticker to show it is registered with The Equipment Register?

☐ Note the chassis number _____
and check with TER, the manufacturer and/or Trailerwatch (see Chapter 3).

☐ Can the vendor prove its age?

- [ ] What use has it had?
- [ ] Check for internal and external damage/corrosion.
- [ ] Is it reasonably clean?
- [ ] Do the lights work?
- [ ] Are the tyres in good condition?
- [ ] Check tyre tread depth.
- [ ] Are ramps in good condition?
- [ ] Does the floor appear sound from above (lift mats)?
- [ ] Does the floor appear sound from below?
- [ ] Can you feel grease under the plastic gaiter behind the hitch?
- [ ] What servicing has it had?
- [ ] When were the brakes last adjusted?
- [ ] When were the wheel bearings last greased?
- [ ] Can you test tow it? (Check insurance first.)
- [ ] Does the vendor appear to know their way around the trailer? (A thief might not.)
- [ ] Will they give you a land-line phone number? (A thief would not.)
- [ ] Do you feel good about the trailer and vendor?

Buying a Towcar

The horse's/horses' weight

The trailer's unladen weight

Total trailer weight

Car's maximum towing weight

Car's 85 per cent weight

☐ Are the above weights safe?

☐ Looking at the brochure specification, does the car appear to have a good towing engine? (See Chapter 3.)

☐ How much is a towbar and associated electrical connection, including fitting?

☐ Can you afford the insurance?

☐ Is it comfortable?

☐ Does it have sensibly sized door mirrors?

☐ Does it have enough boot space for tack?

☐ Can the 4WD be used on the road? (Not just for pulling away.)

☐ Do you like it?

Used Cars

Note numbers: Registration _____

Chassis _____

Engine _____

☐ Can the vendor prove its mileage?

☐ Can they prove it is theirs to sell?

☐ Is there a full service history?

☐ Do the numbers tally with the registration documents?

☐ Check for interior and exterior damage/corrosion.

☐ Does the car have ABS (anti-lock brakes)?

☐ Are tyres legal and sound?

☐ Do all interior electrically operated systems (windows, mirrors, heated screen) work?

☐ Do the lights work?

Are there any leaks from:

　☐ Engine?

　☐ Transmission?

　☐ Cooling system?

　☐ Fuel system?

　☐ Brake system?

☐ Is interior wear and tear reasonable for the mileage?

☐ Are there any signs of water leaks inside?

☐ Does it appear cared for?

☐ What use has it had?

☐ Is there a towbar fitted?

☐ Is the towbar sound and does the socket work?

☐ If buying from a dealer, can they show you that a history check has been done?

☐ Does the vendor object to waiting for checks?

☐ Has the vendor given a land-line phone number? (A thief won't.)

☐ Did they insist on meeting away from home? (A thief would.)

☐ Does the vendor know their way round the vehicle? (A thief may not.)

☐ Do you feel happy about the vendor?

☐ Do a history check or arrange vehicle inspection (see Chapter 4).

Test Drive

- [ ] Can you get a comfortable driving position?
- [ ] Can you see in the mirrors?
- [ ] Can you reach important controls?
- [ ] Can you see the instruments?
- [ ] Does it start easily?
- [ ] Does it smoke excessively on start up?
- [ ] Does the smoke clear quickly?
- [ ] Does it smoke when warmed up?
- [ ] Can you manage the clutch/gearbox?
- [ ] Does the steering feel vague or loose? (Off-roaders do not always feel as positive as ordinary cars.)
- [ ] Is there any difficulty with changing gears?
- [ ] Are there any gaps in the gear ratios where, say, third is too low but fourth is too high?
- [ ] Does the engine seem flexible (not in need of constant gear changing)?
- [ ] If automatic, does it change up and down readily?
- [ ] If manual, does it jump out of gear if you come off the throttle quickly? (Check off-roaders in both high and low ratio.)
- [ ] Do the brakes feel good?
- [ ] Does it pull up straight?
- [ ] Any odd noises?
- [ ] When warm and allowed to tick over for several minutes, does blipping the throttle produce a cloud of smoke?
- [ ] Do you still like it?

Buying a Lorry

The horses' weight
_____

The lorry's payload*
_____

* Payload is the lorry's gross weight minus its kerb
(unladen) weight.

☐ Is the lorry's payload high enough to take your horses, you and everything
else you need to carry?

☐ Can you legally drive a lorry of this size?

☐ Is it high and wide enough for your horses?

☐ If forward-facing, can the breast and breech bars be positioned high/low
enough for your horses?

☐ Can you manage the ramps and partitions?

☐ Is it well finished inside and out?

☐ If this is a converted box-body lorry, has the floor been reinforced?

☐ If you are not viewing the actual lorry you are buying, are there any items
fitted to the 'showroom model' that are extras? (If you are comparing
lorries, make a list of fittings you want and which vehicles have them as
standard or what they cost as extras.)

☐ Does it have a sensible warranty? (New lorries.)

☐ Is the chassis new or used?

☐ If used, how has it been prepared?

☐ Is it taxed?

☐ Does it have a valid MOT/ plating certificate?

☐ Can you test drive it? (Check insurance.)

☐ Is the vendor prepared to haggle?

Used Lorries

Note numbers: Registration _____

Chassis _____

Engine _____

☐ Can the vendor prove its mileage?

☐ Can they prove it is theirs to sell?

☐ Is there a full service history?

☐ Do the numbers tally with the registration documents and test documents?

☐ Check for interior and exterior damage/corrosion.

☐ Are the tyres legal and sound?

☐ Do ramps/doors work?

☐ Do the floor and chassis appear sound from underneath?

☐ Do the lights work?

Are there any leaks from:

    ☐ Engine?

    ☐ Transmission?

    ☐ Cooling system?

    ☐ Fuel system?

    ☐ Brake system?

    ☐ Living section plumbing?

☐ Is cab wear and tear reasonable for the mileage?

☐ Is there any sign of water leaks through the roof, doors or windows in cab/living?

☐ Is there any sign of condensation or mould in living/horses' section?

☐ Does it appear cared for?

☐ What use has it had?

☐ Does it have a current MOT/plating certificate?

☐ If the owner can show previous MOT/plating certificates, do the mileages tally?

☐ If buying from a dealer, can they show you that a history check has been done?

☐ Does the vendor object to waiting for checks?

☐ Has the vendor given a land-line phone number? (A thief won't.)

☐ Does the vendor know their way round the vehicle? (A thief may not.)

☐ Do you feel happy about the vendor?

☐ Do a history check or arrange vehicle inspection (see Chapter 4).

Test Drive

☐ Can you get a comfortable driving position?

☐ Can you see in the mirrors?

☐ Can you reach important controls?

☐ Can you see the instruments?

☐ Does it start easily?

☐ Does it smoke excessively on start up?

☐ Does the smoke clear quickly?

☐ Can you manage the clutch/gearbox?

☐ Is the steering too heavy for you?

☐ Does the steering feel vague or loose? (It will not feel as positive as a car's.)

☐ Is there any difficulty with changing gears?

☐ Does it jump out of gear if you come off the throttle quickly?

☐ Does it smoke when warmed up?

☐ Do the brakes feel good?

☐ Does it pull up straight?

☐ Are there any odd noises?

☐ When warm and allowed to tick over for several minutes, does blipping the throttle produce a cloud of smoke?

☐ Do you like it?

First Aid Kits

Keep copies of these in the kits so that you can tick off any you have used.

Horses

- [ ] Digital thermometer
- [ ] Moist wound gel (e.g. Robinson's Vetalintex and Equine America's Derma Gel)
- [ ] Roll of cotton wool
- [ ] Non-stick dressings to go over wounds (e.g. Melonin or Rondopad)
- [ ] Stretchable conforming bandages (e.g. Vetrap or Kband)
- [ ] Surgical, insulating or duct tape to hold bandages in place
- [ ] Animalintex
- [ ] Cool bandages
- [ ] Good antiseptic (e.g. Hibiscrub or Pevadine)
- [ ] Curved scissors
- [ ] Card with important phone numbers and insurance details.

People

- [ ] A bottle of distilled water
- [ ] Adhesive dressings
- [ ] Large, small and medium sterile dressings
- [ ] Crepe and gauze roll bandages in various sizes
- [ ] Roll of surgical tape
- [ ] Triangular bandages
- [ ] Cotton wool
- [ ] Foil blanket
- [ ] Tweezers, scissors and safety pins
- [ ] Surgical gloves.

Car and Trailer Checks

Pre-drive

- [ ] Car tyre pressures and condition (Pressures: front _____ rear _____)
- [ ] Trailer tyre pressures and condition (Pressure: _____)
- [ ] Engine oil
- [ ] Coolant
- [ ] Washer fluid
- [ ] Brake fluid.
- [ ] Sufficient fuel
- [ ] Clean lights, mirrors and windows.

Hitching up

- [ ] Apply trailer handbrake
- [ ] Remove security devices
- [ ] Raise hitch with jockey wheel
- [ ] Remove covers on car's towball and socket
- [ ] Reverse up to trailer and apply car handbrake
- [ ] Lower hitch onto towball then raise again to check it is locked on
- [ ] Fully raise and lock jockey wheel
- [ ] Attach breakaway cable
- [ ] Fit stabilizer
- [ ] Plug in electrical connections
- [ ] Check the car's handbrake is on and release the trailer's
- [ ] Check lights on car and trailer
- [ ] Load horses
- [ ] Check that doors and ramps are closed
- [ ] Check that tyres and cable ground clearance still look all right under load
- [ ] Check that trailer handbrake is fully off and jockey wheel fully raised.

Unhitching

- [ ] Apply car and trailer handbrakes
- [ ] Drop and lock jockey wheel
- [ ] Disconnect electrical connections and stabilizer
- [ ] Unclip breakaway cable
- [ ] Unlock locking hitch
- [ ] Unhitch by raising it on the jockey wheel and moving car
- [ ] Lower it on the jockey wheel (makes trailer more stable in strong winds)
- [ ] Apply wheel clamp or wheel chocks
- [ ] Release trailer's handbrake
- [ ] Replace car's towball and socket covers.

Lorry Pre-drive Checks

- [ ] Tyre pressures and condition (Pressures: front _____ rear _____)
- [ ] Engine oil
- [ ] Brake fluid or bleed airbrakes
- [ ] Coolant
- [ ] Washer bottle
- [ ] Sufficient fuel
- [ ] Lights clean and working
- [ ] Mirrors and windows clean
- [ ] Tack and living section supplies stowed
- [ ] All external lockers locked
- [ ] All internal lockers latched
- [ ] Load horses
- [ ] Partitions secured
- [ ] Check that all doors and ramps closed.
- [ ] Fold-up side steps raised

Things to Take

- [ ] Horses' first aid kit
- [ ] Humans' first aid kit
- [ ] High-visibility tabard
- [ ] Torch
- [ ] Tool kit
- [ ] Jack and wheel brace for trailer
- [ ] Mobile phone and hands-free kit
- [ ] Important phone numbers
- [ ] Breakdown membership card
- [ ] Road atlas
- [ ] Bridle (even if not riding)
- [ ] Horse rugs
- [ ] Clean tail bandage
- [ ] Water for horses
- [ ] Bucket
- [ ] Tack
- [ ] Show clothes (body protector for cross-country)
- [ ] Grooming kit
- [ ] Riding hat
- [ ] Riding boots (spurs)
- [ ] Gloves
- [ ] Lunge line (if loading difficult or young horses)
- [ ] Horses' feed (long journeys)
- [ ] Food and drinks for humans.

Trailer Maintenance

Keep a note of when maintenance tasks were carried out.

Job	Date	Estimated mileage
Adjust brakes		
Grease wheel bearings		
Clean hitch cup		
Lubricate drawbar		
Lubricate hitch and hinges		
Check floor/ramps		
Disinfect interior		
Check brake shoes		
Clean inside lights		
Clean electrical plug contacts		
Check tightness of bolts		
Check tightness of wheel nuts		

Lorry Maintenance

Keep a note of when you last checked things or when it needs servicing and testing.

Job	Date	Mileage
Next service due		
MOT/plating expires		
Living appliances' next service		
Tyre pressure and condition check		
Check oil and fluids		
Lubricate locks and hinges		
Clean inside side/tail lights		
Drain/clean fresh water system		
Drain/clean waste water system		
Check living section water and gas pipes		
Check for condensation		
Check floor/ramps		
Disinfect interior		

Further Information

Further Reading

J. A. Allen Photographic Guides: *Preparing for the Towing Test*.

The Stationery Office: the *Driver Licensing Information* pamphlet sent with your licence and *Driving – The Essential Skills* for cars and towing, *Driving Goods Vehicles – The Official DSA Syllabus, The Official Theory Test for Drivers of Large Vehicles* and *The Highway Code* available from bookshops or online at www.tso.co.uk.

Society of Motor Manufacturers and Traders' publications department (020 7235 7000): *The SMMT Guide to Towing and the Law*.

Government Bodies

Driver and Vehicle Licensing Agency: Driver inquiries: 0870 2400009. Vehicle inquiries: 0870 2400010. Website: www.dvla.gov.uk. Driving Standards Agency: local offices in the phone book. Website: www.dsa.gov.uk. Vehicle and Operator Services Agency: 0870 6060440 and local offices in the phone book. Website: www.vosa.gov.uk.

Equestrian Breakdown Services

Equestrian Support Services: 01300 348997. Website: www.equestriansupport.co.uk.

Organisation of Horsebox and Trailer Owners: 01488 65765. Website: www.horsebox-rescue.co.uk.

RAC (ESS services can be added to a normal RAC membership for trailer owners) 08000 722822. Website: www.rac.co.uk.

Websites

The ESS and OHTO websites mentioned above include a great deal of useful horse transportation information.

Ifor Williams Trailers' website www.iwt.co.uk and the National Trailer and Towing Association's site at www.ntta.co.uk have general information about towing and the law.

Trailerwatch for stolen trailer checks: www.trailerwatch.com.

The Equipment Register to check a trailer registered with them: www.ter-uk.com.

RAC for general motoring information, route planning, used car inspections and used vehicle history checks: www.rac.co.uk.

AA for general motoring information, route planning, used car inspections and used vehicle history checks: www.theaa.co.uk.

Caravan Club for general towing information and training courses: www.caravanclub.co.uk.

British Horse Society for general equestrian information, a list of lorry and trailer driving schools and bookshop: www.bhs.org.uk.

Bookbrain – if you cannot find the books listed above locally this site will show you the cheapest source online: www.bookbrain.co.uk.

Index

ABS 31, 63, use of 118
Accidents 89
Antifreeze 183
Axle stands 165

Bandages, tail 144; leg 147
Battery 184
Bodywork, artwork 62; choosing
    lorries' 60
Bodywork; lorries 10, 188; trailers 167
Boots, horses' travelling 147
Brakes, anti-lock see ABS
Brakes, lorries 192; trailers 6, 165, 167,
    177
Breakaway cable 8
Breakdowns 86, 90, 208
Breaks on journeys 159
Breast bar 150; law 24
British Horse Society 21, 208

Cleaning, trailers 166; lorries 186
Condensation in lorries 184

Driver and Vehicle Licensing Agency,
    see DVLA
Driving Standards Agency, see DSA
Driving tests 17
DSA 14, 208; books 120
Dual-carriageways 131
DVLA 14, 208

Electrical sockets, see towing sockets
Electronic driving aids 31; use of 118
Electronic stability control: see ESP
Engines, cars 33; checks 96; diesels 33;
    lorries 61
ESP 32, use of 118
Eyesight 17

Fire extinguishers 82
First aid kits 84; checklist 202
Floors 11, lorries 60, 187; trailers 15, 48,
    51, 169
Four-wheel drive, buying used 42; types of
    30; use of 116

Gas appliances 69, 74, 184
Gearboxes, car types 35; use of 114
Gross train weight, definition 5

Headcollars 144
Hitch 8, 98, 101,170
Hitching 101; in driving test 20; checklists
    203, 204

Ice 138

Jacks 83, 91, 165
Jockey wheel 8, 104

Legs, bandages and boots 147
Licence categories 15

Lights 24, lorries 11, 193; trailers 9, 105, 170

MAM, definition 5; trailer test 18; Maximum authorised mass, *see* MAM
Medicals 17
Minibuses 15, 28
Minor roads 129
Mirrors, use of 113, special for towing 113, special for hitching 101
MOT 22
Motorways 131
Motorways, emergencies 88

Navigation 99; satellite 64
Nose weight, definition 5

Oil, engine 35, cars 41, lorries 75, 189
Overtaking 127

Payload, definition 6
Plating 22
Plumbing in lorries 185
Poll guard 144
Problem loaders 155
Punctures 90

Rain 136
Ramps 48, 149, lorries 188, trailers 170
Rest 25, 159
Reversing 107, in driving tests 18
Roadworks 134
Rough ground 140
Roundabouts 124
Rugs 144

Sale of Goods Act 77
Security 79; of lorries 71, 73; of trailers 53, 165
Side winds 135
Snaking 141
Snow 138

Speed limits 121
Spray suppression 136
Stabiliser 39
Suspension 140; on lorries 64

Tachographs 23
Tail guard/bandage 144
Tool kits 83
Towball/bar 9, 37, 98, 170
Towing sockets 9, 38, 105, 173
Town driving 128
Traction control 32
Trading Standards 77
Training 21, 208
Travelling gear 143
Turbo(charger) 34
Turning 125
Tyres, checks 40, 93, 166; checklists 203, 206, 207; minimum tread 94

Unhitching 101; in driving test 20; checklist 204
Unladen weight; definition 5
Unloading 153

Vehicle and Operator Services Agency, *see* VOSA
Vehicle Inspectorate, see VOSA
Vehicle testing 22
Ventilation 66, 160
VOSA 15, 22

Water systems in lorries 185
Websites 208
Weights, calculating horses' 27; definitions 5; when buying towcar/trailer 26; when buying lorries 59
Wheel nuts 92, trailers 173
Wheel bearings, trailers, types 174; servicing 176, 182
Wind 135